Fern Eisner

About the Author

Brad E. Sachs, Ph.D., is a family psychologist and the author of *Things Just Haven't Been the Same: Making the Transition from Marriage to Parenthood* and *The Good Enough Child*. He is the founder and director of the Father Center and has written for numerous periodicals. He is married to Karen Meckler, a psychiatrist and acupuncturist, and together they raise their three children, Josh, Matt, and Jess, and their two dogs in Columbia, Maryland. He can be contacted directly through his website at www.bradsachs.com.

THE
GOOD ENOUGH
TEEN

THE
GOOD ENOUGH
TEEN

Raising Adolescents with
Love and Acceptance
(Despite How Impossible They Can Be)

Brad E. Sachs, Ph.D.

Perennial Currents
An Imprint of HarperCollins*Publishers*

HarperCollins books may be purchased for educational, business, or sales promotional use. For information please write: Special Markets Department, HarperCollins Publishers Inc., 10 East 53rd Street, New York, NY 10022.

FIRST EDITION

Designed by Phillip Mazzone

Library of Congress Cataloging-in-Publication Data is available upon request.

ISBN 0-06-058740-7

05 06 07 08 09 WBC/RRD 10 9 8 7 6 5 4 3 2 1

THIS BOOK IS DEDICATED WITH LOVE . . .

To the blessed memory of my great-aunt,
Dasia Cherson, *z"l* (1904–2003)

To the wondrous family music that my ensemble of
children—Josh, Matt, and Jessica—so exquisitely create

And to their mother and my wife, Karen Meckler,
whose rich and loving harmonies bring
our whole quintet together . . .

*"And she kissed me just right
like only a lonely angel can . . ."*

All changed, changed utterly:
A terrible beauty is born.

W. B. YEATS, *Easter 1916*

I stand between two worlds. I am at home in neither,
and I suffer in consequence.

THOMAS MANN, *Tonio Kröger*

One never knows, do one?

FATS WALLER

CONTENTS

THE
GOOD ENOUGH
TEEN

INTRODUCTION

There are few situations in life more difficult to cope with than an adolescent son or daughter during the attempt to liberate themselves.

—ANNA FREUD

Here's how it is . . .

Perhaps your son has earned A's and B's throughout elementary and middle school, but it has primarily been based on the strength of his excellent memory and his interpersonal charm rather than on his perseverance and steady work habits. You have been warning him repeatedly that, come high school, he'll have to begin buckling down and actually *completing* homework and studying for tests, but he habitually blows you off with an off-handed "Whatever," convinced that he'll continue to glide smoothly by.

Now, in the middle of ninth grade, the A's and B's have gradually melted down into C's and D's. He forcefully resists your efforts to get him organized at home and responds to your mantra-like "Do you have any homework tonight?" with an equally mantra-like "I finished it in school," even though most of his teachers at back-to-school night told parents that students should have at least twenty minutes of homework or test prepara-

1

tion in each subject every night. Worse, you receive a call from the assistant principal telling you that he has missed his world history class on two separate occasions without either a note or an adequate explanation. When confronted with this data, he adamantly insists that he's never missed a class and that there "must have been a mistake at the office." You stare into his eyes, wanting to believe him, but knowing, down deep, that you don't. . . .

Or your 15-year-old daughter, who, since fourth grade, has been hanging around a group of kids you've always felt comfortable with, has started dating a boy whom you simply don't trust. He's three years older than her and goes to an alternative high school program for students with behavioral problems. Since she started seeing him, she's been dressing differently, more gothic, less athletic. You've begun to notice some odd-looking scratches on her arms and legs, which she explains away as "The cat and I were messing around." She's taken to lighting incense in her room, and she set off the smoke alarm once when a lit candle burned down so low that it ignited some papers that were lying nearby. She is constantly on the computer, e-mailing her boyfriend or engaged in Instant Messenger conversations, discussing with him their newly hatched and most cherished dream, which is to open up a Runic tattoo parlor.

Her middle school friends, whom you liked so much, don't call or come around anymore, and the father whose children your daughter babysits for two afternoons a week has diplomatically told you that he won't be having her back anymore if she continues to receive calls on her cell phone when she's supposed to be doing her job. You try to talk with her regarding your concerns about where things are headed, but she angrily spurns you, demanding that you refrain from "trying to choose my friends for me." You resort to spying, attempting to surreptitiously read her e-mails, listen in on her phone calls, and go through her backpack, ashamed, but afraid of what's happening. . . .

Or your son, the mischievous youngster who always had you holding your breath, wondering what he would get into next, has been making it abundantly clear what he's gotten into next. You have found drug paraphernalia in his room; you have learned from an alert neighbor that he has been leaving the house in the middle of the night and sneaking back in before dawn; you have been hearing the telephone ring at all hours of the night; and you have seen the same seedy-looking buddies of his show up on the weekends and congregate sullenly and suspiciously in your backyard.

He has gone from being cheery and playfully irreverent to nasty and downright disrespectful. You haven't had a meaningful conversation with him in months, he's lost weight, he has reduced his 13-year-old sister to tears with his vulgar comments about her sexual development, and he adamantly refuses the help that you and the school guidance office have been offering. . . .

In the three years since my previous book, *The Good Enough Child: How to Have an Imperfect Family and Be Perfectly Satisfied,* was published, I have led hundreds of parenting workshops on the importance of having realistic expectations, both for your children and yourself, and on how to forgive, accept, and love the child that you have, despite all the ways in which he has, and will, disappoint and disillusion you. During these workshops, participants have always brought up a vast range of childrearing problems, dilemmas, and concerns. But I learned early on that I could always count on one particular question popping up at some point in our discussions: "When are you going to write a book on *teens*?"

Initially, this puzzled me. After all, *The Good Enough Child* presented within its pages numerous case studies that involved adolescents. And the basic five-stage process that I developed and explored for readers of that book seemed, to me, to have both relevance and healing powers no matter how old the child was. But in listening to so many mothers and fathers, it soon became clear that the process of seeing your child as "good enough" is, for many reasons, especially daunting when that child becomes an adolescent.

What has also taken place since my previous book was published is that two of my three children have now plunged themselves into the thick of adolescence, and my youngest is poised on the brink of this same precipice. So I am now experiencing the challenges of viewing teens as good enough from both a clinical and a personal perspective, and, rest assured, even psychologists can find themselves unnerved and upended at times! Between my patients and my own charges, I confess that I sometimes find that the only explicable thing about adolescents is how thoroughly inexplicable they truly can be.

The reality is that adolescence, encompassing ages 12 to 18, but often beginning earlier and ending later, represents the most dramatic and highly elaborated passage from one developmental realm to another that we will ever encounter. And this passage doesn't just affect the teen, of course. Just as the lights in your house may dim when a large appliance kicks in, the entire family is affected when your child begins to conduct the massive emotional current of adolescence.

But it's possible, as the parent of an adolescent, to become like Toto in *The Wizard of Oz*—doggedly tugging away the curtain to display the vulnerable, insecure, but ultimately humane individual who hides behind and operates the complex psychological machinery that so terrifies and intimidates. That's what this book will help you to do.

A former patient of mine, a rabbi, told me a funny but revealing story about her own gradual enlightenment as a young clergywoman. After she completed rabbinical training and took on her first job leading a congregation, she thought it would be a good idea to organize an annual workshop for parents. Married, but not yet a mother herself, she boldly titled it "The Ten Commandments for Parents." After a couple of years, she and her husband had their first child, and she found the experience to be so humbling that she renamed her workshop "Ten Rules for Parents." In another few years, they had a second child, a boy who was even more demanding than his older sister, and she renamed the workshop again, calling it "Ten Tips for Parents."

And as her daughter approached adolescence, she went for one final change in title: the parenting workshop came to be known as "Survival Strategies for Parents."

What is it about teenagers that makes it so uniquely difficult to appreciate them, to agonize less about their developmental fits and starts and to gaze more benevolently on their at times clumsy, at times conscientious efforts to differentiate from us and blossom forth into functional young adults?

In *The Good Enough Child* I presented some of the typical stumbling blocks that interfere with many parents' ability to accept their children's flaws and imperfections with patience and equanimity. After all, from time immemorial mothers and fathers have wanted the best for their children. They have imbued their children with their own dreams and desires and insisted that they correct parental errors, heal parental pain, compensate for parental failures, and cleanse parental sins. But for the current generation of mothers and fathers, the pressure to raise the perfect child seems to have expanded exponentially. There are a number of reasons why this is so.

For example, when couples have fewer children, and have children later in life, a trend that has been continuing for years now, this raises the stakes for each child that they do have and increases the share of parental fantasies that each child must shoulder.

One patient of mine, a mother of five, laughingly told me that while raising five children was certainly overwhelming, "It raises the odds that, at any one point in time, at least *one* of them will be doing well and staying out of trouble." But with only one or two children in the family, those odds diminish quickly.

Another growing trend, having children later in life, can affect our tolerance as well. A patient of mine who became a father for the first time at the age of 42, reacted to his 15-year-old son's meandering journey through high school by mordantly commenting, "I feel like I'll be in a wheelchair by the time he marches across that stage for his diploma. I'll be lucky if I can even *see* him."

Also, many parents have invested substantial time, money, and energy in their efforts to start a family. Mothers and fathers who couldn't have conceived a child even a decade ago now happily find themselves birth parents, but only after committing many years and thousands of dollars to this achievement. Couples who can't conceive or are unable to carry a baby to term may embark on the adoption process, which can take more years and more money. When that kind of emotional and financial sacrifice is entailed, it is only natural to expect a high return on one's investment. As one patient admitted to me during a fractious time with her daughter, "If she only knew how hard we worked just to bring her into this world. No child was ever more *wanted* than she was."

Additionally, because of an unpredictable economy and the ever-widening gap between the haves and have-nots, parents worry that without some income-producing skill or talent, their son or daughter will wind up at the bottom of the socioeconomic food chain. Recent economic studies have demonstrated that more than 90 percent of individuals who declare bankruptcy would qualify as middle-class based on income, and that though the modern two-income family earns 75 percent more income than the one-income family of a generation ago, they actually have *less* discretionary income because of the astounding, and continuing, increases in the cost of health insurance, school tuitions, and homes in "desirable" school districts. In other words, a satisfactory "middle ground" in our society seems to have shrunk to near invisibility. That may explain the cartoon that showed a boy sitting in his guidance counselor's office with a caption that read: "So what are we aiming for, Timmy—the Nobel Prize or Inspected by Number Seven?"

Then there's the electrifying change in the cultural expectations for children just in the last generation alone. What was considered to be above average when we were growing up is now run-of-the-mill. What used to be considered extraordinary is now baseline. I recently read an article in my college's alumni magazine by a graduate who, to make a point, resubmitted her identical application 25 years after she had initially submitted it and been accepted. Not only did she get turned down, but she was strongly discouraged from reapplying until she had gained some additional "credentials."

No matter what endeavors your child pursues these days, there are tiers upon tiers of competition, and dozens of ways for her self-worth to be incinerated. She's good at soccer? Well, how come she's only playing for a high school and club team when your neighbor's daughter is playing for the Olympic Development Program? He's a fine clarinetist? Then why is he only performing in the high school concert and marching bands when there's an elite statewide orchestra that his best friend was selected for? She did well in Spanish? Then how come she hasn't gone to Spain for a summer and taken courses while living with a native family in Barcelona? He enjoys the computer? Then how come he hasn't created his own website and started a high-tech company that was recently featured in a national business magazine like your neighbor's son did?

Even though our children's life expectancy will exceed our own by years, and exceed their grandparents' by perhaps a decade or more, we still force them to grow up faster than ever before. We overschedule them in our efforts to "get the most out of them," to outperform their peers and "be the best that they can be," while insisting that they devote their "leisure time" to productive pursuits that will look impressive on their applications to prestigious, hyperselective colleges. From the earliest moments of infancy all the way through adolescence, our children are discouraged from slowly finding their own way because the race is on to produce the healthiest, brightest, most accomplished child imaginable; because billion-dollar industries are happy to reinforce your fears that you are an inadequate parent if you haven't purchased the right toys, games, materials, services, and programs; and because your child will fall hopelessly and permanently behind unless you selflessly devote yourself to facilitating her success and happiness.

In a way we become like King Midas, who was granted the magical wish that everything he touch turn to gold, and in the process, lost the capacity to do the simplest, most important things, like embrace his beloved child: we push and push for our children to experience their (and our!) moments of golden triumph, and then we miss out on the warmth of loving contact when that triumph becomes our sole focus.

But while what we have been discussing thus far are some of the impediments to parental acceptance that apply during any stage of child development, there are others that tend to be more specific to adolescence.

First, of course, there is simply much more at stake during adolescence then at earlier points in child development. As one patient ruefully acknowledged, "When my kids were younger, there were certainly more problems. But now that they're bigger, there are bigger problems." Or, as the Yiddish proverb wryly notes, "Small children bring headaches; big children bring heartaches."

Adolescents' errors in judgment can have lasting or irreversible physical or emotional consequences, such as when it comes to their decisions about drug and alcohol use. Their curiosity, adventurousness, and maddening sense of invulnerability and immortality can place them smack in the middle of harm's way time and time again, living their lives like a game of Russian roulette. The psychological growing pains that many teens experience may lead to their acting in self-destructive ways—cutting or burning themselves, making suicide attempts—as a way to stave off their most discomfiting feelings.

Adolescents' behavioral problems might begin to occur not only at home or in school but out in the community as well, where the law enforcement and juvenile justice systems may get involved. Their ability or inability to be academically focused, organized, and directed will influence where they go to college and what kind of job they eventually get. Their sexual behavior can result in life-altering consequences such as pregnancy or sexually transmitted diseases. Their initial intimate relationships could possibly endure, eventually leading to living together, engagement, or even marriage. All of this makes it understandably that much harder for parents to simply "relax, lay back, and let them mature." We worry that, in the face of all of these lures, threats, and dangerous possibilities, such an opportunity for growth might never even occur.

All parents of adolescents also feel a sense of urgency—after all, it's our final imprimatur, our last chance to put the "finishing touches" on our children, to polish and burnish and transfigure them before we send them out into the world. It's our only remaining opportunity to provide them with the skills that we believe that they'll need, to teach them the lessons that we want them to learn, to instill the attributes that we want them to embody, and to sand away all the defects and blemishes that somehow still remain despite our best efforts to remove them over the years. We know that there will never be another time when we have the potential for any kind of daily, direct influence on them, and that, henceforth, their peer group and other adults will have impacts that equal or surpass ours, so we desperately hammer away and try to shape them into the young adult that we think they ought to be.

A father whose son was in his senior year of high school described his thought process for me in the following way: "It's like I'm in college, cramming for some final exam. All I think about is all of the things that we need to do before he graduates, and all of the things I wish that we *had* done—the trips we didn't take, the talks we didn't have, the projects we didn't work on. So instead of making his last year at home a pleasant one for him and me, I'm probably making both of us miserable." And a 17-year-old girl snarkily commented at one point during our session: "*Now* my mother wants us to be close? We haven't talked in years, and all of a sudden she wants mother-daughter bonding time. Is she completely *wacked*?"

Additionally, by the time our children are adolescents, virtuous, hard-working parents understandably want to see some payoff for all of their valiant effort and sacrifice. After years of providing for their wide-ranging needs—scraping together money to support their interests and pursuits; making meals and doing laundry and scheduling medical appointments; volunteering for teachers and PTAs and fundraisers; driving them to friends' houses and practices and rehearsals and libraries; sitting in parking lots, waiting rooms, auditoriums, and athletic fields—mothers and fathers naturally want to be *rewarded*—most fulfillingly, with an attractive, engaging, well-mannered young adult who earns good grades, high SAT scores, accolades, and commendations in his well-rounded areas of interest, and of course acceptance to several top-notch universities. The possibility that all of our efforts could produce mediocrity becomes more than we can bear and makes it difficult to be charitable when we have to come to terms with our teen's rough, irregular growth.

And don't forget that by the time our children become adolescents, we ourselves are moving into middle age and are having to ask and answer difficult questions about our own lives. At a point when we may be experiencing the deep ache of regret and remorse, feeling a bit like an imposter in our own life as we appraise the unpredictable, unimaginable shape that it has somehow assumed, it becomes difficult, if not well-nigh impossible, to avoid transposing our most precious longings onto our teenaged sons and daughters, entrusting them with the impossible mission of making good on our broken promises to ourselves, our partners, and even our own parents.

As the dancing cheerleaders sang to fans in another cartoon I came across: "Hang your fading hopes and dreams / on your children's high school teams." Or as one mother snapped to her daughter during a tense session: "Look, honey, I know I blew a *lot* of chances when I was younger, and I'm still paying for them now, but I'll be *damned* if I'm going to let you make the same mistakes!"

Another common but anxiety-provoking parental expectation is that we want our teenager to validate the choices that we've made so as to alleviate the insidious parental guilt that constantly bores away from inside of us. If we chose to sacrifice a fulfilling career to be more of a stay-at-home parent, we feel entitled to have a child who will somehow concretely display the benefits of our hands-on parenting and surpass the children of those parents who continued on their professional paths. If we made a decision to allow our son to listen to the misogynist rap music that we found so personally distasteful, we at least want him to redeem us by growing up to treat women with respect. If we begin to take the risk of choosing *not* to pressure our daughter to get good grades, and refrain from constantly going over her assignments and preparing her for her tests, we want to see that she still goes ahead and earns those good grades on her own.

The anguished mother of a drug-dependent young man confessed, "My mother always was home with me and my brothers, and she told me point-blank that if I stayed busy with my own career once I had kids, I'd pay for it forever. But I loved my job, so I stuck with it and did the best I could to strike a balance between work and home. Now that I've learned that my son has gotten so heavily involved with drugs, though, I feel horrible—like her prediction came true, like I've been a terrible mom."

We also like to anticipate that, by the time our children are adolescents, they will have "grown out of" all the problems that so trouble us. The shyness that seemed to make her so isolated and unhappy, the devil-may-care approach to life that resulted in his lack of achievement, the sibling rivalry that has created such family tension, the temper that got him into so much trouble—all of these we hoped, or were reassured, would gradually be shed like an old snakeskin as our children marched confidently through pubescence.

How demoralizing, then, to notice that not only do these stubborn flaws remain, but that in some cases they seem to have gotten *worse*. A father conveyed this to me when he said, "I was sure, by now, that we wouldn't be dealing with his being so disorganized when it comes to his schoolwork—in another month, he'll be eighteen, for god's sake. But his teachers all along said not to worry, that he'll get it, that kids change when they move through high school and start putting it all together. Well, he's in his senior year now, and I'm *still* waiting for these so-called changes to come about—he's still forgetting books, still not doing homework, or doing it but not turning it in, still utterly at a loss as to how to prepare for an exam. And as far as I can tell, we're just about at the same place we've always been and running flat out of time."

Finally, adolescence is a stage in life during which it is crucial for children to begin to develop their own identity, and to start differentiating themselves from us. We have not finished the job of parenting if we have not produced an autonomous, self-sufficient young adult, but the very nature of becoming autonomous and self-sufficient inevitably involves at least a partial repudiation of what we stand for—as the biblical Abraham heralded his adolescence by smashing his father's *idols*, our children herald their adolescence by smashing our *ideals*. So at the very moment when we so desperately want our children to follow our advice—to buckle down in school, to continue with Scouts, to be more optimistic, to break up with their unsuitable paramours—they are, from a constitutional standpoint, a good deal less likely to do so. During these years they will rattle the family walls with their rage for independence, an unavoidable stage that tends not to provide much tranquility.

Is it any wonder, then, that with all of these issues swirling about, seeing our children as "good enough" during adolescence is a taller order than it was at any previous phase in their lives?

Yet despite the fact that so many of these forces seem to conspire against us, there remain very doable, practical ways to raise our teens with acceptance and compassion such that they are able to capitalize on their strengths, come to terms with and compensate for their weaknesses, and launch themselves successfully into the early stages of adulthood.

To do so simply requires the willingness to examine ourselves, to learn more about the origin of the expectations that we bring to this final stage of hands-on parenthood, and to understand our child and his journey through the labyrinth of adolescence. Parents who are courageous enough to take this exploration on and match their nurture to their child's nature are more likely to reap the benefits—not just a child whom they can be proud of, but, more importantly, a child who is justifiably proud of himself.

Without such exploration, parents inevitably wind up feeling and acting like Procrustes, who, in Greek legend, placed all who fell into his hands on an iron bed, cutting off any extending body parts if they were too long for the bed, or stretching them until they fit the bed—not exactly the best recipe for a warm and loving relationship with your teen.

In *The Good Enough Teen*, as in *The Good Enough Child*, I will not be promising you the sky, or guaranteeing that you will create Superchild, the son or daughter that you think you deserve and believe you should have. I will, however, guide you through five stages that will enable you to distinguish between what you want *for* your child and what you want *from* your child.

I will help you to see the hidden strengths in your teen's weaknesses and envision how to handle and respond to her inadequacies and immaturity in ways that enhance, rather than diminish, her self-respect.

I will help you to distinguish between developmentally expected *problems*, and developmentally threatening *crises*, and how to deal with both calmly and effectively.

I will show you how to avoid becoming overly responsible for your teen, and, instead, how to create the conditions that will invite him to become more responsible for himself.

I will assist you in understanding your adolescent's confusing, contradictory, and, at times, overpowering emotional needs and figuring out how to address them in ways that don't make her (or you!) feel awful for having had them in the first place.

I will explain how to create in your adolescent an openness to self-discovery and self-awareness, a readiness to confront his own depths, and even his own darkness, that will serve him no matter which life paths he chooses to pursue.

I will illustrate the methods by which you can express an appreciation and respect for signs of healthy independence on her part, and embody an attitude of flexibility and compromise while still reassuring her that you are in charge and won't allow her more freedom or autonomy than she can reasonably handle.

I will help you find a place to house your adolescent's periodic phases of wandering and stagnancy, of dislocation and slippage, without become overly worried or critical.

I will guide you through the paradox of raising an adolescent, the need to support his becoming his own person and growing up and out while simultaneously maintaining the connections that are necessary for him to feel secure and supported—his ability to be both an I and a we.

I will present the most effective ways to communicate with your teen, ways that increase the likelihood that both she and you will feel heard, understood, and trusted.

I will ask you to consider the possibility that raising an adolescent is not a joyless burden to take on, but an opportunity for a parent to embrace, a fulcrum around which new and more functional individual and family patterns can emerge.

I will reassure you that parent-teen conflict is both inevitable and a necessary nutrient for maturation, and provide you with the tools to formulate the strategies necessary to survive the "battle of the generations" such that your adolescent learns that he can challenge the rules and test the limits without having to harm himself, or the sources of those rules and limits—namely, you.

I will suggest that your parental goals should not be limited to superficial and eternally fluctuating societal definitions of adjustment or sanity or normalcy or success, nor confined to trying to cure, fix, change, or perfect your teen, but instead expanded to enhance her capacity to reach high and deep enough that her life blossoms fully forth in all its unique and unpredictable radiance.

I will relieve you of the burden of having to be the Perfect Parent and assist you in coming to terms with being an ordinary mother or father who more often than not makes decent enough decisions about everyday problems without having to constantly strive for virtuosity.

And, finally, I will affirm that completing our job as parents means creating the opportunity for our children to "walk away" from home, rather than to run away or to never leave, and for them to be able to leave home with a recognition of their freedom to author their own lives without anyone's self-respect feeling sacrificed.

Let's begin this journey by first examining what is happening during adolescence both for your child, yourself, and your family as a whole, and how parents find themselves most adaptively and maladaptively responding to it.

ONE

STRANGERS IN PARADOX

The Inner Life of Adolescents, Their Parents, and Their Families

Go forth from your native land and from your father's house to the land that I will show you.

—GENESIS 12:1

As I mentioned in the Introduction, while the process of seeing *any* child as good enough is a formidable task, there are some exceptional challenges that occur during adolescence that are likely to make this process that much more daunting.

So what is it about teenagers that so bewilders and bedevils parents? Often forced to conclude that adolescents must be some alien life form that was dredged up from the bottom of the sea, we have an unfortunate tendency to oversimplify them, to see them as ambulatory beakers of churning chemicals who will eventually settle and stabilize themselves as they finish their awkward lurch through biologically based puberty—sometime, if they (and we!) are lucky, by their early twenties.

But it is more accurate and, when it comes to understanding and accepting our teenaged offspring, more practical, to amplify our definition of what adolescence is all about and delve into the breathtaking emotional complexity of this stage of life.

15

What is perhaps most important to remember is that adolescence does not only happen to the adolescent, it happens to the entire family. It is a *sui generis* juncture in the family's development, the effects of which reverberate deeply within each member and broadly across each generation. The overlap of the adolescent's individual development, the parents' adult development, and the parallel and ongoing development of siblings, grandparents, and other important family members heats up the family system, magnifying its interactions and intimacies, making its strengths and weaknesses, its tendencies and patterns, more visible and, ultimately, more available for change.

Having an adolescent in the family is a bit like having a canary in the mineshaft. Just as the canary's demise warns the miners that there has been a gas leak, the adolescent's most exasperating behaviors and problems warn the family that changes need to be made if they are all going to survive. Any adolescent worth his salt pounds away at the family's structure, as well as at society, with whatever tools he has at his disposal—his brutal tirades or his deft indictments, his broody withdrawal or his brazen sarcasm—but he does so not in an effort to annihilate that structure but in an effort to revise and rebuild it, to help design a new, more flexible and functional architecture for all.

Adolescence, then, can best be understood as a collective battleground in which all family members—teen, sibling, parent, grandparent—struggle with their desire to cling to what's old and valuable from the past and an equally strong desire to create something new and valuable in the future. It is the stage during which we try to strike a balance between continuity and change, tradition and innovation, equilibrium and evolution. It is a "hinge in time" when one generation begins to hand itself over to the next, when every family relationship begins to unlock itself and seek out new ways of interconnecting.

Teens instinctively perform their part in this transformation with a variety of strategies. They bring a playful, good-natured spontaneity to family life that can enliven, stimulate, and inspire. They question long-standing assumptions, undermine ancient prejudices, bludgeon outmoded myths, and provoke new insights and outlooks. They play the role of ambassador to the great, diverse world that lies in wait outside the family's small, protected enclosure, acting as conduits for new personalities, ideas, values, and information and as bridges linking the past, present, and future. Through this *ex*change and *inter*change, they insist that the family change, and prevent it from becoming stale, redundant, or obsolete.

As we all know, however, their efforts to spur their family's evolution are not always easy to bear, and can make it quite difficult for us to see them as good enough. For example, the profound changes in teens' physical and cognitive development often create concomitant changes in their moods, which may make for kaleidoscopic displays of enthusiastic exhilaration, gloomy lethargy, affectionate attentiveness, surly defiance, mulish stubbornness, compassionate idealism, and searing cynicism, all within the space of a few hours, and without any observable triggers.

Their developmentally appropriate thirst for autonomy and their hunger for new experiences will lead them to try out their wings in ways that are likely to uncomfortably jostle and jolt their parents' values—experimenting with drugs and sex, rejecting long-standing religious practices, espousing extreme political positions, adopting alien (to the family) manners and customs. They will focus great energy on trying to outmaneuver parental authority—highlighting inconsistencies, exposing hypocrisy, exploiting differences of opinion between their mothers and fathers, or between parents and stepparents, and dexterously dancing their way around the rules and limits that are supposed to be adhered to. Immature and inexperienced as they may be, they are still mercenaries, motivated to do whatever it takes to get whatever it is that they want.

At the same time, they need us to remain in charge, and experience waves of anxiety and panic if they're unsure that we will be there, as a consistent rudder, to guide them through the turbulence of adolescence. So their testing of our limits is also a way to calculate with more precision than ever before the firmness of the very family foundation that they are planning to launch from. And if it doesn't feel firm enough, they'll continue to push us in an effort to awaken us from our torpor, unify us with other adults, and rouse all of us into collective and effective leadership. Whatever the reasons behind this incessant assault on parental command, however, rare is the parent who can always tolerate it with equanimity.

To complicate matters, teenagers are constantly experiencing tremendous ambivalence about how independent or dependent they want to be. On the one hand they talk big and boast about their capacity and desire to make it on their own; but they are still prone to feeling insecure and anxious, and often remind us of their remaining dependency. Every spring, for example, my office is filled with very successful high school seniors who have completed their academic requirements and made realistic plans to proceed with their lives after graduation, but who have suddenly gotten very busy engineering extremely inventive ways of announcing that they still need a mom and a dad, despite their apparent readiness to leave home. The out-of-the-blue drinking binge, the unprecedented $200 speeding ticket, the perpetual cough, the unanticipated credit card bill, the chronic headaches and stomachaches, the steadfast refusal to actually choose a college to attend—all of these speak to young adults' ambivalence about releasing themselves from the ties that bind, the very same ties that they have probably spent the last several years straining against.

There are many other irritants, as well. It's hard to see teenagers as good enough when they're busy insisting, as most of them do, that they don't *have* it good enough. No matter how frequently we attempt to remind them how wonderful their lives are compared with ours when we were their age, or with "others less fortunate than us"—we only had three television channels to choose from, we weren't allowed to date until we were 16, we had to work 20 hours a week to pay for our car insurance, not everyone has the money to send their child to private school, etc.—they will insist that their existence "sucks," and, worse, that we don't understand how hard they've got it.

Adolescents also tend not to see themselves as responsible for their own difficulties. It's usually "someone else's fault" when something goes wrong, and most teens will find it infinitely preferable to assign blame than to assume accountability. Their rationalizations and explanations often border on the banal, or even on the bizarre—"The teacher didn't ask for the homework, so how was I supposed to know to turn it in?" "The manager never called me to give me my schedule, so how was I supposed to know that he wanted me to work last night?" "Someone must have left the bong on the back seat of the car. How was I supposed to know that it was there?" These excuses aren't likely to stir deep feelings of empathy and compassion.

And one final obstacle on the road to seeing our teenagers as good enough is their belief that they always know best, and that we have nothing to offer them based on our years of hard-earned wisdom and experience. They refuse to ask for help—or they actively *reject* our help—because it reminds them of their own vulnerability and dependence on us, which they do not, under any circumstances, want to be reminded of.

So all the lessons that we want so desperately to impart to them in an effort to help them succeed, or to at least avoid the same mistakes that we made—the importance of making long-term plans, the connection between work and achievement, the enduring value of good manners, the benefits of exercise or good nutrition or meditation—are summarily dismissed as they felicitously forge ahead with an abiding belief in the redeeming quality of their own, homegrown *weltanschauung*.

As I noted in the beginning of this chapter, however, it is not possible to separate adolescents from the environment in which their adolescence evolves. The family does not comprise a passive passageway through which the teen's travels unfold; on the contrary, it influences and is influenced by those travels. Here are some additional observations about this nodal stage in family life that will help us to make sense of it.

1. Adolescents are in a state of mourning.

> Come, dear children, let us away;
> Down and away below!
> —MATTHEW ARNOLD

To complete the work of adolescence, and to move successfully forward into adulthood, teens must *mourn* for their childhoods. What this means is that they have to begin to separate from and bid farewell to those aspects of being a child that stand in the way of their becoming autonomous, while venerating and preserving those aspects of being a child that may continue to serve them during their developmental voyage.

We often see adolescents "getting" a lot, and feel some understandable resentment about their sense of entitlement, while not always understanding what they are giving up. But every adolescent has to come to terms with certain hard realities, which include:

- Understanding that her parents are not all-powerful and all-knowing

- Experiencing the existential reality of mortality and aloneness—that she came into the world alone and will one day depart it alone, as well

- Giving up her belief in her omnipotence, her ability to control her world and everything about it

- Diminishing her narcissism, her sense that the world exists just for her and revolves around her

- Realizing that misfortunes that befall others can happen to her, too

- Comprehending that privileges are accompanied by responsibilities

- Perceiving that the rules that apply to others also apply to her

- Acknowledging that while she may be unique, she's also ordinary

- Accepting the reality that she won't always be protected, rescued, or taken care of by someone else

The process of mourning—no matter what or who we are mourning for—always entails considerable feelings of loss, longing, and heartbreak, yet unless it is embarked upon and completed, we consign ourselves to living in the past and prevent ourselves from defining and entering the future.

What makes the adolescent's grieving process so complicated is that she is usually not even aware that she *is* grieving, nor does she have more than a fleeting, dim awareness of what she might be grieving for—at least not right away. The "no longer" of childhood and the "yet to be" of adulthood appear as vague, dream-like visions, and she remains torn between who she once was and who she is about to become without any clear-cut notions of how to create a portal that leads from one to the other.

It hasn't yet occurred to her that she does not have to completely sever and obliterate the bonds with her parents to become her own person. It hasn't yet occurred to her that she can choose to preserve what has been valuable from her youth while releasing herself from what has not been, that she can *transform* her experiences—however difficult and disabling—into something wonderfully new and unique. It hasn't yet occurred to her that she can retain some weakness, some incapacity, some dependence, while still becoming strong, capable, and self-reliant. It hasn't yet occurred to her that there might be a way to be true and loyal both to her family and to herself, and that her departure from childhood is not a betrayal of those who love her.

So she remains in a netherworld, a mourner without any guidelines for her grief, desperately trying to find a resting place for that which must be left behind. Yet one of the things that I regularly find so moving about my adolescent patients is the instinctive ways they engage in this mourning process.

After all, what color do many adolescents gravitate toward? Black, the very color that mourners in many different cultural and religious traditions are expected to wear. What about the self-harming that many teens liberally engage in, the piercing and tattooing and carving that so trouble and offend us? Anthropologists will tell you that self-scarification rituals are an important component of adolescent rites of passage in numerous cultures. This is what Mircea Elide meant when she observed, "We are what we display." The adolescent's soul is invisibly etched, and her body is literally etched with signs of the struggle to relinquish herself from her own childhood.

How about the strong tendency on teens' part to turn to drugs and alcohol? Interestingly, so many of the adolescents that I work with who become chemically dependent report that it helps them to "numb the pain." My belief is that this pain they're referring to is, much more often than not, the pain of mourning, of taking leave of their past.

And what about their preoccupation with death, their gravitation toward that which speaks of morbidity and mortality? Often, when I hear adolescents talking suicidally, what they appear to be addressing is not a desire to end their lives but an acknowledgment of the part of their life that has already ended—their childhood. Helping teens to understand the basis for this death grip is crucial to their learning how to loosen its hold on them.

Much about the unique universe that adolescents conjure for themselves—their music, their dance, their language, their clothing, their adornment, their customs—is designed to help them with this mourning process, to soften the loneliness and pain inherent in their departure from childhood as they prepare for a new and different life.

2. Parents are in a state of mourning, too.

> Look in my face; my name is Might-have-been;
> I am also called No-more, Too-late, Farewell.
> DANTE GABRIEL ROSSETTI

Because adolescence happens not just to one family member but to all family members, it follows that the parents of the teen must mourn as well. And what do we mourn for? Mostly, what our child's adolescence and prospective departure signals for us is our mortality—their development as young adults nudges us further along the life continuum and forces us to leave and grieve for our youth and the stage in our adult life—raising children—when we felt most necessary, most relevant, and most idealized. I have often observed, both in my practice and in my family, that adolescents complete us, but in both senses of the word—they fulfill us but they also finish us off and send us away.

Usually our children are hitting adolescence as we're hitting midlife, the point at which we start measuring our lives in terms of how much longer we have to live and whether we'll be able to accomplish what we want to accomplish in what feels like the rapidly shrinking time that is allotted to us. During this stage we are prone to feelings of disenchantment, stalemate, and upheaval in any of the arenas that are important to us—work, marriage, parenthood, family of origin. As Wallace Stegner wrote, "We were going to leave our mark on life, but instead life left its marks on us."

Knowing that this may be the last chance to make significant alterations in our lives—our world whittled quickly down to now or never—we scrutinize the choices we have made and often find ourselves succumbing to the elegiac undertow of doubt and regret as we review our life and consider the roads we traveled and neglected, the doors we opened and closed, the possibilities squandered and dreams deferred or abandoned altogether.

To top it off, we may also be dealing with medical concerns, our own aging parents, and perhaps even a beloved pet or two who are on their last legs, all of which further contribute to our feelings of weariness, pessimism, and desolation.

All of this becomes juxtaposed with the seemingly infinite possibilities, the ever-expanding vistas, that are opening up for our teenager, whose ebullience, hope, and optimism contrast with our shopworn feelings of disappointment and defeat. We long for their vanishing adoration as they nonchalantly knock us from our pedestal with a callous disregard for all that we have given them and blithely march ahead with their lives, pursuing the very promises and aspirations that have remained elusive and unfulfilled for us.

Because of this collision of symmetrical transitions—our child's through adolescence and our own through midlife—we may find ourselves in shock, staring into the dusty ruins and disturbing regions of our weakened spirit while experiencing tremendous turmoil. Sometimes this turmoil is expressed through psychological or physical symptoms—increases in depression and anxiety, decreases in energy and libido, psychosomatic complaints, insomnia, and chronic pain, to name a few. Sometimes it drives us to make abrupt or radical changes in our lives—a job change, a move, a separation or divorce, an affair—that we may or may not find rewarding.

Sometimes it leads us to deal with our teens in counterproductive ways—taking their criticism or rejection personally and responding in kind, diminishing or tainting their success because it rubs against the raw skin of our own fading hopes and failed endeavors, competing with them at tasks and challenges when what they really need is our support, not our rivalry, insisting that they somehow rearrange themselves in ways that will ensure that we feel better about ourselves, wanting to control their lives as a substitute for the loss of control over our own lives, preempting them in an effort to maintain our own diminished self-esteem, or turning them into mere props in our personal dramatic productions.

The impending loss of our child is not as comprehensible or as concrete as other losses that we have encountered or may encounter, but because of its complexity and the ways in which it cuts across our lives, it is always one of the hardest to grieve for, understand, and endure.

3. How parents understand and accept their adolescents is the strongest influence on how adolescents understand and accept themselves.

Informed parents are deluged with research on all of the various internal and external forces that affect teens—their temperament, their peer group, their neuroendocrine system, their socioeconomic status, their high school schedule, their exposure to the mass media, and many others. But in my experience the most profound influence on adolescents is the psychosocial family environment that their parents have created for them.

This is not to say that mothers and fathers are completely in control of their teenagers' values, choices, and actions; nor is it completely their fault if things go awry for a time. After all, raising a child is a bit like planting seeds: if you've got tomato seeds, you're going to grow tomatoes, no matter how much you might prefer cucumbers. But you can still have a tremendous and lasting impact on how rich and tasty your tomato crop becomes based on how effectively you nurture and tend it.

Benjamin, a senior in high school, was referred to me by his internist because of recurrent stomachaches. In my initial meeting, Benjamin told me that while he has been doing well in high school overall, he had a particular interest in the visual arts, especially sculpture. His eyes shone as he spoke about his work and the many artists and teachers who had influenced him.

When I asked his parents, both of whom were physicians,

what they envisioned for Benjamin as he prepared to graduate from high school, his father, Max, spoke in a deceptively benevolent tone: "Look, Benjamin is a wonderful young man, with a lot of talents, but he's almost eighteen now and almost done high school, so it's really his call. At this point in his life, whichever branch of medicine he chooses to go into is entirely up to him." I waited a moment for the smile that would signal that he was joking, but none was forthcoming, either from him or his wife. And when I looked at Benjamin, his earlier radiance had suddenly vanished, and he sat sullenly and slightly hunched over, as if he'd taken an imperceptible shot in the gut.

Despite his grouchy insistence that he "doesn't care" what we think of him, an adolescent's parents remain the most luminescent mirrors in which he views himself. If what he sees reflected back is darkly disappointed, condemning, restrictive, or judgmental, then that will become the basis for his self-image and, to some extent, the basis for his image of others, as well. On the other hand, when what he sees reflected back is a certain measure of optimistic, open-hearted, accepting glow, he will not only bask in that glow but in turn find ways to direct it toward others.

4. Adolescents always worry about their families.

All healthy teenagers dream about leaving home, usually with a mixture of excitement and trepidation, but their ultimate fantasy can come to fruition only if they are able to leave home knowing that the remaining family will remain intact. Adolescents who are having difficulty making their way toward self-reliant adulthood are invariably struggling not just with their own fears about independence but with the impact of their burgeoning independence on those who will be left behind.

Having served long stints in appointed positions that may have ranged from lightning rod to circuit breaker, from mediator to cheerleader, from stabilizing anchor to court jester, they will find dozens of imaginative methods of slowing, sabotaging, or sacrificing their development if they have the sense that one or more family members may not adapt well to their resignation and departure, or that no one else is going to pick up the slack. As one 18-year-old patient of mine stoically commented, after having decided to forego a scholarship opportunity at an out-of-state college in order to live at home and keep a closer watch on his disintegrating family, "It's hard to leave all these hurting people behind."

So one teen may underachieve at school because she's concerned that her parents' marriage will collapse without her there to play the peacemaking role that she has been devotedly performing for almost two decades. Another teen may turn to chemical dependencies to stall his development and eventual leave-taking because he is concerned that guys may take advantage of his younger sister unless Big Brother is there to protect her. Still another may become too psychosomatically ill to proceed with plans to go away to college because she is concerned that her divorced mother will succumb to depression and loneliness without her there to provide support and company.

Adolescents may often astonish us with their capacity for self-absorption and self-centeredness, but I have yet to meet the teenager who, under the surface, didn't worry about her family and try to find ways to put those worries to rest before she moved on.

5. Adolescent behavior does not occur in a vacuum.

None of us can see gravity, but we all know that gravity exists because we observe the results of its impact: apples fall from trees, moons orbit planets, running uphill is physically harder than running downhill. Likewise, in a family, there are unseen forces that affect the behavior of its members, forces that may not be directly visible, but can be detected nonetheless through the results of their impact. Family therapists talk about a family *system* because it is only through looking at the family systemically that we can begin to understand the often mystifying ways in which its forces appear. In a system, the way in which individuals act is never solely internally based, but is always an outcome of reciprocal interactions between individuals.

For example, 15-year-old Jonathan complains that his parents are too controlling when it comes to his social life. It galls him that they want to know where he'll be and who he'll be with, and that he's to call them with an update every couple of hours, or leave his cell phone on so that they can contact him. What he isn't acknowl-edging is not just that his parents have a right to this information, but that his proven tendency to come home after curfew, to leave one friend's house and go to another's without telling them, and to not answer his cell phone when they do try to reach him, elicits in his parents the very rule making that he finds so asphyxiating.

Jonathan's parents, meanwhile, justify these rules based on his history of not having been responsible when he goes out. How-ever, they try to control so many aspects of his life that it's not surprising that, at the age of 15, he has begun to try to break free of their stifling authority. For example, even though he's already in tenth grade they still go over his homework with him every night, attempt to dictate what courses he should be taking in high school, prevent him from getting the part-time job that he wants because "school should be his only priority," and insist that he spend his high school summers working at a camp that he's been attending since he was 8, even though he would rather try some-thing different. What they're not acknowledging is that their overcontrolling behavior is engendering the defiant, underrespon-sible behaviors that they find so troublesome.

So the more Jonathan rebels, the more his parents try to con-trol him, and the more they try to control him, the more he rebels. Each thinks the other started it, and each member of the system then confidently blames the other without taking responsibility for change by examining his or her own contribution to the system within which this cycle of mutually alienating behaviors occurs.

The more we can see both our teen's and our own behavior as circular rather than linear, as a self-feeding chain reaction rather than as simple cause-and-effect, the better able we will be to un-derstand and, when necessary, reconfigure the family's behavioral patterns.

6. Development always occurs in (at least) a three-generational context.

Although the reciprocity that we have just been examining takes place within a two-generational context, it's also important, in order to gain a fuller picture of adolescent functioning, to look at a multigenerational context as well. Our parental behavior has much of its genesis in the ways in which we were parented, and the ways in which we still relate to our parents, in reality or symbolically (if they are deceased). After years of study and clinical observation, I have come to believe that childrearing and child development always take place in the echo chamber that houses the sympathetic resonance between teens, their parents, and their grandparents.

To give an example, in a family that recently consulted with me I gradually unearthed a close linkage between the presenting problem, a 16-year-old's "unwanted" pregnancy, and, among other developments, her grandfather's retirement two months before. In a condensed version, here's how this came about.

Beth, the identified patient, had had a very warm and close relationship with her father, Miles, over the years. But when she moved into puberty and began to mature both physically and socially, she naturally wanted less to do with her father and more to do with her peer group. She began dating a classmate, Stuart, and the two of them became quite serious.

Miles was hurt and angered by this development, which he experienced as an abandonment. He responded by becoming critical of Beth and Stuart's relationship and tried to maim it by putting Stuart down within Beth's earshot and imposing somewhat draconian limits on their freedom to be together, such as insisting that Beth be home by 10 P.M. on weekends.

His other response was to turn to his wife, Cathy, and attempt to suddenly breathe life into their long-dormant sex life. Cathy, at this point, was totally unprepared for and uninterested in his pursuit after years of infrequent and unsatisfying contact, and retreated uneasily from his advances.

Meanwhile, Cathy's father had recently retired from the postal service, and it was discovered, during his final physical examination, that he had treatable prostate cancer. The combination of the loss of his job and the diagnosis of cancer precipitated a grave depression, however, and he began drinking heavily and refusing to shower, eat, or leave the house.

Cathy's mother had, for years, been in the habit of calling Cathy daily and was quite dependent on her emotionally. Miles was of the opinion, in fact, that Cathy was more devoted to her mother than she was to him. Now the situation worsened, as Cathy's mother was calling her four and five times a day, worried about and suffocated by her drunk and depressed husband and constantly pleading for help, support, and advice.

Feeling sandwiched by the demands of her fragile husband, her overwhelmed mother, and her enfeebled father, Cathy tried to backpedal away from this emotional clutter by throwing herself into her work. As an accountant in the midst of tax season, this wasn't difficult to do.

Meanwhile Miles, feeling rebuffed by both his daughter and his wife, consoled himself with late-night assignations on the Internet, which led to the beginning of a clumsy and ultimately disastrous affair with a woman little more than half his age, who wound up calling Cathy and telling her all about her liaison with Miles. This naturally enraged Cathy, who punished her husband by shutting him out to an even greater extent than before.

Sensing the increase in tension between her parents but not understanding its basis, Beth felt more and more estranged from her family. Unable to tolerate the stony silences between her mother and father when she was home, she began spending even more time out with her boyfriend than before, ignoring the curfews that her father continued to futilely mandate.

Knowing she was getting in over her head, but afraid to further burden her already overburdened mother, and angry at her father for betraying her with his unmistakable efforts to impair her first important romance, she was much more vulnerable to her boyfriend's pressure to move their relationship into the sexual realm, hoping to experience with him the closeness that she no longer felt with her family. (To complicate matters, her boyfriend's parents had recently divorced, so he, too, was beset by fear and loneliness and longing for any kind of closeness he could find.)

So it was only a matter of time before Beth returned from the county health department with the news that she was pregnant, her unmistakable way of hoisting the danger flags that served the function of trying to get the family back on track.

Is it possible that this same scenario could have occurred if there hadn't been turbulence in the parental and grandparental generations? I suppose so, but in my experience, it's unlikely. While the problems that adolescents present are notoriously multidetermined, examining them through a multigenerational view-finder will invariably yield useful information.

7. Adolescents project their internal battles onto and into us.

Adolescents constantly struggle with tremendously tumultuous internal battles. Tormented by the discomfort of their own lack of certitude, they seek to ease their distress by taking half of their doubts about a particular dilemma and assigning them to one or both of their parents. Then, they can settle down and comfortably slug it out with an unwitting mom or dad, a process that feels simpler and less disquieting than addressing the multifarious complexities and contradictions of young adult life.

One of my patients, 17-year-old Lizzie, had been invited to go to the beach for the day with two of her girlfriends who were about the same age. Her parents refused to support this adventure, feeling like the two-hour drive was too much for relatively inexperienced drivers. This led them into a protracted battle that they brought into my office.

"My friends' parents are letting them go. Why won't you?"

"Because we think you're too young to be going that far for that long without an adult present," her mother, Minna, calmly replied.

"But what could happen?" Lizzie insisted.

"*Anything* could happen, Lizzie. You'll be a hundred miles away from home, with all that goes on at the beach."

"Oh, come on, Mother. What do you mean by 'all that goes on at the beach'? Do you think we're going to get raped or something?"

"I'm sure the three of you can take care of yourselves, but it just feels like too much," Lizzie's father chimed in. "But I'll give you another possibility. What if I drove the three of you down and just spent the day there, left you guys alone, and you checked in with me a couple of times? That way you'd get to spend the day at the beach with your friends, but someone would be there in case something happened. I'll even treat the three of you to dinner."

"Oh, Dad, that's ridiculous. What's the point of going if you're going to come along? It makes me feel like such a baby."

"Lizzie, we're trying to compromise here, but you're not

budging at all," Minna said, not sounding quite so calm anymore.

"Well, if you don't let me, I'll go anyway. I'll just sneak out early in the morning and meet up with them. You're not going to be able to stop me, you know," Lizzie said, daring her parents to take her on.

This is not an atypical argument between a teen and her parents. I hear debates like this dozens of times a week—and not always just in my office! What was notable, however, was that when I spent a few minutes with Lizzie privately, she was able to acknowledge some of her mixed feelings about her proposed adventure.

"Seems like you're pretty invested in this beach day you've got planned with your buddies," I ventured.

"It would be so neat if they'd just let me go. They're so overprotective, they don't let me do *anything*. They treat me like my twelve-year-old sister," she complained.

"Putting your parents' concerns to the side for a moment, does the trip make you nervous at all?"

"No, why should it?" she responded, a little too quickly, her eyes darting away from me.

"Well, it does sound like it would be a lot of fun, but it wouldn't be surprising if you were a little twitchy about it. Have you ever done anything like this before?"

"No. . . . I mean I've spent the day at the mall with friends, and my father dropped us off at a rock concert once . . . although that got a little weird."

"How so?"

"I guess I never told my parents about this, but there was a guy and a girl near me who were smoking pot or something, and all of a sudden the girl had like a seizure. And they had to call in an ambulance and take her away, and everybody was freaking out."

"That must have been pretty scary to watch."

Lizzie took a long time to answer. "Yeah. I mean it *really* freaked me out. But I couldn't tell my parents about it, because then they wouldn't let me go to any more concerts. I mean, they probably know that people use drugs there, but they wouldn't be very happy to hear that it was someone that I was right next to."

"Is there any more to the story that made you upset?"

Lizzie paused again, then gazed past me. "Yeah, actually there is. My friend Anne and I were smoking the same pot. Anne's one of the friends who's taking me to the beach. And we were really upset, because we thought maybe the pot was poisoned, and that we were going to get sick or die, just like this other girl."

"Tell me about Anne."

"Annie's great, but Annie's *wild*. I mean, she's done things that I wouldn't dream of doing. If my parents knew this they'd never let me hang around with her, which would be a drag, because she's really a good friend, we've been buds forever, since we were five. But she scares me sometimes, she really does."

"So maybe there's a part of you—perhaps a small part of you, but a part of you just the same—that's a little scared of another day with Anne when the last time you did something together it could have had some tragic consequences."

"Maybe you're right," Lizzie acknowledged, reluctantly.

In this case, it seemed to make more sense for Lizzie to dogmatically insist that she should be allowed to go to the beach, and then assign the counterargument to her parents, than to take into account her *own* counterargument about the trip and what might happen.

However, once she was able to let herself in on the possibility that she too had some mixed feelings about going, she was much more amenable to discussing it with her parents. They went back to the drawing board, and she agreed to have her father drive the three of them down. Of course, the other advantage to her projecting one-half of the conflict onto her parents is that she was able to save face with her friends. Rather than telling Anne that she was uncomfortable going, thus risking her friendship or appearing skittish, she was able to melodramatically roll her eyes and inform her, "I'd *love* to go, but my dumb parents won't let me." As it turns out, Anne didn't mind having someone else drive (particularly because her car didn't have air-conditioning, and Lizzie's father's car did!), and their revised adventure worked out fine.

8. Anger and fighting are necessary precursors to healthy separation.

While not every family with teenagers is beset by vicious or violent conflict, just about every family experiences frequent tussles,

often around issues that appear to be more mundane than profound. The fractious battles about everything from chores to curfews, from study habits to summer plans, fray everyone's nerves
and can get tiresome indeed.

However, these fights are usually a good sign, and they tend to
serve a healthy function. To me, they're kind of like manure—
unpleasant, but still a stimulant for growth. For one thing, fights
remind us how important we are to each other. After all, none of
us fight with someone that we feel indifferent toward or unattached to—we just ignore them or blow them off. Plus, it's usually through our fighting that we tend to expose and express our
inner thoughts and feelings in a more intense and less censored
way. In a marriage, for example, a couple may experience ho-hum
sex, but there really is no such thing as a ho-hum fight. So family
members always get to know each other more intimately through
the fights that erupt between them.

Fights also help to create the friction necessary to facilitate the
adolescent's departure—because when it comes to raising teenagers, conflict is really a sign that everyone in the family is doing
their developmental job well. Adolescents are fighting for their
separateness and autonomy, as they *should* be doing, and the parents are fighting to stay in control until they can become more
certain that their children can manage reasonably well on their
own, as *they* should be doing. Fights fuel the differentiation process that both generations have legitimate fears and concerns
about, and provide some of the motivation required to propel this
process forward despite these fears and concerns.

As I've told many frustrated parents, teens *defy* in order to *define* themselves. Just as a toddler's first word may be "No!" because it's the surest, most instinctive way he knows how to
construct the first, fragile boundary between him and his parents,
a teenager's "No!" is rarely rooted simply in stubborn opposi-
tion, but is part of a multifaceted effort to distinguish himself
from his family, to reassure himself and remind his parents that
he's a separate being who knows where his selfhood begins and
ends and how it can intersect and interact with others.

In fact, perhaps the most noteworthy lesson I've learned from
mediating thousands of family fights over the years is that the
most devastating conflicts are usually the result of our assiduous,

long-standing efforts to *avoid* conflict. Sometimes family fights can be hurtful and dangerous, and fighting is certainly not always the only or best way to resolve conflict. But those parents who can understand and frame age-appropriate squabbles as normal and acceptable are often less affected, and less afflicted, by them than parents who become apprehensive at the first sign of conflict. The view that the end point of conflict must be either bitterly "cold shoulders" or hazardous explosions, rather than self-awareness, resolution, and closeness, sets the stage for even more damaging combat down the road.

Parents of teens are faced with a paradoxical job. They must encourage their children to grow up while simultaneously strengthening the bonds that keep them close—promoting their "I-ness" along with their "we-ness." The family skirmishes that we would just as soon not have to deal with are actually one of our best ways of building the bridge between the "I" and the "we" so that our teenaged children can feel both separate and connected, both independent and interdependent, as they struggle toward healthy adulthood.

9. Adolescents understand everything that we're not saying.

Carl Jung once wrote that it is the "unlived life of the parent" that has the most influence on the child, and never is this more true than during adolescence. Teens have an unerring capacity to tune into the parts of their parents' lives that are least exposed, and, perhaps because of this, most crucial. They wound us where we're most vulnerable to being wounded. We may have tried desperately to hide certain unpalatable or unsavory aspects of ourselves both from others and from ourselves, but our son or daughter will always find a way to go below the family's protective radar and track these vulnerabilities down in a devoted effort to understand us and themselves better.

Marcelle, a single mom, met with me to discuss her concerns about her 15-year-old daughter's drug use. "Rebecca's been drinking, she's been using pot, I'm sure I don't even know half of what she's doing. Worst of all, it seems she's begun dealing, as well. Last week, in the back of her closet, I found a bunch of small plastic snack bags and a scale. What else could those be for?"

"How have you responded?" I inquired.

"Oh, I've tried to talk with her, and let her know how much trouble she could get into, all about the health risks—but it doesn't seem to make any difference. She doesn't want to hear it, and nothing seems to be changing."

In continuing our discussion, however, one of the things that became evident to me was that Marcelle, a sales rep for a pharmaceutical company, had become addicted to painkillers during her recovery from abdominal surgery the year before. Her narcotics habit, distressingly easy to maintain as a result of her job, was something that she had been struggling with and trying to hide from her daughter.

I wondered if Rebecca might not have picked up on what was going on and begun doing what many teenagers do, which is to act in ways that seem strange or worrisome to us because they're trying to bring something to light, something that's unacknowledged yet known just the same. Adolescents should never be underestimated. They may not always know the content of a secret, but they're usually aware that a secret is being kept, and it can make them a little nutsy. Sometimes they act provocatively in an effort to flush the secret into awareness so that at least they have a better handle on what's going on.

It was also noteworthy that both mother and daughter had not only become hooked on drugs but also become involved with drug dealing (Marcelle doing so legally, of course, while her daughter operated illegally). The more I got to know this family, the more I had the feeling that Rebecca's behavior was unconsciously directed toward trying to identify with her mother and getting them both to address their respective dependencies. And it was only when Marcelle finally began to acknowledge her drug problem, both to herself and to her daughter, and to take her recovery more seriously, that Rebecca's behavior began to improve.

Parents often complain that their teenagers don't listen to them, but often they are listening quite well. It's more that we don't necessarily enjoy or feel proud of the internal frequencies that they seem most interested in listening to.

Just as adolescents don't always respond to adolescence in the way that we would like them to, we parents have our flawed penchants and proclivities as well. When we're consumed by disappointment and feel disillusioned by our teens for any and all of the reasons noted above, we tend to react in one or more of the following self-defeating ways.

WE BECOME HYPERACTIVE

Sixteen-year-old Rosemarie, who was in the middle of her junior year in high school, was a fine student who had earned a 3.5 GPA and scored over 1200 on her SATs the first time she took them. She was also a talented artist, having worked diligently on the graphics for the school newspaper and yearbook since ninth grade, and participated in numerous summer art camps and programs. Her parents, Ginny and Aaron, felt that it was definitely time to begin preparing for the college application process, but Rosemarie wasn't quite as motivated as they were.

Ginny and Aaron adopted a "take the bull by the horns" approach, nonetheless. They scheduled her for two separate college fairs that were in the area during the next several months. They planned college trips both for spring break and for summer vacation. They arranged for her to meet with her guidance counselor at school and fill out a computer-generated profile that helps to match students with colleges that would meet their needs. They developed a filing system for all the unsolicited college brochures that arrived in the mail and responded for Rosemarie whenever a college e-mailed an inquiry or any information.

The more they did to lay the groundwork for college decision, the less Rosemarie did. In fact, the more they did, the more she appeared to circumvent their efforts. She overslept and missed the first of the college fairs, and begged out on the second one, saying that there was a yearbook deadline that required her to be at the school all day. She met with the guidance counselor and filled out the computerized profile, but seemed never to find the time to stop by and pick up the results. She showed no interest in the college materials that her parents so carefully filed for her, and while she went along with the college tours, she appeared bored and disinterested, lagging behind and never displaying any curiosity or interest.

Of course, the more Rosemarie resisted, the more Ginny and Aaron intensified their campaign. They hired a consultant who specializes in college searches to work with her, signed her up with an SAT tutor to raise her scores, and constantly asked her to sit down with them and discuss possibilities. By the time Rosemarie began her senior year, they were no further along, so it was two very exasperated parents and a blasé-looking daughter who entered my office for help.

The potential advantage of the hyperactive approach is that there is the recognition that a problem may exist, and there are conscientious efforts being made to solve the perceived problem. The potential disadvantage of the hyperactive approach is that sometimes the perceived problem isn't really a problem at all, and in fact becomes a problem only because it's being *treated* like a problem. In this case, for example, Rosemarie's parents, despite their good intentions, were actually making it less likely, rather than more likely, that their daughter was going to begin doing the necessary planning for life after high school, because they were inadvertently engendering her passive defiance.

WE BLAME OURSELVES

Fifteen-year-old Fred had dug himself into a deep hole. Suspended from school twice already during his tenth-grade year for aggressively threatening other students, he lost his temper in chemistry class when a classmate teased him about a girl who had recently dumped him. Enraged, he wound up breaking two of his tormentor's ribs by shoving a desk into him full-force, resulting in the victim's parents charging him with assault and the administration considering his expulsion from the public school system.

Surprisingly, however, Fred's father, Gerald, seemed angrier with himself than with Fred. "Fred's mom and I had a terrible marriage, and we finally decided to separate a couple of years ago," he explained patiently. "Of course, we get along just as poorly now that we're separated as we did when we were married. But poor Fred's borne the brunt of this, and I feel so awful for him. It's no wonder he gets into all of this trouble at school."

"You're correct in assuming that it's been a hard road for Fred, but are you saying that the difficulties between you and his mom excuse his violent behavior in school?" I asked.

"Not exactly," Gerald replied, tentatively. "It's just that who could blame him for being so angry? He's just heard argument after argument between us over the years. Even now, my ex- and I still wind up saying nasty things to each other, often in front of him and his brothers, and I'm sure it's taken a toll on him. We tried to spare the kids, but apparently we weren't very successful."

"But you're still leaving out the possibility that Fred might have to learn to regulate his behavior *despite* having to continue to witness a conflictual relationship between his parents."

"How's he supposed to learn when we really haven't done our jobs?" Gerald pleaded. "We just haven't given him the tools that he needs to work with."

The potential advantage of the self-blaming approach is that it does acknowledge that actions do not occur in a vacuum, and that how parents and others behave has an impact on how teens behave. The potential disadvantage is that it takes the onus of responsibility off the adolescent, thus diminishing the odds that he's ever going to develop the resources necessary to move ahead with his life successfully, no matter what his parents have or haven't done.

WE BLAME OTHERS

Tawonda, a 14-year-old ninth grader, had been given an alcohol citation and was suspended from school for forty-five days when a police officer caught her and some friends passing around a bottle of rum in the school parking lot during the homecoming dance. Her mother, Monique, was incensed, but, surprisingly, not at her daughter.

"I don't know why she got the same penalty that her friends got when she wasn't even drinking," she complained to me, initially.

"Well, she may or may not have been drinking, but as you've learned, even if you're in the vicinity of alcohol on school grounds, the citation and the suspension are invoked."

"But a *forty-five-day* suspension?!?" Monique hissed. "What purpose does *that* serve? I don't know how she'll keep up in her classes, and she won't even be allowed to attend basketball practices, which hurts her *and* the team. It all seems ridiculous to me."

"You're free to appeal the suspension," I commented, "but you don't seem to be addressing the reason that you're in my office, which is that Tawonda was involved—perhaps indirectly, but involved nonetheless—with alcohol consumption when she's only fourteen years old."

"Well, that's ridiculous, too. She says she wasn't even drinking. One of her friends, Lisa, brought it along, just to show off. If Lisa hadn't have been such a fool, Tawonda wouldn't be in this mess."

"What do you believe that Tawonda should have done once Lisa showed up with the bottle of rum?" I asked.

"What's she supposed to do? I was proud of her for not drinking. It's not her fault that the cops came and rounded everyone up like common criminals. My daughter's a good student, a good athlete—she's no alcoholic and she's no troublemaker. It bothers me that they're all treated the same when they didn't act the same."

The potential advantage of the blame-others approach is that there is some loyalty toward and defense of our child—she's not being singled out, ganged up on, or ostracized. The potential disadvantage of this approach, as with the self-blaming approach, is that the teen doesn't learn to take responsibility for her own questionable behavior and modify it so that it becomes more acceptable.

WE BLAME THE CHILD

Desson, a high school freshman, seemed to be watching helplessly as his grades plummeted from the A's and B's he had earned in middle school to C's and D's.

"I study, I really do," he told me, his eyes moist and his cheeks reddening. "But I just don't seem to get it. I'm spending more time studying than any of my friends, and they're still getting better grades than I am."

"If you're so busy studying, then why are you failing tests?" his father, Wade, angrily inquired.

"That's just the thing, I don't *know* why I'm failing! I read my American government chapters over and over last weekend, looked at the worksheets, went over my quizzes—and I *still* got a D."

"Well, that's just inexcusable, son," Wade continued, disgustedly. "You must not be studying. Maybe we ought to take that computer out of your room, maybe that would help. Or maybe you shouldn't be wrestling anymore. Hell, at this rate, you're probably not even going to be allowed on the team anymore, your grades are so low."

"Has Desson ever had an evaluation that might help us to know more about his learning style, his strengths and weaknesses?" I asked.

"You mean testing? We did ask about that when we saw how much he's been struggling, but the school said that his grades weren't really low enough for him to qualify for testing," Desson's mother answered.

"Would you consider going outside of the school system so that we have a better assessment of his cognitive abilities and what strategies he might use to capitalize on his abilities?"

"What, spend *more* money to figure out that he's got to work harder if he's going to do well?" Wade jumped in. "There's no substitute for hard work, that's really the answer. I don't need to pay someone big bucks to tell me that my son is lazy."

"You're right, there isn't any substitute for hard work. But Desson seems to feel that he's already working hard, but without the results that he, and all of you, would like to see. Maybe if we learned a little more about how his mind works, we could teach him some ways to work not just harder but smarter. He wouldn't be this upset about things if he were lazy. And he certainly couldn't put up with wrestling practices if he were lazy, either."

"Frankly, I think this is all a waste of time," Wade insisted. "To get A results, you've got to give A effort. And my son is just not giving A effort."

The advantage of the child-blaming approach is that we absolve ourselves of any misplaced or exaggerated guilt or responsibility for the presenting problem. The disadvantage is that we severely diminish our child's self-worth when we attribute his failures solely to a fundamental and ineradicable defect in his character.

WE DISTANCE OURSELVES

Thirteen-year-old Alan seemed to worry about everything. He worried about his grades in school, about his health, even about his *friends'* health. He fretted about political conflicts, global warming, and the possibility that tornadoes and hurricanes would annihilate his community.

His mother, Annette, had great difficulty dealing with his constant anxiety. "It's always something with Alan, always something. As soon as he walks in the house he's busy reporting all of the dire events that have occurred—a classmate almost choked in the cafeteria, his science teacher said that the rain forests will have disappeared in another fifty years, and he thinks that he failed his math test. I don't think he's ever failed a math test. In fact, I don't believe he's ever gotten anything below a C on a math test! But it's just one thing after another, a litany of worries."

"How do you respond to him when he's like that?"

"First of all, he's always like that, it's not just now and then— that's what's so difficult. Second of all, there really is no good response. Nothing I say seems to make him worry less. God knows I've tried. I've begged him not to worry so much, I've tried to point out that the things he worries about are unlikely to happen. But it never seems to change things."

"So if nothing seems to be working, how have you been handling things?"

Annette thought for a moment, then commented, "I guess I've basically just given up. I don't even listen anymore, really. I kind of just tune him out."

"And how does he handle your tuning out?"

She paused again, then chuckled softly. "I guess I'm so tuned out, I don't even notice how he reacts to my tuning out. I really

can't remember the last time we had a meaningful conversation
with each other. It's so much easier to talk with his sister that I
think I just direct everything to her. Even *she* ignores him, at this
point, he's such a bundle of nerves."

The potential advantage of the distancing approach is that the
teen does not have to bear the unbroken brunt of parental anger
or criticism. The potential disadvantage is that the child feels as if
his parents have given up on him, that he's no longer worthy of
their efforts and initiatives. And when children no longer believe
that their parents have faith in them, it becomes easy for them to
lose faith in themselves.

WE USE DENIAL

Fourteen-year-old Denise was caught sneaking back into her
mother's house at 2:30 A.M. through a window in the basement.
Confronted by her mom, Fran, a single parent, Denise said that
she had just wanted to "get some fresh air and look up at the
stars." Satisfied, and not curious as to why she didn't simply depart and return through the back door, Fran let it go.

The next week, she received a call from the mother of one of
Denise's girlfriends who said that she had learned that when
Denise was sleeping over at their house that weekend, she had left
the house without permission in the middle of the night and had
inadvertently locked herself out. She had found Denise in the
morning, huddled under a blanket on the deck.

Only two weeks later, Fran awoke to the sound of murmuring
downstairs and discovered Denise and a boy Fran had never seen
before entwined on a couch in the basement, half-dressed. In
shock, she sent the boy packing, grounded Denise, and scheduled
an appointment with me.

"I'm not exactly sure what's going on here, but I'm starting
to get worried," Fran concluded, after filling me in on Denise's
escapades.

"Well, it sounds like you know pretty much *exactly* what's
going on here, and that you have good reason to be worried," I
remarked.

"But I don't understand it. I can't believe she's involved with a guy. She's only fourteen! When I was fourteen, I wasn't even dating!"

"To what extent have you spoken with her about sexuality and responsibility?"

"We've had the birds-and-bees talk, if that's what you mean. She's already had her period for a couple of years, and she knows all about that. But she's always been kind of immature—still is, really—so I don't think there's any point in going into detail about sex and dating or anything when she's really not ready for that."

"What do you mean by immature?"

"You know—not very social, not very interested in guys, kind of silly and giggly, still."

"But that's really the problem with adolescent sexuality. They're maturing physically, but they're still immature emotionally. And that discrepancy between their physical and emotional maturity is why they sometimes take risks and make mistakes during this stage of life that can have enduring consequences."

"But I just don't think she's able to really understand a sexual relationship."

"She probably isn't. Which is exactly why it's important that you speak with her about it, so that she doesn't get caught up in one that she may have a hard time getting out of."

"I don't know, I don't think she's there, yet."

"Even though she's sneaking a guy into your house in the middle of the night, and may be sneaking into his house as well?"

"She's my *baby,* she's only fourteen. . . ."

The advantage of denial is that you don't have to deal with your discomfort about whatever it is that is making you uncomfortable, and you don't overreact to a problem, unintentionally making it worse through your reactivity. The disadvantage of denial is that you are incapable of meeting your child's needs if you are unable to see clearly what she is contending with and join with her in addressing it.

So with all of the changes that are occurring within adolescents and their families, and with all of the problematic parenting tendencies that we are all unavoidably vulnerable to, is it any wonder that viewing our teenager as Good Enough seems like a Sisyphean endeavor, unlikely to ever be attained? Fortunately, there are numerous approaches, maneuvers, and tactics that can make this endeavor more feasible. Let's continue the process of creating the Good Enough Teen by examining some of them more closely.

TWO

UNCOVERING

What lies behind us and what lies before us are tiny matters compared to what lies within us.

—RALPH WALDO EMERSON

Odd as this may sound, the parents that I see in my practice, both mothers and fathers, have already given birth twice to each of their children. And the job that I immediately set out to do from the moment that they make contact with me, whether they know it or not, is to discover the ways in which I can be a psychological midwife for a third birth.

The first birth is the birth of the fantasy teen. The fantasy teen is the adolescent of our wildest imaginings, the one who gratifies our most cherished wishes, who fulfills our most dearly held dreams, who effortlessly meets all of our expectations, who makes us feel warm and whole, soulful and complete. We begin this initial birthing process well before we actually become parents, well before we even become adults.

Because even when we were children, we were devising a vision of ourselves as the perfect parent of a perfect child. When we were playing with dolls or action figures, we were not only trying to address important issues and work out troubling conflicts, we were also laying the groundwork for the kind of relationship that we would one day have with our own children. When we stroked a soft blanket, we were not only receiving comfort, but offering it as well, rehearsing the habits of nurturance that we would one day bring to our spouse and offspring.

And when we were adolescents and young adults, one of the things that helped us through this turbulent time was our insistent vow that we were going to be a different parent to our own teenager than our parents were with us. In creating this idealized parent-teen relationship, we helped ourselves to navigate the white waters of puberty, when our mental, physical, and emotional lives felt so churned up.

So, internally, we all have spent years imagining the blissful connection that was certain to emerge and sustain us when we had children of our own. We pictured our teen as the studious, thoughtful scholar, or the attractive athlete, or the creative, accomplished *artiste*, or the crusading, courageous activist, or simply the affable, kindhearted friend—the adolescent that we were, that we imagined we were, or that we (or our parents) wished that we had been.

The gestation that precedes the birth of the fantasy child lasts our entire lives up until the very moment that we become a mother or father, through birth, adoption, remarriage, or foster care. At this point, we experience the second birth, the birth of the actual flesh-and-blood child.

This child is no longer an inhabitant of our treasured dreams and fantasies. In fact, she is destined to disappoint us, usually many times, at various points along her developmental spectrum. Sometimes this disappointment occurred during pregnancy: she did not grow robustly enough to put our obstetrician's, or our own, concerns to rest, or prenatal evaluations indicated the possibility of a physical defect. Sometimes disillusionment happened right at birth: the baby's gender did not conform to our wish, or there was indeed a congenital abnormality that altered her appearance or abilities or threatened her health or her future.

Sometimes our discontent emerged during her first weeks or months: she refused to nurse well and required bottle feeding, or she didn't return smiles or babble happily like the other babies in our playgroup, or she squalled incessantly whenever she was put down. Or our displeasure arose during early childhood, when we noticed that she didn't like to be read to, or she got sassy with us and other adults, or she resisted interactions with anyone or anything other than her stuffed animals.

Once she began school, our potential for disenchantment may have multiplied: Why wasn't she invited to any birthday parties? Why wasn't she in the top reading group? Why was she so much heavier than everyone else? Why was she having so much trouble with math? How long would she have that annoying twitch? How come she never liked her teachers, and vice versa? Would she *ever* practice her violin without a fight?

But if, by some miraculous dispensation, we have been spared the experience of these feelings of disappointment and disillusionment with our child prior to adolescence, I can guarantee you that they will find fertile ground in which to take root and flourish once she hits puberty. She may pierce body parts that you didn't believe could be pierced, or use absolutely clownish logic in her efforts to convince you to let her stay by herself for the weekend while you go away, or slavishly commit herself to a punk-rock aesthetic, or cut essential classes, underprepare for her SATs, date complete yo-yo's, quit her perfectly fine job before she's embarked on finding another one. Somehow, one way or another, she will find a way to arrange for the fantasy child's gruesome death, bury her, and then dance deliriously on the grave, declaring that she is the sole victor, the survivor, the one that you must now contend with.

In fact, parents' disappointment during their children's adolescence is so common and so appropriate that if you continue to feel perpetually pleased with her during this stage, it's not because she or you are so terrific, but because she doesn't see you as strong and competent enough to handle her flaws and imperfections, or because you're not involved or attentive enough to notice the fact that she's essentially selling her youthful soul in her desperate desire to please you and keep your fantasy alive.

So with these two births—the birth of the fantasy teen and the birth of the actual teen—having occurred, where does that leave us? As I said, my job is to promote a third birth, and that is the birth of the Good Enough Teen. The Good Enough Teen is a synthesis of the fantasy child and the actual child, and draws from both our dreams and our reality.

When I present the notion of a Good Enough Teen, I am not

talking about *resigning* yourself to or *settling* for the adolescent that you have while still secretly wishing that she was your perfect niece or your college roommate's enchanting daughter or your daughter's multi-talented best friend. It means gratefully accepting your child for being exactly who she is, with all her strengths and weaknesses, all her assets and liabilities, all her flaws and contradictions and inconsistencies.

It means seeing her with new and loving eyes as an individual who exists for reasons other than to please or gratify you, an individual who can be loved and accepted for being who she is, not for doing what she does, an individual who has a destiny that is all her own, one that can be meaningful and successful and satisfying even if it doesn't exactly follow the blueprint that you have so carefully drawn up for her.

So how do we make this journey from the first birth to the third? How do we relinquish the fantasy teen, come to terms with the actual teen, and finally bring forth into our world the Good Enough Teen?

In my practice, ferrying family after family across these familiar yet tempestuous waters, I have found that there are five stages along the way, a discussion of which constitutes the essence of this book.

1. *Uncovering* the origin of your expectations for your child, the source of what you anticipate for them

2. *Acknowledging* the ways in which you contribute to the creation of the very behaviors, attitudes, and outlooks that so trouble and disappoint you

3. *Understanding* that what you identify as your teen's problems are actually his *solutions* to his problems

4. *Forgiving* your adolescent for not having fulfilled the impossible expectations that you have laden him with

5. *Changing* how you respond to your teen so that both you and he can see and fully accept him as Good Enough

What I have seen time and time again is that the parents who are able to work their way through these five stages inevitably experience a tremendous sense of liberation, joy, and relief. It is as if they have finally commuted a self-imposed life sentence and released themselves and their families from a prison of their own making. What felt impossible now begins to seem achievable, what felt oppressive now begins to seem bearable, what felt ossified now begins to seem malleable.

As one mother said to me at the end of treatment, "It's as if my husband and I were these frozen parents of frozen children, all of us stuck here like big chunks of ice, unable to move or reach out to each other. And now it's like everything is thawing, and we can all flow together a little bit. I guess it's finally feeling like we're a family."

Let's continue by exploring the first stage, Uncovering, and taking a closer look at the origin of the expectations that we bring to parenthood.

I'm frequently both amused and intrigued when different families come to me with the same situation, but with completely different reactions to it. The discrepancies in their respective responses often reveal important insights about the nature of and basis for the designs that parents always have for their adolescents.

For example, the weeks during which high school students receive their SAT scores are always tense ones in my practice. Recently, two separate patients had earned almost identical scores, but the scores had elicited quite dissimilar reactions from their parents.

Carl Broadus, a 17-year-old senior in high school who had only recently prevailed through a frightful battle with leukemia, strode in and plopped down in his usual chair in my office before his parents, Tad and Anna, had even made their way from the waiting room. Eyes shining, he pulled a creased form from the pockets of his strategically torn jeans and held it aloft, announcing: "I broke 1100!" As his parents settled into their seats, he burbled forth happily about what this score meant to him: "My guidance counselor says that this means I'm basically a shoo-in for the college that I really want to go to. Plus, there's a scholarship sponsored by the American Cancer Society that I've got a shot at now that will pay for two years of tuition at the college of my choice if I can keep my grade point average above a 3.0. This *rocks!*"

Carl's parents were clearly delighted as well. "We're really tickled," Tad began. "I mean, when all of the other kids were busy taking SAT courses and getting tutored to get ready, Carl was busy getting chemotherapy. Frankly, we're just so thrilled that he even got to the point of *taking* the SATs, let alone doing as well as he did."

Meanwhile, Anna was beaming. "He has a future now, what with college and all, and it's so amazing because a couple of years ago, when he was first diagnosed, we weren't sure what the future would hold—or even . . ." Her voice grew soft, and her eyes moist: "or even if he would have a future."

Carl got up out of his chair and went over to hug his mother, while his dad reached his hand over to hold hers. I felt a little lurch in my chest, and my eyes began to glisten as well.

"I think it's going to be okay, now, Mom," Carl said, pulling back from his hug. "I think it's going to be okay."

Having seen this family through such a terrible trial, and having witnessed their coming through it intact, I could not imagine being happier for them if they had been my own family.

So what an emotional contrast it was when, at the tail-end of that same afternoon, the Kurtz family, led by 16-year-old Douglas, soberly took their seats in my office.

"Douglas got his SAT scores back today," his father, Emmanuel, began drily. "Why don't you tell Dr. Sachs what you got?"

Douglas stared at the floor, expressionless. "Douglas, it's not the end of the world," his mother, Daniela, added, albeit not very convincingly.

Slowly lifting his eyes to meet mine, Douglas said, quietly, "1110—530 Verbal, 580 Math," and then lowered them back down. From the way in which he spoke, you would have thought that he was announcing that he had an incurable disease.

"This means we've got problems," Emmanuel stated flatly. "This means that those top-notch schools that he's been dreaming about are probably out of the question. This means we're talking about his going somewhere in-state and not earning much scholarship money. *That's* what this means."

"Honey, we don't know that yet, we really don't," Daniela

countered. "He can take them again, he's got a good, solid 3.0 GPA, and the SATs don't count for everything, you know."

"What I know is what I've seen," Emmanuel answered, irritably, "and what I've seen is that unless you are heading up into the 1400 or above range, with a 3.75 GPA, you can kiss those Ivy League schools good-bye. There's just too much competition. I think it's time for us to adjust our sights, rather than go after something that can't be gotten."

Meanwhile, Douglas continued his visual encounter with the carpet, completely still, except for one knee jiggling slowly up and down. It felt to me that this restless movement was the only sign of life he felt comfortable exposing.

Two young adults, the same gender, the same age, with almost the exact same scores on the same college preparatory exam. But with the Broaduses, there was an abiding and contagious sense of triumph and joy, while with the Kurtz family, I almost felt like I was attending the funeral that the Broaduses feared that they had been heading towards. Why?

The answer, of course, is that each family had very different sets of expectations for their adolescents. In one family, expectations were not only met but greatly exceeded, leading to a feeling of success. In the other, expectations were *un*met, leading to a feeling of failure.

Let's take a closer look at each of these families' histories to see what we can learn about how these expectations came about.

When the oncologist reported that Carl's bloodwork pointed to a diagnosis of leukemia, "It was like all of the air got sucked out of the room," Tad had told me during our first session. At the time, Carl was in the middle of ninth grade and hadn't been doing well in school or elsewhere.

"We knew something was the matter," he went on. "We just never thought it was going to be cancer. At worst, we thought maybe he had mono. But we felt so bad, because we were really getting on him. He wasn't staying on top of his schoolwork, and he had been a pretty good student, not great, but at least turning his work in and preparing for tests. Now he was tired and listless all the time and hadn't really hooked in to high school life in the way that we had hoped he would—no sports, no activities, no nothing."

"I think both of us felt very guilty," Anna admitted. "I mean, here we were, egging him on, egging him on, trying to light a fire under him, get him moving with his life, and then we find out he might not even *have* a life!"

The next couple of years were consumed with medical appointments, tests, evaluations, and treatments, including, eventually, a successful bone marrow transplant. "A living nightmare that I wouldn't wish on my worst enemy," Tad had said to me, shaking his head, innumerable times during those harrowing months.

But even when they were out of the woods medically, Carl was struggling to catch up. While the school had been very flexible when it came to providing missed work, and his parents had arranged for private tutoring during his hospitalizations, he had been absent for a tremendous amount of class time, and his energy level was still quite low.

"He used to be a big reader—sci-fi, fantasy, all that stuff—but for ninth and tenth grade, I don't think he picked up a book. It was all he could do to get to all of his doctors, take his medications, and try to keep up with his classwork."

Starting to feel a little better, he signed up for the PSATs at the beginning of his junior year but barely scored over 800. Nobody was surprised or upset with him, but Carl did admit to me that he was disappointed. "I know I've been sick and all, but the fact is, I'm intending to have a long life, and it'll be hard to get into the colleges I'd like to go to if I don't improve my scores, even if they know what I've been through."

With his energy slowly increasing, however, the family rehired the tutor that they had used when he was sick in order to help prepare him for the exam, and he gave himself plenty of time and worked steadily for the next year, studying vocabulary lists, working on math problems, and taking practice tests.

In the fall of senior year, he took his SATs and was thrilled to raise his score by almost 300 points. And his parents couldn't have been more proud.

"The thing is, and of course it's easy to say this now that we've hopefully gotten through the worst of this, the leukemia really forced Carl to grow up," Tad explained. "I mean, he was a good kid before, but he hadn't ever had to deal with anything difficult. He was an easygoing guy who didn't take anything too seriously, and once he had this life-and-death experience, life started to feel a little more precious."

"But it changed us too, Tad," Anna added. "You hate for something like this to happen to help you appreciate what you have, but the fact is, we *did* have a tendency to focus on Carl's weaknesses before he got sick. I would constantly complain to you about his being so messy around the house, leaving a trail of clothes and books and CDs wherever he went, and you were pretty impatient with his lack of involvement, his reluctance to try an activity or go out for a team."

"She's right," Tad recalled. "I did feel that Carl kept himself on the periphery more than he should have, and I was on his back plenty, trying to encourage him to do things when he was clearly content to just hang around with his friends, playing video games and watching TV.

"Now, the irony is that we've backed off of that stuff entirely, and he's taken charge of his own life more than he ever did when we were bugging him. *He* was the one who thought it would be a good idea to prepare more diligently for the SATs, *he* was the one who suggested we call Sharon, his former tutor, and of course *he* was the one who put in all of that time studying. Mostly, we just kind of sit back and marvel that he has a life, while he's gone ahead trying to do something with his life.

"Of course," he said with a wink toward Anna, "we still see the line of clothes, towels, books and CDs heading into his room, but even that is kind of a reminder that he's still with us, and hopefully will be for a long time. So we just kind of roll our eyes and look the other way now."

Tad and Anna's capacity to adjust their expectations as a result of the medical ordeal that they all had had to undergo not only enabled them to take pride in Carl's test scores, but, just as importantly, allowed Carl to take ownership of those scores so that he could feel some justifiable pride as well.

· · ·

Emmanuel Kurtz was a journalist who felt that others with less talent had been promoted ahead of him. "I know the quality of my work, but somehow, when editorial positions become available, I'm overlooked," he said angrily. "It's either some sort of latent racism"—the Kurtz family was African American—"or it's because I didn't go to one of the Cadillac journalism schools that the old-boy network all seem to have attended."

He went on to explain more about the organizational hierarchy that existed at work and how, to his way of thinking, it worked against him.

"So that's why it's imperative that Douglas ace these tests. If you're African American in this country, you have to do better than everyone else if you're going to succeed. And you have to grab whatever edge you can grab. At this rate, he's going to be stuck behind the same eight-ball that I've been stuck behind, the victim not only of his race but of his alma mater. His race, he can't do anything about, that's for sure. But his college—well, that's up to him. My father was a bricklayer, so there was no way I could afford to go anywhere but to community college for two years, and then to the cheapest state school I could find. But we could put together a financial package for him to go *anywhere* he wants to go. He's got a chance for something better and we're here to help him make it happen, but he's gonna blow it if he doesn't get moving."

I asked Daniela to share her thoughts about Douglas's future. "I guess I'm not as convinced as my husband that his race and where he goes to college have to work against him. I think it really depends on what field you go into. I'm a nurse, and I think it's a fairly color-blind field, at least in my experience. And when it comes to these test scores . . . well, I just think Emmanuel is placing too much emphasis on them."

"You're a fool to think they're not going to matter!" Emmanuel thundered. "His future starts right here, right now. These scores affect where he goes to college. Where he goes to college affects where he goes to graduate school. Where he goes to graduate school affects where he's going to work and how high he's going to go. And 1110 simply isn't going to do the trick. He's not a great athlete, he's not a great musician, he's not the president of the student government, and his GPA isn't a 4.0, you know. So it's going to come down to his SATs, and they're not looking very pretty right now."

Douglas, who was sitting so quietly that I had almost forgotten about him, finally spoke up. "I'm sick of you telling me what I have to do to succeed. Just because *you're* not city editor doesn't mean that *I* won't succeed. Just because I'm not getting 1600 on my SATs doesn't mean I can't get into a good college. Minority students have an advantage, you know."

"Don't give me this 'minorities have advantages' business, son," Emmanuel replied acidly. "Don't even *start* with that. Sure, they may give you a little bit here, a little bit there, but I can promise you, you'll pay for it down the road. I have more experience than you, I know what I've seen, I know what's out there. You can quote all the statistics you want, you can believe in affirmative action, but trust me—being a minority is *not* a plus, not in this country."

"So screw it, then, Dad. If that's the case, why should I even bother applying to college? Why not just forget the whole thing and become a bricklayer like Granddad? Isn't that what you're saying? Isn't that the point?"

"Now, Douglas, the point is that your father's just trying to help you understand some things," Daniela offered.

"Yeah, right, what he's trying to get me to understand is that I'm a failure, and I'll probably wind up being one just like he is."

"Your father's not a failure!" Daniela countered, sounding desperate, while Emmanuel looked like he was going to explode. "He's a successful journalist who believes he could have been even more successful if he'd simply had some of the privileges that we're trying to provide for you."

"So I'm a bad son because I can't blow away the SATs and make it into the colleges that he thinks *he* should have gone to? Is that what you're saying?"

It was evident that Emmanuel's disappointment in his son's scores was not likely to abate on its own. His desire to create possibilities in his son's life that he felt that he had been deprived of made it difficult for him to accept his son's current level of achievement and build from there. Daniela was gamely trying to balance things out, but she was probably feeling just as stuck and unsuccessful as a mother as Emmanuel was as a journalist.

And in our session, Douglas was beginning to make it clear that lower-than-hoped-for SAT scores weren't going to be the only problem if his parents didn't begin to handle things a little bit differently.

All parents have expectations for their children, and all parents struggle to find a way to calibrate their expectations in ways that promote their child's growth. After all, when the bar is set too high—when it seems like nothing is good enough, no matter how much they do and how hard they try—we can guarantee that our teen's self-respect will suffer, and chronic and mutual feelings of resentment will ensue. On the other hand, when the bar is set too low—when we don't expect enough from our offspring—we deprive them of the chance to summon their strengths and resources, to take on challenges and excel in ways that result in a deep and abiding sense of accomplishment and self-assurance. Ironically, then, the same result ensues: a teen with fragile self-esteem and a steady family climate of reciprocal irritability. So what can parents do to find a workable balance?

The answer, always easier said than done, is to establish realistic expectations, expectations that acknowledge and take into account who our adolescent is and is not, what his strengths and his weaknesses are, what he is and is not capable of. Reasonable, balanced, and realistic expectations enable our child to incorporate our faith and belief in him and his capacities such that he can surmount obstacles, recover and learn from defeats, overcome fear of failure, and pursue his most dearly held ambitions and objectives with conscientiousness and confidence.

While there may have been one or more stages in our child's development when we felt as if our expectations for him were optimal, meshing well with his needs, there will always be other stages that are characterized by an imbalance, when it seems like he is constantly letting us down because he is unable to meet our impossible-to-fulfill expectations, or we are letting him down by not adjusting our expectations upward and asking him to capitalize on his potential. Incongruent parental expectations are particularly likely to occur during our child's adolescence, and one way to adjust them to more appropriate levels is to take a closer look at the germ of these expectations. This is a crucial first step in the journey toward seeing him as Good Enough.

We all like to envision the transition into parenthood as a completely instinctive, effortless one. After all, the urge to raise a child, to have become a parent in the first place, is among the most, if not *the* most, natural urges of all. Why, then, shouldn't the building of a relationship with our child feel innate and natural as well?

The reason lies in the very nature of the parent-child relationship itself. While the desire to bring up a child is a very familiar one, the child herself is a stranger. And what we are asked to do—to commit our lives to the nurturance of this stranger, to devote unimaginable mental and physical energies to her care, to embark on a lifetime of fears, worries, and concerns, all without the slightest bit of certainty that what we do will pay off in a currency that is meaningful to us—is perhaps the most dramatic, demanding, and unbreakable contract that we will ever agree to sign.

How do we manage to live with a covenant that seems so one-sided? One of the most effective and common ways is to make this stranger less strange. In other words, if we can provide this little "alien" with an identity that we can identify with, it can seem a little less irrational to make all of the sacrifices and compromises that are necessary for her growth.

But the process of formulating this identification is a complex one indeed. While we might like to believe that our child's identity is the simple summation of her traits, characteristics, and temperament, the reality is that her identity evolves in a complicated equation that is the result not just of who she is but, often more importantly, who we imagine her to be.

Without even knowing it, and from the very inception of our relationship, we begin to assign attributes to our child—attributes that may or may not be relevant or accurate—in an effort to make her more recognizable to us. This is one of the essential elements of the process of bonding with our child, but it's a process that has complicated, and often unpredictable or even unwanted, consequences.

Sometimes the attributions that we make are benign or positive. We look at our newborn's physical characteristics and try to link her up with someone that we're already connected with. "That's her mother's nose, that's for sure," we comment, or "Look at those long legs—he'll probably be tall, just like all the other men in this family," or "You've definitely got Grandpop's barrel chest!"

Or we might take note of some psychological or temperamental traits and use those to give this for-now-unknown entity an identity. "Boy, she and her father—they're both so easygoing," we marvel, or "He could sleep all day, just like I can," or "Look at her smile—she's such a flirt!"

Even the timing of our child's entry into our family can lead to a matrix of attributions. "She was born on her father's birthday, and it's like they're the same person," we note with astonishment, or, "We got the news that we could adopt our son the same week that my mother died. It's like her beautiful soul magically migrated from her right into him!"

Sometimes, however, these early attributions have a more negative tint to them. "I know where he got *that* temper—he's just like his grandmother," we conclude. "She's so chubby. She'll probably turn out to be overweight, like me," we might silently muse. "I'm starting to believe in astrology. She was born under the same sign as my sister and *both* of them are impossible to please," it occurs to us.

While the attribution process may begin during infancy, it certainly doesn't end there, but continues on through childhood and into adolescence, influencing the parenting behaviors with which we respond to our children, which in turn influence their behavior. One mother, for example, may view her 5-year-old's fascination with television as an act of imagination, reminding her of how absorbed she was in the shows she watched when she was young, and how this became, to her way of thinking, the impetus for her eventual career as a set designer. Another mother might view her 5-year-old's fascination with television as a sign of depression and loneliness, reminding her of her woeful mother's obsession with soap operas and the embarrassment of returning home from school each afternoon to find her sitting on the couch in her bathrobe, staring vacantly at the tube.

One father might see his 10-year-old's decision to switch from sport to sport as versatility, signifying his willingness to take risks and try out new things without worrying about failing or seeming like a beginner. This is a quality he envies, and wishes that he himself embodied to a greater extent. Another father might view his 10-year-old's decision to switch from sport to sport as a sign that he is a quitter, lacking stick-to-it-iveness, unable to hang in there when life gets difficult. This is a quality that he abhors, because, in his eyes, it is so reminiscent of his father, who abandoned his mother and the family rather than "stick it out," leaving them destitute.

One parent might discover a bag of pot in her 15-year-old's backpack, react with alarm, but also be able to see this as an effort on her daughter's part to subtly let her parents in on the secret, and prompt them into helping her stay out of trouble and use good judgment, which, this mother knows now, is why *she* brought pot into her house when *she* was in high school. "She wants me to know what's going on in her life, or she never would have brought it into the house, just like me," Mom says, assuredly, to herself.

Another parent might discover a bag of pot in his 15-year-old's backpack and see this as an effort on his son's part to be secretive, to "get away with something without being caught," which, he believes, is what his twin brother used to do when they were in high school. "He's a sneak, trying to pull the wool over my eyes just like Tommy used to do with Mom and Dad," this father thinks, warily.

Whether the attributions we make are positively or negatively slanted, we create them so that our child becomes an individual that we can identify with, good or bad. Once this identification takes place, the stage is set for an emotional bond to be established between us, a bond that will link us forever and help us to lay the foundation for our relationship through childhood and adolescence. This bond may turn out to be rewarding or disappointing, rejuvenating or demoralizing, but there has to be some bond in place for us to summon and justify the vast physical and psychological resources required to successfully raise a child.

And so it is through examining the process of how we attribute qualities to our children and attempt to make sense of their behavior that we find the origin of our expectations for them, and the ways in which we impose these expectations. How we inter-pret and make sense of our children's most obvious or subtle, most significant or innocuous, behaviors, traits, and characteris-tics reveals with great precision our conscious and subconscious fears, dreams, hopes, and wishes, which in turn become the basis for what we demand of them.

Let's take a closer look at how parental attributions predict parental expectations, and how to modify the attribution process so that it results in the development of the realistic expectations that contribute to healthy teenage development.

Glynnis was a wonderful cellist, so good that she had always been first chair in her school orchestra. She was also selected first chair in the county orchestra and, last year, even in the state orchestra, even though she was still only a sophomore. For years, she has been repeatedly told by her teachers and conductors that she had the talent and diligence to "go all the way." Now a junior, how-ever, she performed poorly at this year's audition for the state or-chestra and wound up being selected as fourth chair, rather than first. Her commitment to practice had begun to drop off, and she had recently decided to go out for the volleyball team this year, rather than playing in the county orchestra.

Her mother, Ingrid, contacted me because she and her daugh-ter had been arguing constantly, not just about her indecision re-garding the cello and her sudden keenness for volleyball, but about "everything else, as well—these two just go at it every day about one thing or another, and it's making me nuts," Ellis, In-grid's husband, announced wearily during our initial session.

"He's right," Ingrid assented. "We used to have such a great relationship. Everybody would talk about how unusual it was to see a mother and a teenaged daughter so close with each other, like we were best friends. She was never embarrassed to be seen in public with me, like most of her friends are, and she always in-vited people to the house and made sure that I met everyone. It's like she was proud of me, and I was proud of her!

"But now, everything has gone downhill, starting with her changing her mind about the cello. It's like she's taken a wrong turn, and now she's nasty and irritable all the time, and we can't even talk about the weather without her winding up in some kind of snit and storming out."

"Has it been the same with you, Ellis?" I inquired.

"Well, I've noticed a shift, too, and while I was never as close to her as her mother was, we still got along pretty well. Mostly, though, she just keeps her distance from me and her mom, and I guess I can't blame her, because whenever those two even get near each other, sparks start to fly. I'd keep myself far away, too, if I were her."

I invited Glynnis, who had been listening attentively, to share her perspective as well. "Dad's right—I keep to myself because no matter what I say, there's a fight. Mom's just gotten impossible. Maybe it's menopause or something, a lot of my friends have talked about this with their mothers, but she's different now."

"Were the two of you as close as she says you were?"

Glynnis paused for a moment and stared up at the ceiling, almost as if she had to remind herself about the past. "Yes, I think we were. We did stuff together, she's right about that, and I liked our having the house where all the kids would come to hang out, watch videos, and stuff."

Then, it was as if she had awakened from a trance. Her tone suddenly sharpened and her green eyes flashed: "But it hasn't been that way for a while. Now it's her picking at me, nagging at me, constantly wanting to know what I'm up to, what I'm doing, where I am, where I'm going. And whatever I tell her, she's always got a problem with it. I'm not *neat* enough, I'm not *practicing* enough, I'm not *studying* enough—well, I've *had* enough!"

"Your parents told me that you're kind of at a crossroads when it comes to playing the cello. What are your thoughts about this?"

Glynnis's tone and posture softened again. "Look, I really love the cello. I've always enjoyed playing, I never had to be told to practice, and I have a great teacher, he's really *so* cool. But what my mom doesn't seem to understand is that I'm *tired* of it. It got to the point where I was practicing two hours a day, and I'm just tired. I've been playing steadily for seven years now, and I'm just not sure I can keep it up."

Ingrid impatiently jumped in. "But why stop now, Glynnis?

Why stop now when you've had such success, and when there's so much that could come your way? You've aced every audition you've had, your teacher has said that you're already playing at the conservatory level. How can you give it up when you have such a future ahead of you?"

"Mom, I'm not saying I'll never play the cello again. I'm saying that I'm sick of playing as much as I'm playing right now. That's *all* I'm saying."

"But don't you see, honey, that if you stop right now, you'll miss out on all of the wonderful opportunities that are awaiting you. If you stop now, you might not get a music scholarship. If you stop now, you may not be accepted into a conservatory. There are plenty of other cellists who are going to continue working hard their junior and senior years, and they're going to get the scholarships and the conservatory spots."

Glynnis's previously calm façade began to quickly dissolve. "And what makes you think I want a music scholarship? And what makes you think that I want to go to a conservatory? You want those things more than I do!"

"Oh, Glynnis, you want them, too, I know that. I saw how excited you were when you made first chair in the state orchestra! I saw how thrilled you were when you earned a 1 at the adjudication last year. You can't hide that from me, and you shouldn't hide it from yourself."

"Mom, you see what you want to see, not who I am! Listen to me, for once in your life! I don't want to be a professional cellist! I may not even want to play cello in college! Who said I wanted to go to a music college in the first place?"

"*You* did! You were the one who brought it up, not me, after your teacher suggested that we think about it last year."

Glynnis skillfully backtracked. "Well, maybe I did, but I've changed my mind. You don't care about what I want, all you care about is whether you can brag about me to your friends. I'm not Yo-Yo Ma, I'm Glynnis, and if you don't like it, you can kiss off!"

"I know that you're Glynnis, honey," Ingrid pleaded.

"Then how come you don't come to any of my volleyball games, huh? How come you're always busy reserving the best seats in the house whenever I'm in a concert or a recital, but you're nowhere to be found at the gym?"

"Glynnis, I didn't know it was important for you that I show up at your games."

"Well, that's just what I'm talking about, Mom. You didn't know it was important because you've never listened to me! You never want to hear about my practices or my games. It's like you don't want to believe that I even *play* volleyball."

"Look, if it's important to you that we get to your games, we'll get there," Ellis reassured her.

"Yeah, right," Glynnis said, glumly, her energy level suddenly sagging, while Ingrid looked at me helplessly.

I asked Glynnis to have a seat in the waiting room so that I could have some time alone with her parents. During our conversation, I learned that Glynnis was the second of three sisters, both of whom were very athletic. "Our eldest daughter, Nicole, was a nationally ranked swimmer in high school and now swims up at college, where she's a sophomore, and our youngest daughter is an *amazing* softball player," Ellis enthused. "She's been invited to play on a regional team, and her coach says that she's got one of the best arms he's ever seen in a thirteen-year-old."

"What about Glynnis's interest in sports?" I asked.

"She didn't seem to have the same physicality that her older sister seemed to have, right from the start," Ingrid replied. "I mean, her older sister was a real tomboy, very active, always moving. We didn't even have to teach her to swim, we just put her in the water and she was like a little wind-up toy, instantly churning her arms and legs. She just loved it."

"And the same thing was true with our youngest, Marabel. She threw everything—it's like she's been in training to be a pitcher from the word go," Ellis recalled, grinning.

"What interest did the two of you have in sports?" I wondered.

"Well, I was a real jock, still am, really," Ellis answered. "I was never much of a swimmer, I have to admit, but I ran track and loved baseball, and I still play in a softball league, even though I'm one of the oldest players on the team now. But I can hold my own."

"Not me," said Ingrid, laughing. "I just know that Nicole and Marabel got their athletic genes from their father, not from me. I never liked to play sports, was never good at sports, never had any interest in sports."

"What did hold your interest when you were a child?"

"Music!" Ingrid answered, her eyes shining. "I always loved music—I was in the chorus, I played clarinet in the school band, I even taught clarinet when I was in college to earn money."

"What was it like for you when Glynnis started to become musically engaged?"

"Oh, it was like a breath of fresh air! I mean, it was hard for me early on because Ellis had all of these sports connections with Nicole and Marabel, and I really did feel closed out. I couldn't connect with the other parents, either, who all seemed to know each other, while I couldn't even connect with Nicole and Marabel. But I knew that Glynnis had the music thing going, early on. She was always humming to herself, even as a baby, and she always responded instantly to classical music whenever I played it for her. She'd get very still and very alert. She had a steady diet from the time she was a baby—not just Mozart but contemporary stuff, too, Gershwin, Ellington, Copland. And while the other two were more than happy to be plopped in front of the TV for entertainment, she'd always prefer to listen to these audio tapes we had that told fairy tales with musical backgrounds."

"Plus, don't forget, she was the one who you'd sit with at the piano," Ellis reminded her.

"Oh, yes. One day I came downstairs and there was Glynnis, couldn't have been more than two or three, and she had hauled herself up on the piano bench and was plinking away at the keys. So I sat down next to her and we played our first duet!

"Once she began elementary school, we gave her piano lessons, and then she moved on to the cello when they started giving lessons at school, and from there she's just gone like wildfire. Her teachers have always been amazed not just at her skill, but her ability to emote, to make the instrument sing. That's something that can't be taught—you've either got it or you don't."

It was beginning to become clearer to me why the tension level between Ingrid and Glynnis had been rising so steadily over these last months. Ingrid had difficulty establishing a bond with her firstborn, Nicole, because they didn't have a common interest in sports, and the same thing happened with her youngest, Marabel.

But when Glynnis was born, her mother chose to select and interpret certain specific behaviors—her humming to herself, her response to classical music, her interest in audiotapes—as signs that she was musical, a characteristic that Ingrid could instantly identify with, based on her own history.

In this case, of course, the attribution had some accuracy to it: Glynnis was, indeed, a gifted musician. But what was just as significant was that her musicality was the link that Ingrid needed so that she could feel connected with her, a connection that she hadn't been able to so easily establish with her other two daughters, who bonded more easily with their father through sports.

So, not surprisingly, once Glynnis began to move away from music and toward athletics, it was a profound source of disappointment for her mother. Ingrid felt that she was going lose the primary source of attachment she had with the daughter she felt most attached to. And the fact that one of the things that she was turning to as she drew away from music was athletics, the activity that Ingrid felt so alienated from, made this transition even harder.

Ingrid's hurt feelings came out in her criticism of Glynnis for not doing "enough," which began to erode the closeness that the two of them had enjoyed, and prompted Glynnis to distance herself from her mother, which led to more hurt and more criticism on Ingrid's part. A ceaseless cycle of acrimony had begun, and none of them were finding it particularly enjoyable.

In an effort to break the cycle, I had a couple of suggestions for Ingrid and Ellis. One, it was obvious that just as Ingrid was hurt by her daughter's temporary departure from the cello, Glynnis was hurt by her mother's neglect of her involvement in volleyball. With that in mind, I recommended that Ingrid begin showing more of an interest in this part of Glynnis's life by making sure that she attended some games and by listening more attentively when Glynnis shared stories about her practices or her teammates.

Second, just as Glynnis was demonstrating a healthy desire to broaden her definition of herself by refusing to confine her interests to one endeavor—music—I asked Ingrid to take a closer look at her youngest daughter, Marabel, and see if there were any dormant or nascent aspects of her identity that she might be missing. As long as Ingrid felt that she only had one "true" daughter, it would create the highly pressurized relationship that made any disagreement the basis for a battle royale.

The family returned a couple of weeks later sounding like something had shifted. "I took your advice, and went to a scrimmage that Glynnis's team had with another school, and I had to say that I was impressed. Glynnis surely isn't one of the top players on the team, but she's only been playing for a little more than a year, and she still did pretty well.

"I couldn't help but shudder as I watched her hit the ball, or dive for it, thinking about how broken fingers would ruin her cello playing—couldn't she have taken up soccer and at least protected her hands?—but I could see how into it she was.

"And I also had an interesting conversation with Marabel, who told me something that I hadn't heard before. I asked her if she ever thought about doing any other activities besides sports, and she said, yes, that she'd been thinking about—of all things!—learning how to play the drums. I was really floored, but in a way it kind of made sense. She's really gotten into hip-hop, which is very rhythm-based, and she used to take dance lessons before all these sports activities gobbled up her time.

"So we decided that we'd get her one of those little drum synthesizer sets to begin playing around with, and maybe when the summer rolls around, we'd invest in a few lessons to see what comes of it."

"How have things been for you, Glynnis?" I inquired.

"Actually, a little better since we were here last. Mom's been a little easier to deal with, I guess, and we're not fighting so much."

"What was it like having her at your game?"

Glynnis smiled, and her eyes darted over to meet her mom's for a moment before she looked back at me. "It was kind of neat to have her come to my scrimmage. One of the girls on the team said she looked up at one point and Mom was really into it, clapping and cheering!"

"It's funny," Ingrid added, "I *was* very excited, and a little surprised at how much I got into it. And what was interesting was that I drove home remembering that we used to have a badminton court out back when I was growing up, and that was a sport that I really did enjoy. In fact, I was actually quite good at it. So seeing Glynnis bopping that ball over the net reminded me of bopping that little birdie over the net and how much fun I'd had."

"You know, there's a co-ed volleyball league that my boss and his wife play in," Ellis said. "Maybe we could put your old badminton skills to good use."

Ingrid chuckled at his suggestion, without making any kind of commitment. But what was clear was that she had begun to find another avenue down which her relationship with her middle daughter could travel. Through coming to appreciate Glynnis's new interest in volleyball and not relying so heavily on music for them to feel connected, and by realizing that she could share her musical energy with one of her other children, Ingrid had, in effect, opened a relational valve that released some built-up emotional steam. This allowed her and Glynnis to revisit some of the closeness that they had temporarily lost and begin to perform a more variegated duet.

Interestingly, I ran into Ingrid almost a year later at, of all places, the gym. She chuckled as she told me that, while she hadn't taken her husband up on his volleyball league suggestion, she had decided it was time to get in shape and begin taking better care of herself, and that Glynnis had joined her a few times to work out together. "It's good to have a partner for this kind of stuff," she remarked, a statement which, in this case, had multiple levels of meaning.

Meanwhile, I learned that Glynnis had decided to continue studying cello after all, but had chosen not to apply to any music conservatories. However, she was going to attend a college that had an excellent music program and that allowed non-music majors to participate in their performance groups.

Ingrid admitted to still harboring some residual mixed feelings: "The son of a good friend of mine applied to the Peabody Conservatory and was accepted, and she's just been crowing about it to everybody, and, frankly, it's hard to listen to her. I want to tell her, 'You know, my daughter could've gotten in, too. She just elected not to try.' But I know that Glynnis really had to make her own decision, and that once I gave her some room to do this, things got really good between us again—and that was worth it, right there. She'll always have music, but it's got to be on *her* terms, not mine."

In the case of Glynnis and her family, tension resulted from expectations that were rooted in positive attributions that Ingrid made at the earliest stages of her daughter's life. However, as I discussed above, the process of assigning qualities to our children, and interacting with them based on these assigned qualities occurs throughout our children's development and doesn't always depend on the attributions being positive ones. Let's take a look at a family in which difficulties were the result of negative attributions that did not have as long a history to them.

Forty-seven-year-old Marla was three years into her second marriage; her first husband had died nine years earlier from cancer. She had two sons from her first marriage, Kyle, 14, and Nathaniel, 12. Her husband, Larry, who was in his mid-fifties, had been married once before as well, a marriage that had ended in a hotly contested divorce. His only child from that marriage, 27-year-old Simon, was living on his own in another state.

"I'm caught in the middle," Marla began. "I really love Larry, and I'm much happier being married than when I was single. But the fighting between Larry and Kyle, my oldest, is just getting worse and worse. I try to side with Larry, because I know it's important to present a unified front and show Kyle that we're solid, but that upsets Kyle so much, he acts like I don't love him anymore. And if I try to take Kyle's side, Larry gets upset and tells me that I'm choosing my son over him."

"But Marla, we've been over this again and again. We know that Kyle is going to test us, we know that he's going to try to figure out if we're going to stay together, and it's essential that we remain a team in these matters or he'll take advantage of us," Larry countered.

"I agree with that, Larry, really I do . . . but the fact is, sometimes you're so ridiculous with him. I mean, the things that you get on him for, it's just one thing after another."

"What, like coming home on time? Like being presentable when he goes to church? Like doing his homework? Like speaking to me with respect? Is that what you mean by ridiculous?"

"Of course not, dear. They're all important things, I know. But it's like you don't let up, you're on him for *everything*. Yes, he's been late coming home from being out with his friends. Yes, he fights getting dressed up for church. Yes, he tries to avoid doing homework if he can. And yes, I wish he spoke to you more respectfully. But you sure don't seem to respect *him* very much these days. Do you think he's the only ninth grader who acts like this?"

"And you're forgetting about all his good points. He's got good friends, even if they stay out too late, he'll eventually relent when we stay on him about his appearance, and while he's not on the honor roll, he's really doing all right in school—B's and C's are just fine with me. If you took a stand on just one or two things, it would be all right, but it seems like you can't go ten minutes without finding a reason to criticize him."

"I criticize him when there's something to criticize, I praise him when there's something to praise. I don't know, Marla, I think he's got you hoodwinked into believing that I'm the devil and he's an angel."

"But you weren't always this way, Larry. When you first met Kyle, you had such a good relationship with him. He really looked up to you, and you were so understanding with him. I think you knew how hard it was for me to raise two boys without a father, and I think he knew that you weren't out to replace his father. It seemed like you went out of your way to be kind to him, not to attack him. I was so happy for both of my boys, I felt like I had hit the jackpot, a wonderful husband who was also a wonderful stepfather."

"Look, I'm kind to him as long as he does his job. When he starts falling down on the job, then I'm going to attack. Isn't that a parent's job? And why is it always *me* who has to do it?"

"You don't give me any *room* to do it, Larry. You're telling him what to do so often that I never have the chance to make a comment. And then the two of you get into it, and he storms up to his room and you go down to your workroom, muttering, and both of you want me to take your side, and I'm left feeling awful, just awful."

"How long have you felt that you're in this no-win situation, Marla," I asked, trying to get a handle on how deeply entrenched they all were.

"I guess it's been pretty much this whole school year, since Kyle started ninth grade—so about six or seven months, now," she replied.

"Does that sound about right to you, Larry?"

"Yeah, I guess. I mean, I saw some signs last summer, after middle school, when he decided not to go to camp, but didn't really come up with anything else to do. I was sort of annoyed that we let him just hang out for two months without having to do anything. And I can guarantee you it's not going to happen again this summer."

"But this is just what I'm talking about, Larry. All you do is remind him, 'You better come up with something for the summer, don't think you're just going to sit around and watch TV again,' and it's just getting on his nerves—and mine, too! If you want to get in there and come up with some ideas, great, but don't just *threaten* him."

"But if I don't, you won't either, Marla, that's the problem. That's how we got into this situation last summer, and I don't want another repeat. He sold you a bill of goods, telling you he didn't want to go back to camp, and then we all just hoped he'd magically find a job or get involved with something, and we waited the whole summer, and it never happened."

What had transpired over these last months that had brought to such a sudden end the honeymoon that this blended family had been basking in? Clearly, some shift had occurred that had set into motion a rapidly accelerating breakdown in trust.

Looking for hypotheses, I obtained some additional history. Marla told me that she had been devastated by her husband's death, but that she and the boys, who were only 5 and 3 at the time, had made as good an adjustment as possible, with the help of her parents, her in-laws, and a very strong network of friends and neighbors. "I worked hard not to put Kyle into the position of being the man of the house, but it was difficult, especially because he looked so much like his father—they're spitting images of each other."

She didn't date much, but when a good friend set her up with Larry, who had already been divorced for 12 years, she knew that the relationship was going to be a good one. "He was solid, and he was caring, and he was secure enough that he understood that at times I would still miss my first husband, and that he'd have to be very patient building a relationship with the boys. And he was so good with them, he just allowed them to get to know him slowly, without expecting too much from them, and by the time I told them that I was going to marry Larry, I think it was anticlimatic. They already saw us as a couple."

Larry's first marriage was a "train wreck from the start," he noted, sadly. "My first wife, Sally, was a good person, but we were so young. We met in high school, got married a year after we graduated from college, and then things just fell apart once Simon was born a couple years later. We weren't even ready for marriage, so we certainly weren't ready to become parents.

"But unfortunately our separation was a very divisive one, and we fought and fought, and the result was that I didn't get to see Simon much at all. Simon and Sally kind of bonded together and left me out of the loop, and when he hit adolescence, well, that was another train wreck right there."

I learned that once Simon entered high school he became involved not only with drug use but also with drug dealing. "It was hell. I've lost track of all of the doctors and therapists and lawyers and judges who tried to help. But unfortunately Sally and I could just never get our act together. She was too angry with me, and I was too angry with her, so no matter what anyone recommended, we were always working at cross-purposes. And Simon just got worse and worse."

Eventually, after three years of disastrous behavior, his mother was able to arrange for Simon to become court-ordered to a three-month inpatient drug rehabilitation facility, and he left the program clean but completely unwilling to even speak to, let alone see, either of his parents. "He lives alone clear on the other side of the country. It's like he associates his mom and me with his drug use, like they talked him out of having any contact with us at the rehab. I really think that he has concluded that as long as he doesn't have any involvement with us he won't have any involvement in drugs," Larry observed, shaking his head as if he were still dumbfounded by this turn of events.

What was notable to me about Larry's narrative was that he remembers Simon as having begun to go downhill right when he started high school, which was exactly the time that Larry and Kyle had begun experiencing more conflict eight months before.

"Based on what you learned from your experience with Simon during his adolescent years, what do you want Marla to know about teenagers?" I asked, trying to elicit a better understanding of his parenting philosophy.

"Look, I believe that if Sally had allowed me to be the father that I had wanted to be, my son would never have gotten involved with drugs, and he and I wouldn't be completely estranged from each other. Simon needed a dad, a man who could step in and take charge and keep him off of and away from drugs—and a dad was the very thing that Sally deprived him of by turning him against me. It broke my heart to see this terrific kid get involved in such a mess. And it was all preventable if only I had been allowed by his mother to be the man that he needed me to be. I think he's angry at me for not being there, and angry at her for not letting me be there, plain and simple. I hope to god he gets over this one day and that we can have a normal relationship, but I don't know that that's ever going to happen."

It was easy to speculate that Larry saw his marriage to Marla as an endeavor that would provide him with another chance to parent a son successfully through adolescence, an experience that might heal the wounds that still remained open from his hurtful relationship with Simon. The problem was that he was merging his memories of Simon with the realities of Kyle, and assuming that what he believed would have helped Simon—strong, autocratic fathering—was exactly what Kyle was needing now, as well.

To my way of thinking, that was why he had begun jumping on Kyle "for every little thing" when Kyle began high school. It was his chance to inoculate Marla, Kyle, and himself from the nightmarish problems that Sally, Simon, and he had been infected by years before. Naturally, Kyle reacted to this abrupt swerve in the family road with surprise and resentment: "How dare this man start telling me what to do—he's not even my father!" were the words that might have been going through his head, especially since, from everyone's perspective, things had been going pretty well up until he had begun high school.

So of course he turned to his mother for help, a mother who then felt paralyzed between her loyalty to her new husband and her love for her son, the son who reminded her so much of her first husband. Her sense that Larry was being too hard on Kyle made it difficult for her to join with him around what she felt to be his unreasonable expectations, a divide that reminded Larry of the counterproductive relationship he'd had with his first wife. This prompted him to be harder still with his stepson in an effort to compensate for Marla's lenience with Kyle, and keep him in line, leading Marla to be even more lenient with Kyle, and more distant from Larry. No wonder the family's hitherto healthy climate had begun to decline.

The priority here seemed to be helping Larry see Kyle for who he really was—a basically well-behaved, fairly responsible young man who had some maturing to do—rather than who he feared he'd become—a delinquent drug dealer enduring a prolonged and self-imposed alienation from his family.

"Between now and when we follow up, I'd like you to do a little homework," I said to Larry. "I want you to make a list of the ways in which you think that Kyle is similar to and different from Simon when Simon was his age, and I want you to make another list of the ways in which Kyle's family life is similar to and different from Simon's family life when Simon was his age. When you're done, I want you to share your lists with Marla so that the two of you can discuss them together."

Larry and Marla returned for their next session with a different perspective. "I think I knew where you were going with this when you asked me to do the assignment," Larry began, with a smile, "because once I sat down and started to compare Kyle and Simon, I knew instantly that they're different kids, with different families. I mean, here's Kyle with his mom and dad in a good marriage for the first part of his life, and then even after his father dies he's got all of these grandparents on his side, while Simon never really had the benefit of any of that kind of support. Almost from the day he was born his mom and I were in battle, and we remained that way every day of his life.

"And I realized that they're different kids, too. Simon was always a spit-in-your-eye guy, the kind of kid who didn't take no for an answer and was always pushing the envelope, but Kyle's always been much more of a go-with-the-flow guy."

"I was so relieved that you gave Larry that homework and that we talked about it," Marla added, "because I wasn't aware that Larry was taking such a hard line with Kyle because he was so afraid that Kyle was going to turn out like Simon. But what I also realized was that I have really turned over the hard part of parenting to Larry. I haven't raised a teenager before, and I know that Kyle's smart enough to dupe me into agreeing with things that I shouldn't agree to.

"So it's really not such a good idea for me to continue to absolve him of responsibility while I sit back and criticize Larry for being so critical. I'm starting to understand that Kyle can't be—*shouldn't* be—my pal anymore, like he was during the first few years after his father died. He needs to grow up some, and some of what Larry's been asking of him is legitimate and important."

Over the next few sessions, I helped Marla and Larry to develop a set of mutually agreed upon expectations of Kyle. And not surprisingly, once they were able to present more congruent leadership and demonstrate that they were in league with each other, Kyle's disrespectful behavior began to drop off, as did the fights between Kyle and Larry.

Larry's capacity to disentangle his stepson from a web of miscast attributions rooted in his relationship with his son freed Kyle and him to have a less conflicted relationship and enabled him to reestablish his previously positive collaboration with his wife.

As these two case studies show, our inappropriate expectations for our teenagers have their roots in the attributes that we assign to them, an assignment that may be old or new, positive or negative. But if you think that the way to establish more appropriate expectations is to eliminate the process of making attributions, you're in for a rough road. After all, these attributions are not only unavoidable, since it is in our nature, going back to Adam and Eve, to give the creatures in our universe recognizable identities. They're also indispensable, since they provide us with the rationale for establishing a bond with our children, the bond that enables us to invest in the hard work of parenting without ever being certain we'll receive any meaningful returns.

While you can't simply block the assignment of attributes, however, you can make yourself more aware of them. And once you are more aware of them, they'll be less likely to impair your judgment and expand or shrink your expectations of your teen in ways that interfere with his growth and self-respect.

The following exercise will help you to uncover the often invisible process of attribution such that you can more clearly see the labels that you have attached to your adolescent and assess the ways in which these labels may be affecting your relationship with him, and what you expect of him, for better or worse.

EXERCISE 1

The process by which we ascribe qualities to our child is one that has very deep roots, and thus is not always easy to unearth. This exercise will help you to do so.

First, describe some of the behaviors that your teenager displays that trouble or disappoint you. Next, take a look at how you typically explain these behaviors. Then, try to develop some alternative explanations for these behaviors, ones that might have a more neutral, or even positive, slant. Your alternative explanations may or may not be accurate—that can be assessed later on. What's important now is simply contemplating the possibility that there are, in fact, alternative ways of understanding why she does what she does. Finally, see if you can find some exceptions to the negative conclusions you have come to about your teen based on your initial attributions, even if the expectations are rare.

Feel free to use the blank sheet at the end of the chapter to guide you. Here's an example of how one parent in my practice completed it. Peninah found her 15-year-old daughter, Hannah, to be a great source of aggravation, mostly due to her "attitude."

Peninah's Chart

Behavior:	Bitchy
Attribution:	She's a bitch!
Alternative Explanation:	She needs space and being bitchy is one way to get it because we all back off from her when she's like that.
Exceptions:	She's well thought of at her job—they think the world of her there.
Behavior:	Gets angry when we give her advice.
Attribution:	She thinks she knows everything already and doesn't need our help.

Alternative Explanation:	She feels insecure about what she doesn't know, and our suggestions make her feel more insecure.
Exceptions:	She was fairly open the other night when I tried to help her sort out something that happened with a customer at work.
Behavior:	Won't take no for an answer.
Attribution:	She's spoiled and self-centered, can't handle being disappointed.
Alternative Explanation:	She knows how to persist, and has seen the value of persistence because we haven't always held our ground.
Exceptions:	When we told her that under no circumstances would we allow her to have a co-ed sleepover, she didn't push it (possibly because she was relieved!).

In working on this assignment, Peninah came to several important realizations. One, she had gotten into the habit of seeing Hannah in a negative light and explaining her more annoying behaviors in an unrelentingly pejorative way. Two, in viewing all of Hannah's behaviors through this negative filter, she was likely to miss, ignore, or minimize the moments when Hannah was acting differently, which meant that she was losing the opportunity to try to amplify or "balloon" these small moments into something larger or more frequent.

Finally, in exploring this, Peninah began to realize the extent to which her feelings about Hannah mirrored her mother's feelings about her younger sister, Sarah. "My mother used to criticize Sarah incessantly, and I certainly didn't mind, because I was always seen in a good light compared with her. But I also felt guilty, and there were times I know that I set Sarah up, knowing that Mom would come down on her and I'd get off scot-free. I'm not proud of this, believe me, and I think it's contributed to some of the tension I still feel with Sarah, even though we're both adults now and have a decent sisterly relationship. But one of the reasons I believe we *have* a better relationship now is because, once we grew up and left home, I was gradually able to see her differently than my mother had chosen to see her."

As we talked, it began to dawn on Peninah that perhaps she had tended to see Hannah in a negative light as part of her replication of the relationship between her mother and her sister long ago. "It's like I almost felt cursed to have a daughter who reminded me so much of my sister, like I was being paid back for all the times I took advantage of the situation when we were kids.

"But knowing that this isn't good for Hannah or for me, I've got to change things around. It's funny, when you asked me to think about exceptions to how I see her typically act, I was sure I wouldn't be able to come up with any, I was so convinced that Hannah was this *tyrant*. But how nice it is to be able to see that she's more than a bitchy teen with a bad attitude—she's a whole person, difficult at times, to be sure, but a whole person nonetheless."

As you complete this exercise, see if you can determine the *origin* of the negative interpretations you use to explain your teen's behavior, and whether they are really echoes of another time, place, or person. Also, try on the alternative explanations to see if they might have some relevance, and look carefully for the exceptions to her behavior that might disprove the conclusions that you may have prematurely and/or mistakenly come to.

Behavior:

Attribution:

Alternative Explanation:

Exceptions:

Behavior:

Attribution:

Alternative Explanation:

Exceptions:

Behavior:

Attribution:

Alternative Explanation:

Exceptions:

THREE

ACKNOWLEDGING

One doesn't discover new lands without consenting to lose sight of the shore for a very long time.

—André Gide

One of the first lessons that the parents who visit my office learn is why, often without their knowing it, and certainly without meaning to, they find themselves making life with their teenager worse, rather than better—how they travel at warp speed, with their own hands on the wheel, away from the green hills of "good enough" straight into the barren desert of "just terrible" as if there were no other destination available.

Just as insanity can be defined as "doing the same thing over and over again while expecting different results," ineffective (but not atypical!) parenthood can be defined as "doing the same thing over and over again and watching your relationship with your child deteriorate, and then continuing to do the same thing, anyway, but with even greater intensity."

We are bright, thoughtful, caring parents who love our children and only want the best for them. So what infernal mechanism prompts us to make our children into the instruments of our own dissatisfaction? Why do we find ourselves conscientiously contributing to the very family impairments that so upset us? How is it that we persist in monotonously traversing the same bleak street of ineffectual interactions without slowing down, stopping altogether, or choosing to take what is clearly a more scenic and satisfying detour?

Discovering the answers to these questions will help us to change the grimly inflexible patterns that so vex us and lay the groundwork for creating a new, less conflicted, more gratifying relationship with our adolescent. There are two good places to look for these answers. We need to look at our past experiences as children and how they influence our present encounters with children. And we should also look at our present experience as adults at a midlife crossroads and how it influences the parent-child relationship as our children approach the threshold of their own young adulthood.

In my previous books I have written about the "reverberating journey" that all parents embark upon when they begin a family. This journey takes us on a tour of our unguarded, ungovernable past, an interior netherworld that swarms with conflicts and dilemmas, memories and fantasies, thoughts and feelings that have been buried for years, happily or problematically, out of our conscious awareness.

Disorienting and disquieting as it may be, the reverberating journey is a necessary and crucial one, because all of the psychological energy that churns up from our dark emotional depths can then be channeled into managing the profoundly complex responsibilities required by childrearing.

By revisiting what are both the unrememberable and unforgettable landmarks from our childhood and adolescence—triumphs and defeats, sorrows and losses, dreams and wishes, conflicts and fears—we gain greater access to our inner strengths and resources, heighten our potential for creative renewal, and find ourselves better able to understand ourselves, our teenager, and the astonishing algebra of the relationship that has gradually emerged between us.

Because what we will inevitably discover as we undertake this excursion is the confusing yet common parental instinct to recreate with our children in the present some of the complex narratives from our near or distant past. This is accomplished, often unconsciously, by assigning to them important parts in scenes from a drama that we feel compelled not simply to reproduce but to rewrite.

The motivation behind this staging is not to self-indulgently exploit or manipulate our children, but to help us mourn old losses, heal old wounds, repair old injuries, and forgive old hurts such that we can put the past to rest and begin to author new, more satisfying narratives for our family and ourselves, with enhanced plots and happier endings. Through directing our adolescents in these rehearsals of our personal passion plays (and for most of us, there's plenty of passion!), we strive to eventually understand ourselves, and, in the process, understand our children, better than we were ever understood—to discover and claim, or rediscover and reclaim, who we and they truly are, and ultimately can be.

The noted pediatrician and psychoanalyst D. W. Winnicott had this in mind when he wrote, "There's no such thing as a baby." Whether it's an infant or a toddler, an elementary school student or an adolescent, a child's identity does not exist in and of itself, but comes to fruition in the context of the entire family's multi-generational history and perception. This psychosystemic heritage that we pass on tends to have far more impact on how our children grow and develop than any genetic lineage and accounts for the myriad ways in which parents and their offspring interact with and influence each other.

There are two major reasons that our personal sagas expose themselves so dramatically during our children's adolescence. One is that we tend to remember our adolescence much more vividly than any other stage of our childhood, both because it was more recent than any of the prior childhood stages and because it was so freighted with the conflict and emotionality, the turbulence and uncertainty, that our own teens are in the midst of. The second is that when our children are adolescents we are generally going to find ourselves in the midst of an important developmental transition as well, so it's not just our past but also our present that is being reviewed and reevaluated.

How natural, then, for us to induce them into participating in psychological pageants that illuminate highly charged themes that are salient once again after never having been quite put to rest, ones that clamor for a more enriched resolution that we can then carry forth into the rest of our adult lives.

The way to reconfigure in more positive ways the scenes that may initially cast us and our teenager into needlessly repetitive and restrictive roles is to understand more about our own personal philosophy of adolescence. In Chapter 2, we saw how the specific attributions that we make as parents from early on— attributions that are a necessary ingredient in the formation of an emotional bond with our child—influence how we view, and respond to, our child's behavior.

Now that our children are adolescents, however, we need to also examine our general understanding of the adolescent transition, and how it affects the evolution of that emotional bond with our offspring as they enter their last stage of dependence on us. For whether we are aware of it or not, every one of us has a parenting template that shapes how we will experience our child's adolescence, a template that can be a complicated amalgam of where we're at in our lives now and where we were at when we were teenagers.

As we noted earlier, one of an adolescent's primary developmental tasks is to differentiate from her family, to begin to separate from her parents and consolidate her own unique identity as a young adult. Our teens' efforts at differentiation usually fall into one of two categories.

1. They began *doing* something that we wish they *wouldn't* do, such as experimenting with drugs or engaging in premarital sex.

2. They began *not doing* something that we wish they *would* do, such as not taking their school performance seriously or refusing to clean their room or dress appropriately.

The way in which we interpret and react to our teen's differentiation is less the result of the nature of their differentiation, however, and much more the result of the template that we bring to the family table. Having worked and spoken with hundreds of parents of adolescents over the years, I've seen the ways in which many of the natural parental responses to adolescent differentiation can be classified.

1. Differentiation signifies our success as a parent.

Some parents are able to experience their teenager's growth away from the family as a sign that they have done their job of raising an independent-minded young adult. In their eyes, they see their adolescent son or daughter not as "oppositional" or "rebellious" or "defiant," but instead as a courageous freedom fighter whose strivings for autonomy are a brave and time-honored insurrection against a stagnant status quo that could stand a bit of a shake-up. Adopting this template allows parents to appreciate the hard work that they've done as caregivers, and manage their adolescent's damning denouncements and tonic honesty without losing their confident authority, affection, flexibility, and, perhaps most importantly, sense of humor.

Micah, for example, was a committed member of his local synagogue; he taught in the religious school there and had recently begun studying part-time with a vocal coach to become a cantor, a vocation he hoped to pursue when he retired from his position as chemistry professor at a local university. As a young girl, his daughter, Shera, had enjoyed going to synagogue as well; she had enthusiastically participated in her religious education, becoming a bat mitzvah, and singing in the youth choir.

However, around the time that Shera entered her junior year of high school, she began to criticize the religion that she had previously been so enamored with. "Sometimes, Judaism feels like a repressive regime, Dad. All of these rules and regulations, and this God who's always sitting in judgement of us and who smites us and others if we don't do what he says—what kind of faith is that?"

She began refusing to go to services and instead started joining a friend of hers who attended Quaker meetings at a neighbor's home. While she agreed to be confirmed at her synagogue, she chose not to continue with a postconfirmation class and joined a newly developing Quaker study group devoted to the exploration of pacifism. And rather than singing Hebrew hymns and folk songs in the synagogue choir, she got involved with organizing a benefit concert for Peace Now.

Micah wasn't exactly happy that the religious connection that he and Shera had shared for the first 14 years of her life was fraying. But he also understood that this was part of her development as an independent-minded adult. "It's not easy for me when the rabbi asks where she is and why she's not coming to services anymore. She was so well liked and well thought of, and it was a great source of pride for me. I kind of wish she had been more direct with him about her disenchantment, rather than just choosing not to go anymore, but I guess that's a lot to ask of a kid her age.

"But I also remember when I was in high school, and how strange it was for my parents, who weren't very religious at all, that I had such a strong interest in going to synagogue. They were always trying to figure out where I got the 'religious gene' because nobody in the family was particularly observant. In fact, most of them kind of looked down on religion, like it was some sort of crutch for the weak and unfortunate. Especially because my mother was a Holocaust survivor, being Jewish was seen as nothing more than another source of persecution and misery.

"Yet, I never got the sense that they were really disappointed in me. Granted, it's not like I was going off to abuse drugs or live in a commune, but just the same, I always had the sense that they knew this was part of my development as a young adult.

"And my mom and I had an interesting conversation recently in which she told me that she came to appreciate my shift toward religion because it sort of emboldened her to pursue her own spiritual life with a little more energy than she might have otherwise. And that's been a big help to her now that my father has Alzheimer's—the daily prayers and the support of the sisterhood at her synagogue all have really helped her to survive this ordeal.

"Now, I'll tell you, I certainly wouldn't be so understanding if Shera were coming home insisting that Jews were responsible for the death of Jesus, or if she were part of some destructive cult. But the reality is that she's developing a spiritual identity and a social conscience all at the same time, and while I wish that were taking place in synagogue, I guess I'd prefer that it take place *somewhere,* rather than no place at all. So I kind of give her credit, and

I give myself and my wife some credit, too. After all, who knows where this is all going to take her."

The understanding response that Micah received from his own parents as he made his first efforts to distinguish himself from his family enabled him to see his own daughter's efforts in the same, benevolent light, and not only to be respectfully appreciative and supportive of her but, just as importantly, to be pleased with himself.

2. Differentiation signifies our freedom.

Other parents see their teen's separation as a source of liberation: as less is asked of us as parents, more energy is emancipated for other, often long-deferred endeavors. Sometimes this can lead to feelings of excitement and rejuvenation. For example, Chet had been his son's soccer coach from the time that he was in kindergarten until he completed eighth grade. But now that Armon is preparing to enter high school and try out for the team, Chet is no longer needed as coach. While he experiences some feelings of loss, there's also a healthy amount of relief.

"I feel like I really put in my time all these years, running practices, going to coaching clinics, scheduling tournaments, dealing with the parents. I wouldn't give it up for anything, but I have to say, I'm looking forward to going to my son's games now without having to worry about who's going to play where or who's going to substitute or which parent's going to be angry with me. Just being able to sit back and watch. . . .

"And it's time that he got a different kind of coaching, anyway. It probably wasn't always such a terrific thing to be the coach's son. He's already told me that he doesn't want me hanging around his high school practices, and I told him I've got no problem with that. In fact, I'm kind of celebrating my 'retirement' by joining a men's soccer league, now that I'll have a little more time on my hands. All those years of coaching and watching, I feel like it's finally my turn to get out and play around a bit.

"It's kind of like how my parents responded when my youngest sister graduated high school. I was a senior in college at the time, so I was supposed to be having the time of my life, but I had nothing on them. All of a sudden, with no kids at home, they were going on cruises and signing up for golf tournaments and seeing every movie that came out. I was envious, but I think I see, now, why they were doing all that. It's like they were let out of prison!"

Chet's ability to see Armon's appropriate distancing as something that had value for both of them resulted in his capacity to respond graciously when it was time to acknowledge he was less needed by his son.

3. Differentiation signifies danger.

Many parents feel that they have no choice other than to see their teenager's departures from the family's norms through a filter of fear. Adolescence, to them, feels like a minefield—one false step, and you can lose a limb, or even your life.

Doreen seemed able to remember her older sister Anika's adolescence better than her own. Drinking regularly by the time she was 11, addicted to pot by the time she was 14, abusing heroin at the age of 16, and giving birth to two children by two different fathers before she was 20, Anika barely survived her adolescence, and she wasn't doing a whole lot better as an adult. Now on her third husband, both of her children lost to their birth fathers in custody battles, she was living a hand-to-mouth existence, still hitting Doreen up for loans that would never be paid back and making excuses for her inability to break her addictions and live more honorably.

It was no wonder that Doreen's personal memories were so unavailable to her—everything in her own life had shriveled under the hot glare of her sister's self-destructive behavior. But when her 15-year-old daughter, Karly, was arrested because she was a passenger in the car when her friend was pulled over and a carton of beer was found in the trunk, it was also no wonder that Doreen was overwhelmed with terror.

"Why else would she be driving with someone who had beer in the car unless she's been drinking too? How long do you think she's been drinking? Do you think that she's an alcoholic? Does she need to go into rehab? Do you think we can still save her?"

These were all good and legitimate questions (albeit somewhat unanswerable, for now), but you would have thought, from the tone of Doreen's voice, that her daughter had been found lying unconscious in an alley with a needle stuck in her vein. Clearly, as I eventually learned, the many frightening images from her sister's adolescence had been unleashed by Karly's citation and were already at work influencing how she was interpreting her daughter's behavior.

4. Differentiation signifies abandonment.

While parents like Doreen bring a fear-based template to their teens' separation, afraid of what will happen to their children, other parents bring an anxiety-based template to this separation, afraid of what will happen to themselves.

Gloria had earned a college degree with a major in English literature, but she had never embarked on a fulfilling career, flitting from job to job with little professional satisfaction for almost a decade. When she finally gave birth to a son after a long struggle with infertility, she was relieved to have an excuse not to work outside the home anymore, and her husband was happy to take over the breadwinning role while she focused on raising the family, which eventually came to consist of three more boys.

Now that her youngest, Andy, is in the midst of his senior year of high school, however, and the older three are all living away from home, she is filled with a nameless dread. "I wander around the house in a fog, walking from one empty room to another, wondering what I'm going to do with myself. I had no career to speak of, and it feels too late to start one now. The women my age who have continued working all this time are already planning their retirements, while I haven't set foot in an office in over twenty-five years!

"My husband's very encouraging, he tells me there are all kinds of things I can do. I could go back to school, I could get a job, I could volunteer somewhere—but mostly I just feel so sorry for myself, and I can't imagine who I'll be without the kids to raise. What am I going to do when we drop Andy off at college next September? It's less than a year from now, and I haven't the faintest idea who I am without the kids around.

"And of course Andy's not really around much as it is now, anyway. He's a senior, he's always out with his girlfriend or with his football buddies, and he has a job. Worst of all, I used to get along with him so well, but now we've been fighting a lot. We had a huge falling-out just the other night, with me telling him he needs to at least be home every night for family dinners and Andy telling me that it's not really a family anymore, it's just the three of us, and he doesn't need to be home for that, and I was so upset that I threw a salt shaker at him. I almost hit him, my own son, I've never done anything like that before! And then, when I realized what I'd done, I went upstairs to bed and just sobbed."

Andy's gradual departure seems like a desertion to Gloria, leaving her feeling lonely and rejected, and resulting in the loss not only of her youngest child but of her entire self-definition. It's no wonder that her initial response to his preparing to leave home is one of hurt and rage.

5. Differentiation signifies our being surpassed.

Observing our adolescent's budding life is always a bittersweet experience for parents. We may feel happy for them, but we may just as likely feel sorry for ourselves. The limitless possibilities that seem to open up for them may contrast depressingly with the limitations that we are feeling as we contend with remorse and misgivings about what may be the stale, stalled-out status of our lives, our work, and our relationships.

Hal's son, Alex, seemed to have an excellent chance of getting into a top-flight university. A near-4.0 GPA, sky-high SAT scores, and sterling successes on his high school math and "It's Academic" teams that had led to his participation in national competitions were going to make him an attractive applicant to any college in the country.

Although Hal had taken pride in his son's accomplishments over the years, when it came time for Alex to start making selections and preparing applications, he appeared ambivalent. He craftily avoided his wife's attempts to pin down his work schedule so that they could arrange some campus tours and interviews for Alex; he avoided contacting his investment adviser regarding the status of Alex's college fund despite his accountant's suggestion that he do so; and he "misplaced" a couple of the bulky college catalogs that Alex had asked him to look over in the hopes that his father might help him narrow down his options. It seemed that Hal was doing everything within his passive powers to delay or obstruct his son's application process.

As we talked, it became clear that anticipating Alex's potential triumphs was a process fraught with complicated feelings for Hal. "I didn't have my sights set very high when I was in high school. I did all right, but nothing at all like Alex. And the same thing was true in college—while some of my friends were heading off to law school or business school or medical school, I was content to just chug along and get started with a decent job in the work world.

"Now, with hindsight, I wished I'd taken things more seriously, because most of my college friends are more successful than I am. I never went ahead and earned an M.B.A., like I should have, and like everyone told me to, and so now I'm stuck as this mid-level manager in a bank with zero chance of promotion. I've topped out before I've even reached the age of fifty, with nowhere to go but down."

Rather than being able to enjoy Alex's accomplishments vicariously, Hal was instead suffused with regret and rumination, seeing his son on the verge of achieving what he was unlikely to ever achieve himself. But because he was having difficulty acknowledging his ambivalence, it leaked out in his indifference and inertia, the subtle but unmistakable ways in which he was trying to derail Alex's differentiation and his subsequent prospects for success.

6. Differentiation signifies our becoming powerless.

Parents try to survive parenthood by remaining in control, but the nature of adolescence is that we must gradually relinquish control if we are to prepare our children to become self-reliant. The balance of power that was so predominantly and necessarily in our favor during early and middle childhood must shift to one that is more even (while we still, of course, reserve the right to issue non-negotiable vetoes over behavior that is clearly excessive or destructive). But that shift doesn't occur without a battle, since power is addictive to both generations, and some parents have more difficulty giving up their addiction and surrendering their power than others. In these families, the Battle of the Generations becomes the commanding template that guides their childrearing.

Monty had been raised by weak and ineffectual parents and felt that he had paid the price for the lack of discipline in his upbringing. "I didn't have any control over myself, and, unfortunately, my parents didn't either—they let me run wild, and, believe me, I ran wild. I was on a first-name basis with the police officers in my town by the time I was fifteen, and it was years before I was able to straighten things out. By then, I had lost a lot of time."

Intent on not repeating the pattern, he saw just about every interaction between himself and his 15-year-old daughter, Chelsea, as a winnable power struggle: "She's gonna fight, but *I'm* gonna win." For Monty, there was no demilitarized zone—everything Chelsea chose to do or not do was part of the war, not just the "big issues" like the friends she hung out with or the grades she earned, but also the music she listened to, the color of her hair, how clean her room was, how much jewelry she wore, even the shade her toenails were painted! He policed his daughter and the family as a whole like an ever-vigilant dictator, constantly on the lookout for the next incipient uprising.

"My job is to stay in control as long as I can, and if that means taking all these things on, I'll do it. I'm not one of these pantywaist parents who let their kids push them around and make decisions for themselves. She'll toe the line or she'll have to find another place to live."

Not surprisingly, Monty's efforts seemed to be backfiring. The harder he tried to stay on top of things, the more this motivated Chelsea to find some pocket of empowerment. She was a master at finding the exception to every rule, or just circumventing the rule and devoting herself to evading the consequence. For every insistent demand on her father's part, there was an equally insistent "Make me" from Chelsea.

The constant escalation of impose rule, break rule, followed by impose consequence, fight consequence, was one that Monty had met his match for. His daughter was just as strong-willed and militaristic about "winning" as was her pugnacious father.

7. Differentiation signifies the death of our dreams.

Children are the ultimate vanity project. We invest them with our ambitions and project onto them our fantasies, hoping that they will make good on them, thereby honoring and immortalizing us. They're our second (and until we have grandchildren, our last!) chance to make our dreams come true.

But an adolescent's successful differentiation results from finding ways to shrug off the shackles of our wishes for them, and create and make good on some of their own. If we become too preoccupied with what we are losing when they do this, we will have difficulty appreciating all that they've gained.

Dean was a high school English teacher who had always dreamed of being a writer. He had written several novels, but none had been published, something that he confessed had been such a great disappointment to him that he no longer wrote at all. Naturally, he took great delight in his 15-year-old daughter, Avery, who was a fine poet and essayist whose work had already been published in a couple of newspapers and the school literary journal.

For the summer after tenth grade, he encouraged her to apply to a writing program for high school students held at a prestigious Midwestern university. Avery applied and was selected right away, but then did an about-face and decided that she'd rather spend the summer at home working as a lifeguard at the neighborhood pool.

"Why should I waste my vacation by going to school and *writing* all day?" she asked indignantly. "Summer's for hanging around the pool, making some money, being with my friends. Why can't I have a *normal* vacation like everyone else?"

"Because you're a great young writer, Avery, and this is a golden opportunity," Dean pleaded. "You're going to be with other young writers, learning from terrific, renowned faculty—you'd be foolish not to take advantage of this."

"Forget it, Dad. I'm not interested anymore, and I'm not going."

"Well, you have to get parental permission to get a job as a lifeguard, you know. You're still only fifteen."

"Dad, you wouldn't really prevent me from working at the pool, would you? Because if you did, I would never forgive you."

"We still have the right to decide what's best for you, Avery, and you can't convince me that working at the pool is best for you when you have a wonderful chance to really improve yourself as a writer."

"Look, Dad, if spending my summer in school is your idea of improving myself, then maybe I don't want to improve myself. Maybe I just won't do anything all summer, how about *that*? Would *that* meet your approval?"

As I listened, it appeared that Dean was equating his daughter's differentiation—in this case, her wish to spend the summer at home rather than at college—with the demise of his own dreams of being a successful writer, an equation which predicted the doomed intolerance with which he was responding. Only when he eventually began to come to terms with his sense of having disappointed himself was their conversation able to become a more constructive one.

8. Differentiation signifies our having failed.

"Where have I gone wrong?" is the spoken, or unspoken, plaint that all parents of teenagers at times find themselves asking. As we saw in Chapter 2, one of the most natural things to do when our children show signs of blossoming with different colors than we had intended is to point the finger of blame directly at ourselves and assume culpability for whatever discrepancy exists between our wish and their reality.

When Julie's 14-year-old daughter Sabrina began dating a boy who was less achievement-oriented than her, and from a less affluent neighborhood than theirs, it made Julie feel like she hadn't made the grade as a parent. Even though the relationship thus far appeared harmless, and the dates consisted mostly of hanging around together after school, and talking on IM at night, Julie couldn't help but see her Sabrina's new bond as a denunciation of her mothering.

"What kind of low self-esteem must she have to be going with a boy like Curtis?" she implored. "I raised her to respect herself, to see herself as attractive and intelligent, and her first boyfriend is a kid who isn't in a single GT or AP class in her high school. What does she *see* in him? Why can't she date someone who's her equal? Do you think this is because we haven't given her enough attention? What are we missing here?"

My initial efforts to help her gain some perspective were all for naught, so intent was Julie on skewering herself: "It's not un-usual for adolescents' first boyfriends or girlfriends to be individ-uals who are very different from their parents. It's a way for them to establish their own identity, and to try out the beginnings of in-timacy with someone who they're unlikely to stay involved with, which lowers the risk of hurting and being hurt."

"But I can't help thinking that this means we haven't done our job," said Julie. "Her best girlfriend has a boyfriend who plays lacrosse, just like she does, and is in all of the GT classes. So there must be something about how we've raised Sabrina that accounts for this. Why else would she feel so comfortable with someone who's beneath her in so many ways?"

"He may be beneath her in some ways, such as in his course selection in high school, but it doesn't sound like you know him all that well at this point. Chances are she doesn't, either. He may just be a good-looking guy with a decent personality."

"Or a manipulative scumbag who's out to jerk my innocent daughter around to get what teenaged boys want. The point is, kids hang around with kids who are their equal, and if she thinks Curtis is her equal, then we must not have done a very good job teaching her to feel good about herself."

Julie's insistence on seeing Sabrina's first love relationship as an imputation of her talents as a mother severely limited her abil-ity to handle things with more calm and objectivity.

The reality is that all of us will at times find ourselves responding in unproductive, if not counterproductive, ways when our teens begin the important process of separation and individuation. Be-cause our responses are usually determined by the aforemen-tioned templates, and thus more about us as parents than them as adolescents, our job is to learn more about these templates and to increase our awareness of their impact, so that we can begin to create room for new and better responses to emerge. These tem-plates are like heirlooms, handed down to us in one form or an-other by the previous generation with the expectation that they be cherished and centrally placed on our parental mantelpieces. But *we* are the ones who ultimately have to decide whether it is truly in the family's best interest for these heirlooms to be given a place of honor or, perhaps more appropriately, respectfully packed away out of sight.

Rare is the parent who fits neatly into just one of the categories noted above. But let's take a look at a real-life case in which a parent's willingness to examine and revise his parenting template changed things for the better.

Doyle's complaints about his 15-year-old son, Chad, could be summed up with one simple phrase: "He's lazy." When I asked for specifics, Doyle was quick to comply: "He doesn't get the trash out on time. He doesn't get the recycling out on time. He doesn't clean his room when we ask him to. He doesn't clean the bathroom, even though it's mostly *his* mess in there. When I'm doing yard work, he'll help if I insist, but I have to watch him constantly or he'll slink off into the house, and I'll find him in front of the computer playing those damn online fantasy games."

Not sensing a great deal of patience on the part of this father, I quickly checked in with Chad and was not surprised to hear his impassioned defense: "No matter what I do, it's not going to please him. The trash has to be done a certain way, the recycling has to be done a certain way, my room has to be cleaned a certain way. It's like I'm in the Army or something!"

"What happens when you try to do it his way?" I asked.

"What's the point? He'll find something wrong with the way I do it no matter what I do."

"If what you mean by 'doing it my way' is that I'd like you to have the trash out the night before so that it's ready to be picked up in the morning, then I stand guilty. Is that such a tremendous imposition?" Doyle interjected, his voice drenched with sarcasm.

"Dad, I can do it before I head off to school, it's not a problem. They never come before seven o'clock to pick it up."

"They sure do, Chad. How many times have I come home from work and seen the trash bags sitting out there next to the street?"

"But it's not just the trash, Dad, it's *everything*! If I do the recycling, you yell at me because the bottles haven't been washed out. If I clean the bathroom, you yell at me because I missed a spot around the toilet. If I'm mowing the lawn, you come running out of the house just to point out all the areas that I've missed."

"I don't think it's so much to ask a fifteen-year-old to do these simple chores, Chad," Doyle insisted. "You're an intelligent young man, surely you can see for yourself that you've missed spots in the yard or that the trash has to be out early or that there are still pee stains on the floor near the toilet. I wouldn't have to point all of this out to you if you'd simply take care of it yourself in the first place."

"Sure you would, Dad. Or you'd find something else to complain about."

"This is where I start to feel like it's hopeless," Doyle sighed, looking at me.

No wonder, I thought to myself, as I searched for a way to intervene.

"What positive or negative consequences have you used to help motivate Chad to do things the way you believe they ought to be done?"

"Well, I'm certainly not going to schedule a parade simply because he's doing chores that he ought to be doing in the first place. These are baseline contributions to the workings of our household, and I don't think he should be rewarded for doing them. He gets plenty in return, believe me."

"How about on the negative end?"

"Well, he still gets an allowance, and sometimes I withhold that if he's been particularly unhelpful."

"Dad, you don't give me my allowance whether you think I've been helpful or not. You never have the money available, and when I ask, you just get annoyed with me, like I'm asking for something I don't deserve."

"Is that true?" I wondered.

"Yeah, I guess it is," Doyle said, defensively, "but I still don't think a fifteen-year-old boy should feel like he deserves to be paid just for doing some very menial jobs around the house that even a chimpanzee could do."

"Any other negative consequences that you've implemented?" I persisted.

"Not really, unless you consider my yelling at him a negative consequence," he answered.

"You mentioned earlier that you often find Chad in front of the computer. Have you ever held computer use in abeyance until he's completed his jobs successfully?"

"Yes, now that you mention it, I've tried that, but it's impossible to stay on top of it. I can't follow him around the house, I've got other things to do, and before I turn around, there he is back online, with his games and his Instant Messenger."

"How many computers do you have at home?"

"Just one."

"So have you installed any kind of password or gatekeeping system such that he can't be on it without permission?"

"I did that once, but he figured it out pretty quickly."

I glanced over to see Chad grin and look down at the floor.

"So you feel as if you have no leverage right now. You have expectations for Chad that you believe are reasonable, but he's not meeting them to your satisfaction. And you haven't yet figured out how you might motivate him to do so."

"You got it," Doyle agreed.

"You feel helpless?"

"Yes, that's it—completely helpless."

Very often, a recurring feeling, or matrix of feelings, that we have as parents is an echo of that same feeling from another time in our lives. In this family, helplessness seemed to have a particular resonance for Doyle. In fact, what was interesting me was that he seemed to be going out of his way to engender the very feelings of helplessness that he was so frustrated by.

First of all, he hadn't addressed his son's abiding and clearly articulated feeling that there was no way his father would ever be satisfied, which was inducing in Chad the same feeling of helplessness that Doyle was experiencing. Also, it puzzled me that he hadn't somehow figured out a way to hold Chad more accountable if doing chores "the right way" was indeed so important to him. Neither withholding Chad's allowance nor restricting his use of the computer had had much impact, but in both cases this seemed mostly due to negligence or lack of initiative on Doyle's part.

After all, when it came to the allowance, because his father rarely had the money available anyway, Chad had apparently grown not to expect it, so it wasn't much of a loss for him when it wasn't forthcoming. And when it came to the computer, Doyle had never made it a point to monitor the situation carefully enough to successfully limit Chad's use. If completing chores appropriately had such high valence for Doyle, why wasn't he using consequences more effectively? This was, for now, as big a mystery to me as Chad's perceived indolence was to his father.

With this in mind, I thought it might be useful to get a better understanding of the template Doyle was bringing to his son's adolescence. I began by obtaining some history, believing that Chad might benefit from listening in as well.

"My childhood was a pretty normal and happy one until my father died of a heart attack when he was only forty-one years old. It was a complete surprise to everyone because he was active and healthy, and it caught my mom entirely off guard.

"I was the oldest, with two younger sisters, and, frankly, my mom was a mess for the first year. This was a woman who hadn't even written a check in her life, and now she was supposed to make a go of it alone with three children to raise. Over time she really rose to the occasion, and I'd have to say that she did a tremendous job. But at first, of course, she turned to me. I became the instant man of the house, and she made it clear to me that I would really have to work with her on keeping things afloat.

"And I think she'd tell you I did a pretty good job, as well. I took care of my sisters after school once she went out and got a job. I handled just about all the chores and yard work at home. I even got a part-time job at a grocery store and saved up all my tips in a jar, in case we needed extra money. It never got that bad—my grandparents helped us out a lot. We even moved in with them for a few months at one point, but I was that kind of kid."

"What did you have to sacrifice in order to fill your father's shoes so effectively?" I asked.

It was the first time I noticed him hesitate before answering a question. "Just about everything. I had been planning on going out for the baseball team the spring of the year he died, but that was out of the question because I had to be home for my sisters after school. And I really just lost my whole social life. When you're fifteen years old you want to go out with your friends, you want to go out on dates, you want to *do* stuff, and the only stuff I did was around the house. My friends were good guys, but they had their own lives to live, they didn't want to have to hold back just because I was stuck with all of these responsibilities."

I couldn't ignore the highly significant fact that Doyle had revealed—his father had died when Doyle was 15, the same age that Chad was now. How complicated it must be for him to raise his son at the same age that he was when he had endured such a sudden and traumatic loss. And, of course, how helpless he must have felt.

"Have you ever found yourself comparing your life at fifteen with Chad's life at fifteen?" I wondered.

There was another pause, and his eyes closed for a long moment, then opened. "You know, it's funny, until you just asked that, I didn't put together that he's now at the age that I was when my dad died." He was quiet again.

"What are you thinking, Chad?" I asked.

Chad's tone of voice had lost the irascible edge that I had heard at the beginning of our meeting. "I knew that my grandfather had died when my dad was young, but I didn't put it together either, that I'm as old as my dad was when his dad died."

"So what goes through your mind now that you're realizing this?"

"I guess I'm realizing how different things are for me than for him. I mean, I've got a mom and a dad, I don't have to get a job, or take care of my younger brother, or any of that stuff. I even get to go out for baseball." Doyle smiled warmly at Chad, the first exchange of affection between the two of them that I had seen thus far.

"Doyle, it must be awfully difficult for you to tolerate Chad's lack of responsibility when you had no choice but to be so responsible yourself when you were his age," I commented.

"That's just what I was thinking," he responded, looking as if he had just awakened from a reverie. "I guess I'm expecting Chad to be just like I was, and maybe I'm angry at him for not having to deal with as much as I had to deal with."

"I think you're right. But I also think that you may still be angry at your father for having abandoned you and left you with such a load to carry," I added.

"It wasn't *his* fault," Doyle protested quickly.

"I'm not saying it was. I'm sure he would've preferred to still be alive. But it's natural to feel angry with someone who deserts you without good reason, even when it's not in his control. And your father, through no fault of his own, *did* desert you. The problem is, there was probably no room and no time for you to experience and deal with that anger, because you had to get right to work bolstering your mom and helping your sisters to cope."

"Well, you're right about that, too. I remember at the funeral my mom was just sobbing, and I was the one who was keeping an eye on my youngest sister, she was only three at the time and didn't really know what was going on."

"So, in some ways, you never got to grieve for your father and come to terms with his departure. Perhaps whatever hurt and anger that's left over from that time is coming out with Chad now that he's the same age you were and, in your eyes, old enough to handle it."

"But if all this is true, how do I get Chad to do what needs to be done?" Doyle, to his credit, hadn't gone so far back into the past that he had forgotten about what had brought him to my office in the present.

"Two things come to mind. One, you do have to examine whether your expectations for how these chores are to be done are realistic. A sure way to diminish someone's motivation is to criticize him for the help that he does offer, and that seems to be Chad's opinion about how things usually go. And a second is to be firmer about the consequences if there are clear lapses on Chad's part."

"What do you mean?"

"It could mean making sure that you come forward with his allowance the weeks he's earned it, so that it means something to him when, through his lackadaisical attitude, he *hasn't* earned it. Or it could mean not just imposing restrictions but following through on them, such as more vigilantly monitoring his computer use or limiting his time out of the house with friends."

"But I've tried that," Doyle insisted.

"You've tried it, but I think that you've been half-hearted about how you've tried it. If you really wanted to limit his use of the computer, you could—there are ways to do it. But I believe that you may have mixed feelings about sticking with these consequences."

"Why would I have mixed feelings about getting him to do what he needs to do?"

"Maybe because you wish that life had been a little easier when *you* were fifteen," I proposed. "Part of you is angry at Chad for not having to do all that you had to do after your father died. But perhaps part of you is *glad* that he doesn't have to do everything you had to do, because you want him to have a more enjoyable adolescence than the one that you were saddled with."

"So you mean by not sticking to my guns, I'm giving him the pass that I wished someone had given me?" he speculated.

"Exactly. And Chad, you might want to give some more thought to the ways in which your life as a teenager is different from your father's as a teenager, and how that might explain some of the arguments the two of you wind up engaging in."

"Will do," he nodded.

"One more thing, and this is for both of you. I want you to make a father-son visit to your father's gravesite, Doyle, and spend a few minutes introducing Chad to him, being that your father never had the opportunity to get to know him."

"You know, it's odd that you mention that, because I go to the cemetery on my father's birthday and death day, but I always go alone. I don't think I've ever taken Chad to see where he's buried."

"You haven't, Dad," Chad acknowledged, with a hint of sadness in his voice.

"I think, as part of this process, that it's very important for you to symbolically create the connection between the generations that wasn't able to occur due to your father's early death. Some of the mourning that you didn't get to complete when your dad died needs to be completed now. It's never too late."

Doyle and Chad returned a couple of weeks later sounding a good deal more positive.

"I did what you said," Doyle began. "First, I outlined on paper exactly what chores I wanted Chad to be doing and how I wanted them done, and we discussed it together and came up with an agreeable set of criteria for a 'completed job.' And we also discussed some consequences, good and bad, that would be used to motivate him."

"How have things been going so far?" I wondered.

"Pretty decently. I mean, I had to make some compromises, but I guess in the long run, as long as the trash is picked up by the truck, it really doesn't matter if Chad got it out there at seven in the morning or seven o'clock the night before. Same thing with the recycling. And I'm trying to not only stay on top of having money available when it's allowance time, I've built in some bonuses if jobs are done particularly well, such as when he mows the lawn and bags everything up nicely, like he did this past weekend."

"Yeah, I got a five-dollar bonus for that," Chad added, cheerfully.

"How's this all going for you?" I asked him.

"A lot better. I'm glad Dad wrote down his expectations, because that way I don't feel like he's always going to change things around and find something new to pick on me for. We made up a little contract and put it up on the refrigerator, so there's no confusion. And I'm glad that I'm going to get my allowance when it's due. It was kind of annoying when he never had the money to give me."

"What thoughts did you have regarding your father's adolescence versus your own?"

"Well, I thought about that a lot, too, and I guess I had a little more understanding about where he was coming from. It made me feel sorry for him in a way. And it also made me realize that what he's asking me to do isn't all that much compared to what *he* had to do. So maybe it's better that I just do what I'm supposed to do, and that'll make it easier on both of us."

"How about your visit to the grave?"

Chad jumped in before Doyle had a chance to speak. "I'd never seen Dad cry before, but we got there and he said, 'Dad, I'd like you to meet someone you would have loved to have gotten to know,' and then he got all choked up." He patted his father playfully (maybe even proudly) on the shoulder.

"He's right," Doyle admitted, "I guess I'd gotten so focused on all the things that Chad wasn't doing by the book that I was losing sight of what a wonderful kid he is, and how much my father would have enjoyed him. It's really depressing, because my father would've been a terrific grandfather. But it felt good, too—like I finally released something that had been holed up inside of me all these years."

Of course, things didn't go entirely smoothly just because a good deal of healing had occurred. In a follow-up session, Doyle reported with some peevishness that Chad had begun cutting things a little too close when it came to getting the garbage and recycling out, and that a couple of times they had gone out too late to be picked up. But this time he acted swiftly, insisting that Chad bring the bags and boxes back into the garage that night, and restricting Chad from computer use for the weekend.

"How'd you keep him off the computer?" I asked.

Doyle chuckled, opened up his briefcase, and pulled out a couple of computer cords. "A friend of mine at work had the same problem, and she told me that the simplest thing to do if I want him off of the computer is to forget about passwords and filters and all that business, and just unplug the wires that connect everything together and take them to work with me. It's a pain when *I* want to use it, because it takes a few minutes to get everything back together, but I'm getting good at it now, and it's worth it in the long run. Thank goodness we don't have wireless technology in our home yet.

"But the funny thing about this is that my father, believe it or not, was an electrician, so it kind of figures that I'm playing around with wires to get my point across with my son. It's like my dad's right here with me."

The process of revisiting the loss of his father had enabled Doyle to amend the perspective he was bringing to his relationship with Chad and develop a clearer and more realistic game plan. Initially feeling powerless in response to Chad's laziness and then engaging in a power struggle which he paradoxically ensured that he wasn't going to win, Doyle shifted gears and was able to mourn his father and more effectively raise his son.

EXERCISE 2

An adolescent's job is to differentiate from us, and it is impossible for us to embrace that differentiation without some struggle. Otherwise, it's not true differentiation. On the other hand, the more we know about why we struggle with their differentiation, the more effectively we can respond to it. Determining the origin of our struggle so that we can move in a better direction will be the objective of this exercise. Think back to the two main categories of differentiation that we discussed at the beginning of this chapter. Then go through the steps below.

They begin *doing* something that we wish they *wouldn't* do.
They begin *not doing* something that we wish they *would* do.

1. Begin by selecting a behavior that your teenager exhibits that fits into one of these two categories.

2. Which parenting template(s) do you respond to this differentiating behavior with?

> Our success as a parent
> Our freedom
> Danger
> Abandonment
> Being surpassed
> Being powerless
> The death of our dreams
> Our having failed

3. What parenting behaviors are associated with your selection of your template(s)?

4. Now, think back to your own adolescence, and a behavior that signaled your or one of your siblings' differentiation from your parents. Which template(s) did your mother and father use to respond to this differentiating behavior, and what parenting behaviors were associated with their choice of template(s)?

5. What positive or negative impact did their template have on you?

6. In what ways could you revise or adjust your current template so that a more constructive or productive outcome emerges?

Here's how one parent completed this assignment. Gloria, the mom we met earlier in this chapter, was struggling with the impending departure of her fourth and youngest son, Andy. The problem for her was that she was having difficulty experiencing his separation and individuation as anything other than a desertion of her.

1. *I guess it's that he's constantly out with his friends, and not treating us like a family anymore, more like we're a boarding house. If he's not with his girlfriend, he's with his football buddies. If he's not with his football buddies, he's busy trying to work extra shifts at his job. It's as if we don't matter to him anymore—he's used us up and tossed us away like we're a paper towel or something.*

2. *If I had to pick one, I'd definitely pick seeing his differentiation as* Abandonment, *although I feel like I bring a little bit of* Surpassed *and* Powerless *to this as well. Come to think of it, there's some* Death of Dreams *in there, too. I'm starting to realize, now that I think about it, how painful Andy's growing up really is for me.*

3. *I definitely find myself trying to control him. I try to set up schedules so that I can regulate how much he goes out, how much time he's at home, how many family dinners we have—trying to pin him down, and of course he just blows me off. I'm not crazy about admitting this, but I also try to bribe him—like I'll make one of his favorite desserts, hoping he'll want to be home for dinner, or suggest that we all go out to dinner, because he loves to eat out. And now that I think about it, I'm not above using a little guilt, as well—you know, saying things like, "What am I going to do next year when your father is working late and there'll be no kids at home, no one to have dinner with?" All in all, not a terrific way of handling things, I know.*

4. *I was the third oldest of four kids, the only girl, and what I remember is that my mother actually handled our leaving home better than our father did. She was all eager to get us moving with our lives, it*

seemed, but by the time my youngest brother and I were getting ready to leave home—we were only about a year apart—my father was a mess. He was always making comments to my mom, like "This is probably the last time we'll be together for Thanksgiving" or "This is probably the last time we'll go to a movie with the kids." It kind of became a family joke, he was so depressed, and so busy cataloguing every "last event." I think it made it harder for him that my two older siblings went to college in-state, but both my younger brother and I went away to school. My mother was basically okay with all of this, kind of excited, actually, because she had never gone away to college, so I guess for her our separation signified her success, which is the first category. But my father took it on the chin, and, I think, really felt like he was being left behind, so for him, like me, it was more abandonment.

5. I have to divide this up between my mother and father. My mother's approach certainly made things easier for me, that's for sure. I remember liking the fact that she took pleasure in my going away to college, liking the fact that she was so proud and excited, her only daughter going out into the world and becoming a competent woman. And she did begin to branch out some after we had all left home. She got a graduate degree in special education, and became a teacher, and only recently retired, but it made a big difference in her life, she received a lot of praise and acclaim.

My dad, on the other hand—it was like I was sticking a knife in his chest by going away to college. He was all mopey, and it got even worse the next year when my brother was packing up to go away. I think my father was very unsatisfied with his career, and had really worked hard to create a good family, which he had. But the thought of it all dissolving in front of his eyes, even though it was to his credit that he raised four healthy, independent children, well, it's like it was too much for him. I think he felt his life had peaked when the six of us were a family, and it was all downhill from there. Which was kind of annoying, really, because, in terms of our relationship with each other, it really was all downhill from there. He never seemed all that interested in what I was accomplishing at college or at work. But when I finally started a family, it was like I was his daughter again,

*and he could love me—something came alive again. Sometimes I
wonder if I would have allowed myself to get more involved in my career if he had been a little more supportive of it.*

6. *Now that I'm writing about this, it's pretty upsetting for me to consider the likelihood that Andy is probably feeling about me the way
that I felt about my father—irritated, suffocated, angry. I guess I've
been so busy being consumed by my own fears and loneliness, I
wasn't aware of how he might be experiencing me. No wonder he's
away from home all the time. Why would he want to hang around
with me if I look and sound just as mopey and depressed as my father used to?*

*I guess I'm thinking that maybe I ought to be approaching this
more like my mother did—seeing the kids' leaving home as an opportunity to start anew, and looking at it as an opportunity rather
than an abandonment. And I know that my husband's getting sick of
me, too, probably like my mom did with my dad. So I guess I could
see Andy's leaving as a chance to get a little closer to him—with him
having worked so hard all these years, and me busy raising the kids,
there hasn't been as much between us as there should've been.*

FOUR

UNDERSTANDING

It is better to fail in originality than to succeed in imitation.
—Herman Melville

In the previous two chapters, we have discussed the origins of our own behavior as parents, and how this behavior has its roots planted solidly in the psychic soil of our past and present experiences. In this chapter, we're going to shift the focus back to our teens and explore some of the origins of *their* behavior, so that we have a better understanding of why they do what they do. This will guide us toward responding effectively *when* they do what they do.

While adolescents often act in ways that range from perplexing to disturbing to downright harrowing, there is invariably not only a method but also a message behind their apparent madness. Our job is to see through their observable behavior, in whatever form it takes, in an effort to find the impelling motive that lies hidden behind it.

In my practice, I never cease to marvel at how innovative adolescents are in attempting to express and alleviate their concerns. Fortunately, adopting an open-minded, inquisitive attitude is sometimes all that's necessary to ferret out the issue and help them find a more adaptive way of addressing it.

One of the adolescents who taught me this very early in my clinical career was Marquis, a high school junior who was a marvelous vocalist. When he reached puberty, his voice had naturally lowered itself into a beautifully resonant *basso profundo*, and the choir director at his church had contacted the music teacher at his high school, insisting that Marquis be invited to join the assorted vocal music groups there.

Mr. Pattin, the music teacher, auditioned Marquis at the beginning of ninth grade and instantly fell in love with Marquis's rich tone. Soon Marquis was not only in the concert choir and Madrigals at his school, but he was also being considered for semi-professional vocal performance groups as well. Mr. Pattin spent many hours with his prized student after school helping him to prepare for his various tryouts and performances, and Marquis greatly appreciated his teacher's enthusiasm and support.

However, Marquis's mother, Daphne, set up an appointment with me on the school's recommendation because she was told that he had recently taken to mutely standing in an open closet during class and rehearsals, not disruptive, but refusing to participate or talk. At the end of the hour, he would quickly leave the music room without a word. Somewhat surprisingly, this had not been reported to the guidance counselor by Mr. Pattin himself, but by several chorus members, who were unnerved by Marquis's strange behavior. The guidance counselor told me that she had spoken with Mr. Pattin, who had reported that Marquis had adopted this strange ritual at the beginning of junior year for no apparent reason, and that because he had been such an excellent student, he was choosing to just let it go for now and hope that it worked itself out.

Daphne also informed me that Marquis had been getting headaches around the same time he had begun his strange in-class ritual, headaches that, according to consultations with his pediatrician and a pediatric neurologist, did not seem to have any organic basis, and were not responding to any treatment.

Marquis was a tall, thin, ascetic-looking young man who spoke softly and somewhat haltingly despite his sonorous voice. After spending some time learning more about his interest in music, and his hopes to perhaps pursue a career in opera, I asked him about his sudden and silent boycott of music class. He stammered that he'd rather not talk about it and then clammed up. I moved the conversation into some less threatening areas and scheduled a follow-up.

Interestingly, a couple of nights after I had first met with Marquis, I awoke in the middle of the night from a very vivid and disturbing dream that took place in my old high school. It involved my trying to escape from a dark and empty classroom that had been locked from the outside. I hollered and hollered and pounded and pounded, but no one heard or came to rescue me.

In reflecting upon the dream, I found myself revisiting a very anguished experience from my junior year in high school that I hadn't given much recent thought to. As a sophomore in high school, I developed a very close relationship with my English teacher, who had recognized my interest in writing and strongly encouraged me to pursue it. Literate, witty, acerbic, and attractive, her support was as welcomed and as nourishing as manna during my lonely trek through the desert of middle adolescence.

Married, but without children yet, she began inviting me over to her house after school from time to time, where we would talk about art and music, writing and literature, philosophy and politics, and where I would confide to her my (thus far) miserably insufficient and unfulfilled experiences with the opposite sex. One rainy afternoon, in a way that was neither wholly expected or unexpected, our relationship crossed the line and became a physical one.

Still a few months shy of my sixteenth birthday, I was utterly baffled and overwhelmed by this shift in our liaison, and absolutely tormented by the mixture of feelings that arose as a result—desire and guilt, affection and despair, gratitude and shame. One time her husband, a man whom I had already met a couple of times and liked, had even arrived home unexpectedly during one of our assignations, and although we both did our best to cover up the nature of our interaction, I could not imagine being more embarrassed or humiliated.

This disquieting arrangement—one that I both sought and loathed—continued almost until the end of summer, at which point she told me that she would not be returning to teach the next year because she was pregnant (not by me—thankfully, things had not progressed that far). I remember experiencing an enormous sense of relief, knowing that I would not have to see her anymore (I had already been wondering what it would be like to run into her once we returned to school in a few weeks), and hoping that she would become preoccupied with starting a family and less drawn to seek my companionship.

So it was with great shock that I entered my eleventh-grade English class on the first day of school in September to find none other than my former English teacher in front of the room, with her name emblazoned on the blackboard. The school, needing a last-minute replacement for a teacher who had been seriously injured a few days before, had called her in as a long-term substitute until she had her baby, and she had apparently complied. Surely registering my look of surprise and distress when I took my seat, she smiled reassuringly, as if to say that things were going to be all right, that our relationship would remain a secret (or at least that's what I hoped she was conveying), but her efforts did me no good. I felt like I had awakened from one nightmare only to find that I had entered another.

For the entire two grading periods that she taught this class, I contributed absolutely nothing, spoke to no one, and sat with my arms folded, staring at the floor. I tried to complete my assignments as drily and dully as possible, a painful endeavor for someone who so enjoyed writing. My friends and classmates were puzzled. I was usually one of the students who participated most vigorously, particularly in English. Why was I so sullen and unresponsive, and only in that one class, they wondered. Of course, I felt as if I could say nothing and stuck to my vow of silence until, finally, she finished her teaching assignment in January and went off to give birth.

Having followed my dream to what I believed to be its genesis—how desperately alone I must have felt in that "dark and empty" English classroom, how "locked in" I had been—I couldn't help wondering if Marquis was in the same boat. After all, his situation was strikingly similar to mine—a favored student thirsting for a beloved teacher's care and encouragement, who then abruptly changes and inexplicably retreats when he's in his mentor's classroom.

In my next session with Marquis, I gently but insistently pursued this line of inquiry, and the story that he eventually told rang hauntingly true. During one of their afterschool practice sessions,

Mr. Pattin, who often touched Marquis to demonstrate proper breathing and posture, had draped his arms around him from behind and kissed his neck. Marquis was both aroused and appalled by this gesture and could not figure out a way to make sense of it. Because he felt so flattered by and hungry for this attention, and because he did not want to lose his mentor's support, Marquis did not clearly reject Mr. Pattin's advances, however, and continued meeting with him after school, meetings that usually involved varying degrees of sexual intimacy.

This continued until Marquis could no longer tolerate it and broke things off. However, his decision created tremendous tension—tension that he was having a difficult time handling by himself or speaking with anyone else about. His "solution" was to continue to show up for class and in-school rehearsals, but to refrain from participating, a way to make a statement without directly disclosing anything or jeopardizing anyone—almost identical to the solution that I had arrived at a decade before. It was also particularly interesting that Marquis was literally keeping himself "in the closet" in his music class, which was, to my way of thinking, a metaphor for his ambivalence about his sexual identity.

As a result of Marquis's bravely coming forward with what he had been struggling with privately, some good things and some bad things occurred. First, having finally unburdened himself, he felt better and his chronic headaches disappeared. Second, I shared my findings with the guidance counselor, who recalled that something similar had occurred between Mr. Pattin and a different male student a couple of years before. This student had surprised everyone by dropping out of choir entirely, even though he, like Marquis, was quite talented.

Mr. Pattin was placed on administrative leave while an investigation ensued, resulting in two additional former students coming forward and relating like episodes, leading to his eventual dismissal from the school system.

The outcome, of course, was a mixed bag for Marquis. While he was no longer in the terrible bind that he had been in, he did lose a valuable mentor, and it took some time and hard work for him to gain a better understanding of what had transpired, to forgive himself for his role in the direction their relationship had taken, and to sort out his sexual preferences. But he *was* able to recommence his commitment to music, rejoin the choir, and move forward, somewhat wiser for his experience. And what he both taught and reminded me is that problem behavior always originates with the desire to solve a problem, and the more we can appreciate that, the more empathetic and helpful we can be as parents.

While all children are problem solvers, teenaged children, as we discussed earlier, tend to have a wider range of problems to solve. I have categorized these problems in the following way:

- Physiologically based problems
- Socially based problems
- Emotionally based problems
- Family-based problems
- Identity-based problems
- Power-based problems
- Separation-based problems

Let's examine some typical examples of problems from each of these categories to see how adolescents try, in their awkward, sometimes inadvertently problematic ways, to address them. To help families begin thinking in a more solution-focused than problem-focused way, I often ask them to answer the following four questions when they are trying to understand their teen's behavior:

1. What is the problem that the teenager is trying to solve?

2. Is the current solution working to the advantage or the disadvantage of the teenager and the family?

3. Is there a solution that could be substituted for the current one that would solve the same problem but work more advantageously for everyone involved?

4. If so, how can we create or enhance the likelihood that the teenager would consider implementing it?

Physiologically based problems are ones that have to do mainly with a teen's pubertal changes. For example, 15-year-old Gabriel had suddenly become very irritable and belligerent with his 12-year-old sister, Cynthia, when for years they had been quite close and gotten along well. What became evident was that Cynthia was beginning to develop sexually and Gabriel, already sexually charged himself, was very concerned about the arousal he was feeling in the presence of his newly blossoming kid sister.

By creating tension between the two of them through his constant taunting and criticism he was able to diminish their closeness, along with the possibility that any of his sexual urges would be acted out, thereby protecting both his sister and himself.

Socially based problems have to do with the need for adolescents to develop and nourish important connections with others. Fourteen-year-old Nathan had been diagnosed with severe learning disabilities when he was in grade 3, and he and his family had worked closely with the school system over the years to develop a practical and effective Individualized Education Plan (IEP) for him. As a result of their efforts, Nathan progressed nicely in his academic work, compensated for his disabilities effectively, and, in general, had as positive a school experience as most others.

That all changed in high school, however. The ideas that had been implemented so successfully throughout elementary and middle school—being pulled out of certain classes for a one-on-one tutorial, using a laptop in school to do his writing assignments, the in-class assistance of a special-education aide—all became anathema to him. Nathan steadfastly refused to go to any tutorials, regularly left his laptop at home, and shunned the aide despite her best efforts to remain unintrusive.

His parents were naturally quite upset. After having worked so hard to build these interventions into his school life over the years, and seeing them contribute to Nathan's scholastic success, they were understandably reluctant to watch him jettison them, and possibly begin floundering at a point in his life when grades really began to matter.

Nathan did not mince words with me when we met to discuss this. "You know what a SPED is? A SPED is a special-education kid. In our school, SPEDs are seen as dummies. Now I know I'm not dumb. I'm no nerd, believe me, but I'm not dumb. But when I leave for the tutorial, or tap away on my laptop, or have to deal with that stupid aide kneeling beside my desk to make sure I understand everything—well, everyone knows I'm a SPED, and that just about ruins my reputation. It's bad enough being in ninth grade, at the bottom of the heap, but to be a ninth grade SPED—well, I'm not doing it anymore, I don't care what my parents or my teachers think. I'm *done*!"

The problem—Nathan's rejection of the supportive services that had been so effective in the past—was his solution to a more vexing problem involving his social standing as he began high school.

Emotionally based problems result from the extraordinary psychological changes that accompany the physical changes associated with puberty. Seventeen-year-old Dana would go into the bathroom on Sunday evenings and slice her thighs with a pair of scissors until they bled. Eventually her physical education teacher noticed the scars and sent her to the school nurse, who sent her to me.

Amazingly, Dana said that slicing her legs actually relaxed her. "It works a whole lot better than the Paxil that my psychiatrist gives me—the feeling of the warm blood dripping down my leg really calms me down." It seems that self-mutilation was, for Dana, a way to "bleed off" the overpowering feelings of dread and anxiety that she felt mounting as the weekend came to a close and another week of school loomed ominously ahead of her.

Family-based problems revolve around the concerns, issues, or secrets that an adolescent is tuned into that affect the family as a whole. Fifteen-year-old Jason would repeatedly sneak out in the middle of the night and run away from home, staying with friends until his parents figured out where he was and went and got him.

One dynamic that became clear as I got to know Jason's parents was that his runaways generally unified the two of them, and in fact seemed to be the time that they were most collaborative. They would work closely together as an investigative team to expose his latest hideout and strategize ways to have him return home.

Jason eventually disclosed to me that his parents had separated two times before in their marriage, and that he was not certain that it wouldn't happen again. It appeared that his worrisome escapades—events that quite dependably facilitated greater togetherness between his parents—were the best way he knew of to try to keep their marriage afloat during a difficult time.

Identity-based problems are rooted in the daunting task that all adolescents have to face—the need to create and define a persona that is all their own. Fourteen-year-old Lina was in a destructive relationship with a young man who drank heavily, sold drugs, and threatened to kill himself if she ever left him. Her parents had not approved of her boyfriend from the start, and had tried their best to dissuade her from getting more deeply involved with him. But, of course, the harder they tried, the more devoted to him she became.

At the point when I met with her, Lina told me that she was sick of the relationship as well and wanted desperately to end things. However, she felt that doing so would mean admitting to her parents that they had been right all along, and that she had been wrong, an acknowledgment that, for her, was tantamount to an annihilation of her budding selfhood.

So she was, for now, intent on hanging in there with him, her misguided autonomy overriding her awareness of the relationship's dangers, a risky and ill-considered way of convincing herself that she was her own person and could do what she wanted no matter what anybody else said.

Power-based problems emerge from adolescents' craving for and ambivalence about power, their desire to acquire it and their fear of having too much of it. Fifteen-year-old Dante was beginning to use physical intimidation with his mother, a single parent. He'd block her way when she was trying to get upstairs, take the phone from her when she was in the middle of a conversation because he wanted to make a call, and threaten to "stab [her] in the middle of the night" if she didn't give him money when he was going out with his friends.

While appearing power-mad to his mother, Dante seemed anxious to me, violently trying to rouse his beleaguered mother out of her lassitude so that she'd either be able to be more of the rudder that could guide him through adolescence, or so that she'd understand that she had better arrange for someone else stronger than her or him to be that rudder. Already starting to get in trouble with the law, he instinctively knew that he'd need that kind of Gibraltar-like support and limit setting if he was ever going to turn things around.

Separation-based problems develop at the point when an adolescent starts preparing to leave home. Eighteen-year-old Sujong, a senior who had not only earned solid grades, but was a nationally ranked broad jumper, refused to complete any applications to college, despite the efforts of her guidance counselor, her parents, and just about everyone else in her life trying to convince her to do so.

When I asked her during our initial interview who in her family she was most worried about, she muttered, somewhat unconvincingly, "No one—they're all fine." When I commented that I had yet to meet a young adult who didn't worry about *someone* in her family, she begrudgingly acknowledged that her younger sister, Liyong, had started smoking pot and "my parents don't notice, and don't *want* to notice."

Further discussion of this concern yielded the strong possibility that Sujong was not going to go away to college and leave her younger sister behind until she knew that Liyong's difficulties would be addressed and taken care of without her.

As you can see from these examples, the process of determining the problem that adolescents are trying to solve with their problem behaviors can be a fairly straightforward one if you just keep your eyes and ears open and contemplate the notion that problem behavior is *always* designed to express or accomplish something, however maladaptively.

Even better, sometimes the process of substituting a better solution for the original one is just as straightforward as the discovery of the problem. To illustrate this, let's look at an example that resides in the physiologically based realm.

Donovan, a high school sophomore, was diagnosed with a

nonmalignant brain tumor in the spring and underwent successful neurosurgery to remove it that summer. Previously a stellar student, he started off his junior year shakily, which was to be expected. However, through the winter and the following spring, his attitude toward his schoolwork continued to be complacent at best, and the high scholastic average he had consistently carried since middle school was dropping steadily.

His first few post-surgical appointments showed clearly that the tumor was not returning and that he was recovering very well. His neurosurgeon went ahead and recommended a battery of neuropsychological tests just to see if there had been any inadvertent brain damage from the surgery, but the evaluation concluded that there were no notable cognitive deficits, and that his global IQ and achievement test scores remained stable and quite high.

In my initial meeting with Donovan, we talked about the discovery of the tumor and the subsequent surgery. At one point I happened to ask him if he knew of anyone else who had gone under the knife recently, and he mentioned that, during the same summer, his father had had to undergo surgery after he broke his ankle sliding into second base during a softball game. "It was no surprise, really—my dad's an animal no matter what he's playing. He can make *golf* into a contact sport. He's definitely one of those win-at-all-cost guys."

When I asked about his father's recovery, he told me that his dad had been told to take it easy and "not stress his ankle" with any of the exercise or physical activity that he was used to doing. Apparently, however, his father hadn't followed this advice and had gone back to playing in his indoor soccer league sooner than he should have. As a result he sustained a stress fracture to his ankle and faced the possibility of further surgery in addition to a long course of physical therapy.

This prompted me to wonder out loud if Donovan had the same concerns about his brain. Was he worried that if he "stressed" his brain by going back to studying as intently as he had done in the past, that it might provoke the growth of another tumor, requiring more surgery? Perhaps he had even concluded that it was his diligence as a student that had triggered the original tumor's existence, in the way that he had concluded that it was his father's intense physical activity that had resulted in his medical problem.

Donovan smiled, replying, "Yeah, I guess that's kind of gone through my mind. I do feel a little bit like I've got to take it easy, and whenever I get the slightest headache or tiredness or dizziness, all the stuff that was going on that led the doctors to look for the tumor in the first place, I'm figuring that the tumor's coming back. And that's not something I want to have to deal with again."

So what others were defining as a *problem*—Donovan's sudden underachievement in school—was, for him, the *solution* to a problem—a concerted attempt to keep himself in good health and not provoke further neurological risk. A consultation with his neurosurgeon to discuss this was all that it took to reassure Donovan that the tumor was unlikely to return, but that even if it did, it would not be the result of his "using his brain too hard." Having literally gone from "having something on his mind" to "having his mind put at ease," he was able to quickly reestablish his previous academic standing.

At a follow-up session, I asked if there were any other parts of his body that had been affected by his concern that overuse would create difficulties, to which he replied, a little hesitantly, "Not really." As I gently nudged the discussion into the arena of sexuality, I wondered out loud if he had found himself thinking the same thing about masturbating that he had been thinking about cogitating—the more you do it, the more danger you'll incur.

Donovan blushed and admitted that he had been afraid to masturbate since the surgery, and that, while he missed it, there was still a part of him that was reluctant to go back to it for fear of what "damage" would ensue. Again, a short discussion was all that was necessary to reassure him, and free him to return to an erstwhile source of sexual pleasure.

Here is a second example of a problematic solution that was quickly and smoothly replaced by a better one, this time in the *socially based realm*. Fifteen-year-old Roni was a biracial adoptee; her birthfather was African American and her birthmother was white. Her adoptive parents, Bart and Leah, and their biological daughter, 14-year-old Sarah, were also white. They consulted with me because of their concerns about Roni's social life.

"For the last year," Bart began, "she's been hanging around with this 'ghetto' crowd at school, the ones with the rap music and the baggy jeans—and I'm not just judging by appearances, this group really *is* up to no good."

"We knew that there'd be some changes once she became a teenager," Leah added, "but we certainly never expected such a radical turnaround. It's like we've lost our daughter somewhere and can't seem to get her back. Her grades are dropping, her attitude stinks, and she's become absolutely impossible to talk to."

Tall and pretty, with wildly dreadlocked hair and bad acne, Roni displayed the conduct of someone who was offended by everything and everyone.

"I don't know why I'm here, but I can tell you that I don't *want* to be here," was her opening salvo.

"I'd have to say that most of the young adults that I meet with would rather not be here," I concurred. "It's usually not high on their list of fun after-school activities."

"So what do you want from me?" she snarled, not appearing in the least bit interested in my conciliatory comment.

"Nothing, really. But it sounds like your parents are somewhat worried about you."

"My parents worry too much. I'm fine. Why don't they just leave me alone?"

"I'd actually like to help you to *get* them to leave you alone, but first we'll have to figure out why they're so worried."

"Oh, I can tell you why they're worried. They're worried because they don't like my friends, and, let me tell you, they're not going to pick my friends for me. Sure, some of them get into trouble sometimes, but we hang together, we've got each other covered."

"Let me hear more about your friends. It sounds like they're pretty important to you."

"My friends are the best. But my parents are always trying to keep me away from them. They think that my friends are the ones who get me into trouble."

"Do they?"

"Well, sort of. I mean, I was with a group of them when they were caught smoking pot before school. I was just there, not smoking it or anything, but I got hauled in. And then another time there was a big brawl in the mall parking lot, and there were some arrests, and I was there too, and now my parents think I'm in with a bad crowd or something, so they're constantly ground-ing me and putting restrictions on me and not letting me have my friends over. It's like I'm in a fucking prison or something."

"I'm just curious—are many of your friends African Ameri-can?"

She leveled me with a squinty-eyed stare. "Yeah, most of them—why?"

"I was wondering if that was one of the reasons that you felt that your parents were mistrustful of your friends, not so much because they've gotten into some trouble, but because they were of a different race than your family."

She thought for a moment, and then answered. "My parents are hypocrites, *that's* what they are. They talk like they're not racist, but they're racist, believe me—I can see how they look at my black friends. They say that they're color-blind, but, you know what? They're *not*."

"That must make it a little difficult for you, being half African American and feeling like your parents are closet racists."

"You bet it does," she nodded, angrily. "They just don't get what it's like for me. They think that they can raise me white, and they tried, but it's not going to work. There's no bleach that's go-ing to wash away *my* blackness, I can promise you that."

"Of course, I suppose that it probably doesn't make things any easier that your sister is white, too. . . ."

"Exactly! It's like she's their *real* daughter, and I'm some foreigner."

"I'm guessing that most of her friends are white?"

"Right. Not most, though—*all*. And of course she doesn't lis-ten to hip-hop, she plays the fucking oboe or something, and she gets all A's, and she just does every goddamn thing right."

What was becoming clear during our discussion was that Roni was feeling a tremendous sense of estrangement from a full half of her racial heritage. There had been little difficulty finding ways to respect her white lineage—her adoptive parents and sister had taken care of that just fine.

Unfortunately, there didn't appear to have been enough efforts to encourage her to honor, amplify, and explore her African American lineage. As she had so succinctly put it during our dis-cussion, she felt as if she was being "bleached" of her blackness.

The mini-community of African American compatriots that she had been trying to connect with was her first real attempt at discovering and displaying her black heritage. Unfortunately, due to a combination of inexperience and poor judgment, it didn't appear that she was choosing friends very wisely.

I brought Bart and Leah back for a session to discuss this with them.

"So what you're saying is that we haven't helped Roni to develop a healthy African American identity?" Leah asked, sounding at best doubtful, and even a little scornful.

"Basically, yes," I agreed.

"But it's not as if we're racist, you know," Bart commented, defensively. "We're both very open-minded, about as open-minded as people can be."

"I'm certainly not suggesting that the two of you are not open-minded, and I'm certainly not suggesting that the two of you are racist. However, Roni needs for the two of you to be much more than just open-minded and non-racist. She needs to know that her black lineage as well as her white lineage can be a source of pride both to her and to the whole family. She needs to be exposed on an ongoing basis to the richest aspects of African American culture."

"But we've done some of those things," Leah protested. "We live in a fairly integrated community, there are children of all races going to the girls' high school, it's not like we've isolated her."

"All of those things have been important and useful, but at this point in her life, she needs even more than you've already given her."

"Give us some examples of what you mean," Bart pleaded.

"How many African American adults are the two of you connected with?"

Both paused. "None, really," Bart acknowledged. "I mean, there's a guy at work who I enjoy talking to."

"Have you ever had him over to your house?"

"No, I guess not," he said.

"To what extent have the two of you tried to network with the African American community, such as through its cultural activities, its political groups, or its churches?"

"I guess we really haven't thought it was all that necessary to do that," Leah answered. "I mean, isn't it enough to live in the area in which we live? Why must everything take place at home?"

"Because Roni needs to also see that her parents value the parts of her racial identity that are different from theirs. Particularly with a sister who she's already going to feel diminished next to because Sarah is your child by birth, it's even more important that she sense your interest in her black heritage.

"Otherwise, she winds up feeling like an undervalued minority not just in the school and the community at large, but in her own family as well. And the danger of that is that she'll tend to believe that she doesn't have the same rights or the same opportunities as the race that's in the majority and has all the power, which, in this family's case, as well as in our society's case, is white."

"So how are we to handle this?"

"The best way is through a combination of talk and action. You should speak with her about what it's like to be a racial minority, ask her what her experiences have been, and how she has handled, and would like to handle, prejudicial treatment. That way, she'll know you're on the same page as her."

"What about action?" Leah wondered.

"You really have to create a better network of African Americans for her, because, as I said before, if you don't provide substantial role models for her, she'll go out and find her own, and she's not doing such a terrific job of that right now."

Bart and Leah agreed to give this some thought and reported back to me a couple of weeks later.

"I did some research in the school and the community," Bart disclosed. "First, I learned that there's an African American student achievement group at her high school, and it's open to biracial students, so I asked the faculty adviser, Ms. Wagner, to make contact with Roni and see if she could talk her into joining. And then Ms. Wagner told me that there's a diversity program that is asking for adolescent volunteers to help mentor young children. There's a whole racial-awareness training program for the volunteers, and I called them and got some information about it, and told Roni that we thought this might be a good thing for her to do.

"And it felt a little weird, but I did talk with my African American colleague—he's an attorney, too, and even though he does different work than I do in the firm, we still run into each other a lot. And I decided to just be straight with him, rather than inviting him over to our house out of the blue, so I explained the situation to him, and he actually was agreeable. He has a daughter a little older than Roni who goes to a private high school, his older two are away at college—and he said his daughter's on the shy side so he's always looking for ways to hook her up with some peers, especially since most of the girls at her private school are white. So they're coming over in a couple of weeks for dinner."

In the subsequent weeks, Leah and Bart began to note certain changes. Roni became less hostile and more engaged with the two of them and with her sister. Her grades started coming up as Ms. Wagner took her under her wing and pushed her to raise her expectations of herself. She began tutoring an African American first-grader as part of the diversity program, and she became friendly with several of the other tutors, young men and women of color who were solid and high-achieving and who Bart and Leah were more comfortable with.

Through finding ways to help Roni unearth and embody her ancestry, Bart and Leah enabled their daughter to discover a new, more positive solution to the social problems that had been overtaking her.

Over the years I have been able to help numerous teens and their families discover similarly straightforward ways to solve problems in ways that don't create new problems or unintended side-effects. But as you probably know, not all teens' "solutions" are as easy to make sense of or yield so willingly to more adaptive alternatives. Often their problem behaviors seem to be just that, problem behaviors, actions or inactions that wreak havoc with their lives or ours, that seem selfish or willful or malicious, that convince us that they have some innate, immutable defect or flaw that causes them to do the things that make us feel disappointed, angry, worried, and helpless.

In these situations, the answer lies not in giving up, but in more patiently and assiduously believing in their problem-solving approach and broadening the scope of our exploration of the knots that they are desperately trying to untangle. Let's take a more in-depth look at an example which required, and finally responded to, a more creative and persistent approach.

Winston's parents contacted me because of their worries about his complete withdrawal from life. A highly creative 17-year-old who had talked about going to an art institute when he finished high school, he had begun sitting as far away as possible from his fellow students, using class time mostly to mumble softly to himself. He had also impulsively quit his after-school job at the library, dropped out of the art club in his high school, and now spent most of his time at home alone in his room, drawing, writing, watching television, and going online on his laptop. The couple of friends who used to call him or come around to visit stopped doing so, and the art club's faculty adviser, Mr. Watkins, whom Winston had been quite close to, had contacted Winston's parents, wondering why he wasn't dropping in to chat as he used to do regularly.

The only individuals he spoke to at all were his parents, and his conversation with them was usually bizarre and rambling, having to do with extreme religious beliefs and the thought that he needed to be persecuted for his "sinful thoughts." His parents also reported that he had been displaying outbursts of volcanic anger at least a couple of times a week, usually when he was asked to help out or clean up, and in the course of these various eruptions had punched several large holes in his bedroom walls, broken some pictures hanging in the hallway, and put his fist through a window, fortunately not injuring himself in the process.

His mother was concerned enough that she had gone through his room one day when he was at school, thinking that he might be using drugs. Although the search turned up no evidence of drug or alcohol use, she did come upon a series of poems that he had written that had to do with his belief that he deserved to be tortured and some drawings that "looked sort of Satanic—the word 'hell' was written over and over again with various spears and flames going through the letters—the poems and the drawings really upset us."

Upon the recommendation of the school's guidance counselor, who had been receiving reports from Winston's teachers about his eccentric behavior, they had consulted with an adolescent psychiatrist, Dr. Jennings, who had diagnosed him with schizophrenia and begun treating him with antipsychotic medication. She had reassured the parents that they were not to blame and explained that schizophrenia was a chronic, lifelong neurochemically based disease, and that their job now was to help him to cope with his disease and manage its symptoms as successfully as possible.

Unfortunately, while the medication did seem to make his thinking a little less peculiar, not much else had changed. He no longer spoke to himself in class, but he still wasn't sitting or engaging with any classmates. He didn't return to any of his extracurricular activities—his library job or the art club—and he remained sequestered in his room at home. His conversations with his parents continued to be unsettling, often centered around his belief that the government needed his help to catch terrorists, and his explosive behavior still surfaced whenever he was pushed to follow through on a task or chore that he would rather not do.

Madness is, for most of us, the greatest fear of all. We all imagine we can or will cope with the loss of physical capacities, but to not be able to retain one's mental capacities, to lose control of one's own thoughts and thought process, is a grievous fate, indeed. So it was not a surprise to find Winston's parents heartbroken and dispirited about their son's distressing behavior.

From my perspective, Dr. Jennings, a fine diagnostician with an excellent reputation, had been helpful to this family in two respects. She was prescribing medication that was bringing some order to Winston's disordered thoughts, and she had absolved his parents of unnecessary blame. The theory that inadequate parenting creates schizophrenic children is an old and overly simplistic one that doesn't carry much merit or legitimacy these days and deserves to be mothballed along with many other outmoded and disproven clinical hypotheses.

On the other hand, in speaking with Dr. Jennings, it appeared to me that she had framed just about all of Winston's behavior as nothing more than schizophrenic symptomatology that they could not hope to have any more influence over than they could over a diabetic child's capacity to produce insulin. In so doing, psychiatric intervention had thus far unintentionally *limited* the possibilities for Winston and his parents and inadvertently made it difficult for any of them to go about helping him to climb out of this hole and go back to constructing a purposeful life for himself.

Did Winston gradually start experiencing psychotic thoughts that led to his withdrawal from the activities and relationships that had previously been meaningful to him, which in turn led to a more complete retreat into psychosis? Or had he, for whatever reasons, begun withdrawing from activities and relationships, which left him vulnerable to the development of his self-absorbed psychotic thinking? To my way of thinking, it was probably some of both. More importantly, I didn't think it mattered.

Because it was my belief that as long as he remained disengaged from adolescent life, for whatever reasons, his mind would continue to develop its bizarrely creative scenarios in an effort to keep itself sharp and vigorous and to ease the loneliness and isolation that were the true source of his suffering. The delusional relationships in his inner world were a desperately imaginative and barely satisfying replacement for the real relationships that had broken apart in his outer world. Only through assisting him in reconnecting successfully with others would he be able to crawl out of his hallucinatory funk and begin using his hungry, active mind for more constructive projects. In the meantime, the identified problem—psychotic behavior—was, for now, *solving* the problem of Winston's lack of healthy involvement with others.

In my family interviews with Winston and his family, I could see how difficult he made it for his besieged parents to engage and why they had just about given up on his having any kind of normal life. His answers to my questions were usually irrelevant and hard to follow, a gurgling stream-of-consciousness that seemed to flow everywhere but back to where we had begun. How tempting it was to resign oneself to despair and just ignore or put up with him, rather than insist on some kind of appropriate relatedness and responsiveness.

What I also learned was that his parents were no longer holding him accountable in the slightest degree for tackling the responsibilities a young adult should have to take on. His grades had slid, but there was as yet no consequence for his underachievement. He did no chores at home, because his parents feared more destructive blowups, yet he continued to be housed, clothed, and fed without making any contribution to family life. He was no longer expected to join them at church on Sunday mornings as he had been up until this year. In fact, they were relieved not to have him there, concerned that he'd embarrass them with a public display of anger or irrationality. They didn't even push him to join them for dinner anymore, and to some extent, who could blame them? He was hardly an engaging mealtime participant, usually either eating silently or subjecting them to his fantastically tangential maunderings on a wide range of political and religious topics.

It seemed to me that before we could get him hooked back in with the world outside of his family, we would have to assist him in doing so inside his family. I asked the parents to come up with a list of expectations that they felt were appropriate for an 18-year-old, and the consequences, positive and negative, for his having met or not met these expectations.

"But we don't know how much he can handle," Winston's mother, Sherrie, worried.

"I don't, either," I replied, "but I *do* know that he can handle more than he's currently got on his plate. Right now, he's got a pretty sweet deal—free food, free rent, free clothes, free television and computer in his own bedroom, free Internet service. Part of me is tempted to ask you where I might sign up for such an appealing arrangement for myself."

"I know, I know," Winston's father, Emil, admitted. "But, frankly, we don't know what to do with him. He doesn't do what we ask. And when we insist, he goes into a rage and starts destroying things."

"What have the consequences been when he has destroyed your property?"

"We're not sure he should have consequences if he's not in control of his behavior," Emil countered.

"Who has suggested that he's not in control of his behavior?"

"The psychiatrist. He's been diagnosed as schizophrenic—he's mentally ill."

"Even individuals with mental illness have to learn to become responsible and self-reliant."

"So you're saying that we should insist that he do what we ask?"

"Absolutely. Letting him off the hook completely because he's been diagnosed with schizophrenia isn't going to do anything but prevent his recovery from schizophrenia."

"But the psychiatrist said that there is no recovery, that it's a lifelong illness, like high blood pressure or alcoholism."

"Unfortunately, we don't know as much as we'd like to know about mental illness. But I can tell you this. Even conditions that have been *proven* to have an organic, medical basis, like heart disease, can be strongly influenced, for better or for worse, by how we live and how we act. Individuals who exercise, meditate, and eat right, for example, tend to be less debilitated by heart disease than those who don't."

"So we're to treat him like he's normal?" Sherrie asked in disbelief.

"Actually, yes. The more normally you treat him, the more normal he's likely to become. The more you treat him like an eternally handicapped victim of aberrant neurochemistry, the more he'll live like a victim."

"But what consequences are going to have an impact on him? He doesn't *do* anything," Emil asked.

"Sure he does. He's got a television and a computer in his room, and from what you're saying, that's pretty much all he's doing when he's not drawing or writing."

"That's true," he agreed. "But are you suggesting that we should take those away from him?"

"I think the presence of the TV and the computer in his room contribute to the ease with which he isolates himself and diminish his motivation to take the risk of reentering the world. If he's going to retain the privilege of having those options so available to him, he should have to earn them through responsible, engaged behavior."

"He'll really blow up if we take his TV or computer away," Sherrie warned.

"I suspect you're right. But remember that, for him, blowing up and having to deal with the consequences of his blowup are a lot better than retreating into a lonely, hopeless, psychotic state. At least when you're stirring his anger, you're reminding him that he's alive and part of the world, and that there are people in the world who care about him and matter. For now, you will have to decide whether you would prefer that he were belligerent and engaged or crazy and disengaged."

In my ensuing discussions with Sherrie and Emil I learned that there was another, background issue that was also making it difficult for these parents to take a more conscientious approach. Emil's older brother, Claude, had been diagnosed with schizophrenia when he was a teenager and had spent almost all of his adult life cycling dejectedly through psychiatric hospitals, homeless shelters, his parents' basement, and assorted halfway houses.

"My parents have been through hell with my brother, although I guess it's not as bad as the hell that Claude's been through," Emil related. "But, really, nothing ever worked. He's been on medication, but then he stops taking the medication. He'll participate in a psychosocial rehab program and then drop out. He'll get a decent job—he's quite intelligent, a really good writer, and came close to earning an English degree—but then he'll quit or get fired for acting weird. Of course, it hasn't helped that he's abused drugs and alcohol all these years—God knows that's made things worse, not better. My parents don't know whether to support him or let him hit bottom. They've gotten all of this conflicted advice over the years, and now they just take care of him whenever he shows up and pray for the best—basically, he's a fifty-year-old dependent."

"Sounds like it's been an unmitigated disaster," I commented.

"For everyone," Sherrie agreed. "I mean, when I see how awful Claude's life is, and then think about Winston being consigned to the same fate, well . . ." She choked up and looked at the ceiling.

"What Claude and your whole family have been through has been, and continues to be, truly and unimaginably awful," I started, "but that doesn't mean that Winston is headed down those same dark roads. I don't know what went wrong with Claude, although I'll agree with you, Emil, that his involvement with drugs certainly exacerbated an already unhealthy and perilous situation. But Winston is a different young man, with different talents and strengths, and even though he's been given a diagnosis of schizophrenia, his life need not play out so horribly.

He deserves better than to be seen as an insane castaway, and so do the two of you. There are many things we can do to influence his behavior for the better and to raise the odds that he'll come through this very unsettling stage intact."

Being reassured that there was, indeed, some reason to be hopeful seemed to mobilize Sherrie and Emil, and they got down to work developing a list of expectations for Winston, which included earning C's and above in all of his classes, with no more than two C's; participating in at least one nonacademic activity, either in school (such as art club) or out of school (such as his library job or some other job); folding the wash and emptying the dishwasher on a daily basis; giving his dad an hour or two of help in the yard on weekends; and joining them for dinner on any evening that he did not have a prearranged social or work engagement. We also agreed that it was time for Winston to resume the process of getting his driver's license (he had gotten his permit months before) as another method of maneuvering him back into the world of reality.

Finally, we spent some time mapping out the consequences for his having met or not met their expectations, and planning how they would respond should Winston test their resolve, as I strongly predicted he would. In particular, I suggested that they not hesitate to contact the police if he began to show evidence that he was losing control of his behavior.

"The police?!?" Sherrie wondered. "Why the police? If we're going to take him anywhere, shouldn't we take him to the hospital if he's out of control?"

"If a young adult is misbehaving, then I believe that the police are the appropriate ones to call. If he's destroying property, it's not because he's sick, it's because he's not exhibiting the maturity to control himself."

"But his lack of control has to do with his being schizophrenic," Emil countered.

"It's puzzling to me that his schizophrenically based lack of control only asserts itself when he is asked to do something he doesn't feel like doing. When no one's bothering him and he's free to do as he pleases, it seems he has little difficulty controlling himself. That suggests to me that he needs *limits*, such as the police can provide, more than he needs medical attention."

Emil and Sherrie hesitantly agreed to try this out. That night, they had a family meeting with Winston and made it clear to him that if he did not meet any of the aforementioned expectations, he could expect to lose the freedom of having the television and computer in his room. As expected, by the end of the week Winston was clearly putting them to the test. He continued to refuse to join them for dinner, wasn't folding the wash that they had left for him to work on in his room, and showed no interest in the art club, in contacting the library about getting his job back, or in looking for a new job. As planned, his parents went into his room while he was at school one day and removed the television and computer, secreting them away in a carton that they hid in a forgotten corner of their basement.

Winston arrived home, became instantly aware of how his parents had intervened, and hit the ceiling. He demanded that they return everything to his room, insisting that they were "his," but his parents stuck to their guns and reminded him of the agreement. Winston started throwing furniture around the living room, screaming that Al Qaeda was going to make them pay for their offense. Emil warned him that if he continued, the police would be called. Winston dared him to, and Emil followed through.

Two police officers showed up within minutes, saw what was happening, pulled Winston to the side, handcuffed him, and then, after briefly speaking with him, asked the parents if they wanted him taken to the hospital for a psychiatric evaluation, to the police station so that charges could be pressed, or left at home. Emil and Sherrie agreed to allow him to remain at home if he promised to control himself and agreed to clean up. Winston promised, the police released him, and he immediately went up to his room and went to sleep.

"That was probably the hardest thing I've ever done, calling the police on my son," Sherrie confessed.

"Me, too," concurred Emil. "I mean, I felt like we had no right to have our son handcuffed like that in our own living room."

"On the other hand," I reminded them, "he has no right to destroy your property just because he's not happy with the rules."

"We know that," Emil responded. "It's just that it never occurred to us to use the police."

"But you'll have to admit, it worked," I reminded them. "He regained control and went to sleep."

"So are we going to have to contact the police every time he throws a tantrum?" Sherrie asked, worriedly.

"I doubt it. I think calling the police is a statement of faith in his ability to modulate his feelings, and once he sees that you mean business, he won't continue to push it. He may test you out a couple more times, but I don't think it'll go much beyond that."

I asked that Emil and Sherrie insist that Winston clean up the living room and put all the furniture back in place, and bill him for the lamp that he had broken during his rampage. When he asked where he was going to get the money to pay for a fixture that cost almost $100, Emil told him that it would come out of his paycheck. When he reminded them that he didn't have a job, Emil suggested that it was high time that Winston find one. What was notable about this conversation was that even though it was a disagreement, it was the first rational exchange that Winston had had with his parents in weeks.

As we anticipated, Winston did lose his temper again a week later. Having felt like he had made sufficient progress, he had asked for the computer and television back in his room. Sherrie acknowledged that he had made progress but pointed out that he still had some things to accomplish before this privilege would be restored, such as having a job and doing his chores. Winston picked up a plate and smashed it on the floor, then held another one over his head, daring her to intervene. Sherrie told him that if he didn't put the plate down and clean up the one he'd broken, she'd call the police again. Winston didn't hesitate to break three more in succession, at which point she called 911.

The same two officers from before returned, handcuffed him, and provided Sherrie with the same three options as before. She again agreed to let him stay, but this time they made it clear to Winston that should they be called again, for *any* reason, they would be taking him directly back to the police station, where he'd be charged with destruction of property and placed in the juvenile detention facility.

Chastened, Winston went up to his room, where he remained until the following morning. He did not complain when Sherrie told him that he would not be allowed to have breakfast until he cleaned up the shattered crockery, and that $20 would be added to the original bill for the broken lamp.

After these two encounters, Winston slowly began to help out a little more around the house and also began joining his parents for dinner, as they had requested. I told Emil and Sherrie that it would be useful to learn a little bit more about terrorism, since that seemed to be the theme that many of his delusions revolved around, so that they might try to bring his dinnertime conversation back into the realm of reality.

When Winston would commence a long and involved sermon on his favorite topic, I asked them not to just roll their eyes and valiantly try to change the subject, but to take him on more directly and insist that his premises be held up to the light of reason. Again, what was important was not that he *agree* with them or relinquish his beliefs, but that he *engage* with them around those beliefs.

I encouraged Emil to start taking Winston out driving in preparation for his earning his license and suggested that each outing be centered around a job-related activity—scouting out places that were hiring, picking up or dropping off applications, attending interviews.

Driving, too, provided a better context for a more personal interaction. Winston, like most teenagers, had to focus so hard on driving that there wasn't much cognitive room left for any of his bizarre thoughts. Over the course of the next couple of months, he gained enough experience to pass the driving test and also obtained a new job at a pet store.

Both of these accomplishments helped to diminish his propensity to violent and psychotic behavior as well. The reason for the former is that individuals usually deploy violence as a last resort, when they have no better way of expressing or discharging their most discomfiting feelings, when they are without resources or alternatives. Having a license and a job provided Winston with some ways to get out of the house, be more independent, and reduce the buildup of stress that often preceded and predicted his blowups.

The reason for the latter is that Winston was simply forced to break through the loneliness that the schizophrenia had been layering around him. No longer so remote that he had to rely almost entirely on his own brain to replace the people he had cut himself off from, he was now asked to interact more normally, which built up his social self-confidence. The pet store was an ideal job in some ways, because many of his responsibilities involved caring for animals, who were sometimes a good deal easier and less threatening to connect with than people.

Winston never rejoined the art club, but he did start spending a little more time after school with Mr. Watkins, his art teacher. He did not earn high marks for participation in his classes, but he moved back into the mainstream and graduated on time. He eventually decided, with his parents' support, that he was not ready to leave home and go away to college when he graduated high school, but he did register at the local community college, with an interest in becoming a veterinary technician. He continued to check in with Dr. Jennings and take the prescribed antipsychotic medication, which, along with the other changes he had made, helped him to gain better control of his thoughts. And he did make a new friend at the pet store, someone who also went to the community college.

There were two notable addenda to this family's development. One was that Emil spontaneously decided to make more of a commitment to connect with his brother, Claude. Seeing that there was hope for his son seemed to motivate him to find some hope for his brother. "I've decided that I'm going to visit him at least once a month, something that I haven't done probably ever. He's sick and impossible and very disturbed, but he's still my brother, and I owe it to him, to my parents, and I guess in some ways to Winston to see if we can rebuild a relationship with each other."

Another positive result was that, despite the improvements in his behavior and responsibility level, Winston was never given back his in-room television or computer, nor did he even continue asking for it. Emil and Sherrie decided that they just didn't want to give him such an easy opportunity to isolate himself, and Winston eventually grew accustomed to, and probably preferred, watching the TV or using the computer in the family room. It was as if they all knew that the seductions of isolation were still strong enough for Winston that it would be best if they weren't even given a foothold.

This creative young man's first try at solving the problem of loneliness and isolation had, with his parents' dogged help, eventually been replaced by better solutions that more effectively solved the original problem.

EXERCISE 3

One of the things that complicates the process of seeing our teenager's problems as their solutions is the fact that their problem-solving strategies differ from ours. All of us develop an individual approach to solving problems based on the strengths, attributes, and resources that we have at our disposal, as well as the nature of the problem and the environmental response to our problem-solving attempts.

Many times, it's difficult to see teens as good enough because, in our eyes, they do not choose to go about solving their problems in the way that we think would be best. But when you are able to see the logic behind their selected problem-solving strategy and come to at least respect it, even if you don't approve of it, you will be better able to help them pursue substitute strategies that might serve as effective replacements.

This exercise will assist you in this process by inviting you to examine the development of your own problem-solving strategies, as well as your teen's.

Begin by choosing some behavior that your adolescent displays that you see as problematic. You might review the categories that we discussed earlier, within which most problem behaviors seem to fall:

- Physiologically based problems
- Socially based problems
- Emotionally based problems
- Family-based problems
- Identity-based problems
- Power-based problems
- Separation-based problems

Then, answer the following questions.

1. What problem might his problem behavior be solving?

2. Have I had a similar problem in my life? If so, how did I solve it?

3. How is my method of problem solving similar to my teen's? How is it different?

4. What are the advantages and disadvantages of my chosen method of problem solving?

5. What are the advantages and disadvantages of my teen's chosen method of problem solving?

6. What other solutions are there that might address this problem in my child's life?

Mary Jo contacted me about her 17-year-old daughter, Pamela, a senior in high school who was coming precariously close to missing the deadlines for the completion of her college applications. "No matter what I do, I can't seem to motivate her to finish them up. This one needs an essay she hasn't written, another one needs a letter from her coach that hasn't been mailed, another one requires a transcript that she keeps forgetting to have sent out—all seven of them are in various stages of incompletion, and I'm afraid that none of them are going to get in on time at this rate, and she'll be left without any options for next year. And that would be a shame because she seems to really want to go, and I think that she's ready for college, but the rules are, if you don't apply, you don't get in."

Here are Mary Jo's answers to this exercise:

1. *I'm not sure, but I supposed I'd have to guess that maybe she's not so sure she wants to go to college. That doesn't seem right, but why else would she not be filling the applications out and turning them in? And if she doesn't want to go to college, then one sure way to prevent it from happening is not to apply.*

2. I didn't have any doubts about going away to college, that's for sure—I couldn't wait to get away from home. But I do know that I had a terrible time deciding what to do after college. I was really lost. But the way I handled it was to try to create a million options for myself—I was filling out applications for graduate school, for jobs, for fellowships, even for the Peace Corps. I must have been at the post office every day during my last few months of senior year, sending something out somewhere.

3. My method of problem solving was different because I was really making sure that things got turned in. I wasn't dawdling at all—if anything it was like I was shot out of a cannon, trying to make sure that I had something in place. I didn't initially think that there were any similarities to our problem-solving approaches, but now that I think about it, they're kind of related because they kind of lead to the same result. She's not turning anything in, so she won't know what to do, and I had so many things turned in that I didn't know what to do!

4. The advantage of my approach was that I really did wind up with a lot of possibilities. The disadvantage of my approach was that I had so many possibilities, I wasn't able to make a decision, so I kind of boxed myself in and went through a long stretch where I couldn't make any decision at all.

5. The disadvantage of Pamela's approach is that she may wind up with nothing, no options at all. The advantage of Pamela's approach is that she won't be overwhelmed with possibilities, like I was, which, in some ways, may make it easier for her to choose which path to take.

6. Now that I'm thinking about this, I suppose it would be best for Pam and me to talk about whether she really wants to go to college, or if it's a more complicated decision than she is letting on.

Mary Jo's comparative exploration of her and her daughter's problem-solving approaches led her into a fruitful discussion with Pam, during which she learned that Pam was indeed having very mixed feelings about leaving home for college, mostly because she had been feeling pushed by her parents to apply to institutions that were, in her eyes, out of her league.

"She told me that the more she thought about the list of colleges that we had finally narrowed down, the more she felt like they were not places that would be good for her," Mary Jo related in a subsequent session, "so we went back to the drawing board and made sure that we included a couple of schools that hadn't previously been on the list that her friends were applying to. I guess I hadn't realized how much she felt that she was under our influence, and that her not finishing her applications was her way of telling us that she didn't like the choices that she was going to have to select from.

"I was still worried, though, because I thought that the last thing she needed at this point was more applications to fill out when she hadn't even filled out the original ones. But this discussion seemed to be some sort of a breakthrough for her, because she went and downloaded the applications to these other colleges, and then quickly tied up all the loose ends and got everything in the mail from the new and old applications. So now we're finally set."

By looking at her daughter's problem behavior through a solution-focused lens, Mary Jo was able to devise an augmented plan that left Pam feeling better able to complete this essential aspect of the leaving-home process.

FIVE

FORGIVING

We had fed the heart on fantasies,
The heart's grown brutal from the fare

—W. B. YEATS

A story is told of a man being chased by a ferocious tiger. He is barely able to stay ahead of the beast and finds himself approaching a cliff. Knowing that he can't stop, he continues running to the edge and jumps off. As he's falling through the air he sees a small tree extending from the side of the cliff, and somehow is able to grab onto it with both of his hands. A hundred feet below, he sees a raging torrent of river. Twenty feet above, the tiger stands, roaring hungrily.

A lifelong nonbeliever, but now in a more dire situation than he's ever been in before, he finds himself instinctively invoking the name of the Lord. "God, I know that I have never believed in you, that I have never turned to you, that I have never prayed to you, but hear my plea. It looks like certain death above, and certain death below. Please answer me, though I've never asked before. What am I to do?"

To the man's astonishment, a voice rang from the heavens. "Let go of the tree," it intoned.

"What?" he said, wanting to be sure he had heard correctly.

"Let go of the tree," the voice repeated.

"But if I let go of the tree, I'll fall to my death. Isn't there some miracle you can come up with that's better than that?"

For the third time, the voice insisted: "*Let go of the tree.*"

"Is anyone else up there?" the man inquired.

Letting go is surely one of the most difficult aspects of parenting, and certainly not for the faint of heart—how can we possibly release our offspring from our care and allow them to begin making their own way through the world? It can feel as frightening for us to relinquish our hold on our children as it is for the man in the story to relinquish his hold on the sapling, and with consequences that feel just as unfavorable. Yet we are never finished with the job of raising our children until we *can* let go, daunting as it may be to do so. In this chapter, we will look at the process of forgiveness and see how it helps us to loosen our grip on our adolescents in ways that serve them, and ourselves as well.

Seventeen-year-old Malvern had been one of the finest ice-hockey players in the state until he tore his ACL during a summer tournament game and had to undergo surgery. Being that he was young and athletic, his prognosis was quite good, and his surgeon was pleased with how things went on the operating table.

Malvern was working out on a stationary bicycle within a week's time, and in another week had begun thrice-weekly physical therapy with what appeared to be the very realistic goal of reclaiming his previously high level of skating fitness and finesse. After two months of physical therapy his rehabilitation seemed to be complete, and his follow-up with the surgeon revealed no difficulties and a complete recovery.

However, Malvern continued to complain about pain in his knee and seemed reluctant to get back on the ice. His surgeon recommended another two months of physical therapy, which Malvern agreed to, but his parents noticed that some of the checks that they had been giving him to bring to his appointments were not showing up on their register. Following through, they learned from the physical therapy office that Malvern had been canceling just about every other appointment by telephone.

Angry and confused, they set up a session with me and brought me up to date. After learning that he had been skipping physical therapy sessions, they had sat him down and asked him to explain himself. He had replied that he didn't think it was helping, so why should he bother going? They responded that their doctor, whom they trusted, had recommended the physical therapy, and that there wasn't any chance of a full recovery unless he participated in it conscientiously. Malvern had quickly pointed out that they couldn't *make* him go, and he wasn't going to waste his time anymore.

"So where do things stand now?" I asked.

"If he's going to play hockey, he's got to recover fully. And to recover fully, he's got to go to physical therapy," his father, Philip, explained.

"Is that your understanding of things, Malvern?" I asked.

"I don't think it's helping. I don't see why I should have to go," he answered.

"But everyone from your coach to your doctor to your physical therapist has said that you've got to follow through with the physical therapy. You've got the best physical therapist around, he spends most of his time with professional athletes, he knows what he's doing, and you've got to trust him," Philip insisted.

"And you've got to trust *me*, Dad. It's not working and I'm not going."

"Then you can forget about playing hockey, son," Philip threatened, raising the stakes.

"Well, then, I'll forget about playing hockey, Dad," Malvern countered, matching the stakes, and then raising them higher.

"How could you forget about playing hockey? You're great at it, you're one of the best players around. Your team needs you, and you have a real future. Malvern, what are you *thinking*?" Philip clearly hadn't anticipated Malvern's countermove and was frantically trying to regain the advantage.

"I'll tell you what I'm thinking, Dad. What I'm thinking is that for the past four months I haven't had to wake up at five-thirty in the morning to get to practice five days a week. I haven't spent just about every weekend stuck in a car with you driving all over the place to get to tournaments. I think I've finally got a girlfriend, which I've never had before, although you apparently couldn't care less, even though I've tried to talk with you about her.

"I was able to go to the homecoming dance for the first time ever, even though I'm already a senior. I'm able to stay awake long enough to complete my homework and still talk on the phone. What I'm thinking, Dad, is that I've finally got a life."

Philip sat in stunned silence for a moment. But only for a moment.

"I see. So after all of those years of *my* getting up to drive you to those ice rinks at five-thirty in the morning, after all of those years of giving up *my* weekends to get you to Canada and Minnesota and Massachusetts, after all the money *I've* spent on hockey equipment, which you grow out of every year, God bless you, after all of the popcorn and cookies and magazines that I've bought and convinced *other* people to buy so that your teams could have successful fundraisers, after all of this, *you've* decided that *you've* had enough, just because you have a girlfriend and got to go to a dance. Well *good* for you." He shook his head with disgust.

By now, of course, Malvern was livid as well.

"You don't get it, Dad, do you? I'm halfway through my senior year of high school and I feel as if I've never *been* to high school! The only friends I have are on the hockey team, and they're good guys, but, frankly, I'm sick of them, they're the only people I've hung around with for the past seven years, I won't care if I *never* see them again. And, in case you hadn't noticed, *none* of them are girls!" (I had to stifle a smile at that one).

"All I've done is skate and practice and skate and practice and try to stay on top of my homework. And the funny thing is, that was really okay with me—I like hockey, it's a great sport, and I know I'm good at it. But what I learned once I tore my ACL was that there's more to life than hockey." He paused, as if considering whether he dared to go further. "And there's more to life than pleasing *you.*"

"Well, you sure picked a helluva time to figure that one out," his father responded curtly. "Right when college recruiters are contacting you and doors are opening for you. *Now* you decide there's more to life? *Now* you decide you've been doing it all for me?"

"Dad, at this point, I don't even *want* to play hockey in college. What's the point of committing to something that I don't want to do? And I'm certainly not going to make it as a professional, you and I both know that."

"Well, you better take a look at your GPA and your SATs, because they sure as hell aren't going to get you into the schools you want to go to unless you continue to play hockey. And that's not for me, that's for you."

"But what makes you so sure I want to go to those fancy schools? What—do you think I want to sign up for another four years of *this*? Early morning practices, no social life—why should I even bother going to college if it's just going to be a repeat of high school? You're the one who has the image of me playing ice hockey at an Ivy League college, not me."

"All I know, Malvern, is that you're making a huge mistake. Giving up hockey now would be the most foolish thing you could ever do with your life."

"Well, then, I guess I'm a damn fool," Malvern muttered, barely audibly, and father and son glared at each other across the formidable chasm of their misunderstanding.

All of us have some intuitive feeling for what forgiveness means, but trying to put it into words or action is hard work indeed. In fact, we are usually encouraged to envision forgiveness as an offering that is for someone else's benefit. "I will go to the trouble of forgiving you for having hurt me, which means you no longer have to feel guilty for having done so." But forgiveness may better be defined as a gift that we give not only to others but, more importantly, to ourselves. Because through tending the garden of forgiveness we will reap the most important human harvest of all, the capacity to equitably give and receive love. Let's examine how this plays out.

Every individual has an internal gauge that constantly and acutely measures the levels of justice and fairness in our relationships with others. In a healthy relationship, there is an equitable flow of what we import from and export to our partner. We know that there will be temporary periods of inequity and imbalance, but we trust that, over time, things will balance themselves out in a reasonable way.

Of course, we adjust this gauge in different ways for different relationships. In a marriage, for example, we generally set the gauge on Equal, because we expect our partners to be as available to fulfill our needs as we are to fulfill theirs. On the other hand, with an infant, we are better off setting the gauge on Unequal, because we know that we are going to have to give a whole lot more than we're likely to get for quite some time. The same may be true with our aging parents—we should expect to be in the position of providing more than we receive, and in fact can choose to see this as an opportunity to compensate them for the sacrifices that they may have made for us over the years.

When the give-and-take of a relationship matches up with our gauge's "equity setting," we tend to be pleased and satisfied with that relationship. When it doesn't, when what we feel compelled to give is not congruent with what we feel entitled to receive, then the relationship will begin to tilt and wobble, buffeted by the conflicting feelings that are aroused.

In some situations, our gauge tells us that we're giving a lot more than we're getting, which results in feelings of anger. In other situations, our gauge tells us that we're getting a lot more than we're giving, which results in feelings of guilt. When these imbalances occur, we instinctively try to "right" or secure the relationship so that equity can be restored and so that these discomfiting emotions—guilt or anger—can be dissolved. Depending on how we go about implementing them, these instinctive efforts to stabilize our connections with others can be either constructive or destructive.

In a constructive situation, for example, Judd feels that his wife, Hope, is becoming overly consumed with her work and PTA activities, and is neglecting him in the process. He takes the time to let her know that he greatly values what she does at her job and in the school community, and then lets her know that he's feeling a bit like he's at the "bottom of the list" of her priorities.

Judd offers to give Hope a hand with some of the endless phone calls that are an unavoidable part of her PTA responsibilities so that they might have a little more time together in the evening. In return, Hope agrees to try to get some of the other parents to take over the gigantic spring sports banquet that requires months of planning, rather than attempting to manage it mostly by herself, as she's done the past two years.

Judd and Hope also agree, as part of their discussion, that once she is done with the particularly consuming proposal that she is in the midst of at work, they will ask her parents to stay at the house while they go away for a weekend and discuss, in more detail than they have before, the future of their professional life as their children move toward college.

In this situation, Judd's sense of the relational inequity spurred him to address things with Hope in a way that worked to both of their advantage, and both were able to "let go" and rebalance their marriage constructively.

In a destructive situation, Sam finds himself feeling similarly about his wife, Linda's, commitments, as Judd did about Hope's. Instead of addressing it directly, however, Sam grouses silently, and does what he can to interfere with Linda's endeavors. Messages that are left with him for her somehow do not find their way onto her desk. He displays no interest in listening to her complaints about her employees at work and helping her to come up with strategies that might solve some problems, even though he too is a high-level manager and understands to a large extent what she's dealing with.

Feeling unattended to and put off, Linda throws even more of her efforts into her work and volunteer activities. She not only takes over the project of a colleague who has left for maternity leave, with the rationale that "Someone's got to do it," but she also offers to put together the student directory at their sons' high school, a monstrous endeavor that requires hours at the computer.

Not to be outdone when it comes to neglectful behaviors, Sam signs up for a men's basketball league on Sunday mornings, the only morning that both of them are uncommitted and could sleep in, meaning that he has to get up at 7:00 A.M. to get to the games. Hurt and angry, but just as unwilling to back down as her hurt and angry husband, Linda joins the social action committee at their church and agrees to spend her Sunday afternoons rebuilding dilapidated houses downtown, thus completing the process and effectively ensuring that they are apart from each other for just about every day of the entire week.

With both of their gauges registering inequities in the relational balance, each of them were vengefully trying to restore that balance, but in ways that were working at cross-purposes, destructively disrupting their sense of marital fairness and justice.

Now let's take a look at your relationship with your teenager. One of the most complicated aspects of raising an adolescent is that the meter that measures the relational balance between parents and adolescents is in transition. During the initial stages of childrearing you may have been content to be "exporting" much more than you have been "importing," but now that your son or daughter is a teenager, you are naturally going to look for a different kind of balance, one characterized by a more even-handed equilibrium.

The basic, unwritten parenting contract that we drafted well before our child was born—"I will make tremendous sacrifices, compromises, and investments on your behalf, with the expectation that you will grow up to become the young adult I expect you to become"—is one that we reinvoke, directly or indirectly, when our children become adolescents, shoving it under their noses and insisting that they read it over and be reminded of their contractual obligations. Whether it involves losing out on interesting professional opportunities to be more available to our families, giving up on our own hobbies or pleasurable endeavors so that our teenagers can pursue their own, or working two jobs to pay for private school tuition or tutors or coaches, we want and expect something for our efforts.

The problem, of course, is that while teenagers may read the contract that we wave in front of them, they know that they never agreed to sign it, and experience no compulsion to make good on it, no matter how much duress we place them under. In fact, in their efforts to establish their own identity, they may do everything in their power to renege on the contract, *even if it works to their disadvantage.*

When this situation occurs, we will be likely, like the couples described above, to react in either constructive or destructive ways. Philip, Malvern's father, is an example of a father who, for now, is responding in a destructive way to his perceived lack of justice. The sacrifices, compromises, and investments that he has made in time, energy, and money should, in his eyes, result in his being repaid in a coin that is important to him—Malvern's continued commitment to and achievement in hockey, and his subsequent and related success in being granted admission into an elite university. The idea of getting to know Malvern differently, and wanting to learn more about why he is tiring of hockey and desirous of a more normal high school experience hasn't yet crossed his father's mind—he's too caught up in feeling betrayed by, rather than interested in, his son's emotional development and can't let go of his resentment at the unfairness and injustice of it all.

Of course, Malvern is experiencing his own sense of relational unfairness and injustice. It has begun to dawn on him, through his fortuitous rehabilitation period, that life has more to offer than ice time, and that maybe he has sacrificed more than he should have just to please his proud papa. Up until recently his experience of both his own, hockey-based accomplishments and his father's vicarious pleasure in these accomplishments had coalesced and made all of his sacrifices worthwhile. Now, he understandably wants to make up for lost time and is earnestly trying to pack four years of high school into one, astonished by how much he had been missing while going through adolescence with his blinders on.

Many of the parent-teen conflicts that I observe in my practice (or experience at home!) are rooted in destructive responses on one or both generation's parts to relational imbalances. Parents respond resentfully when they perceive that their teenager is not making good on the unspoken agreement that was worked out, without the teen's awareness, many years before. Teens respond resentfully when they begin to feel that they have sacrificed too much of themselves to parental demands and desires over the years, when they conclude that they have been selling their soul to pursue their parents' images of perfection, without the kind of return, in the form of love and acceptance, or rights and privileges, that they feel they deserve.

The main reason that these generational conflicts can become so entrenched and intractable over time is because parent and teen have been going along for years with changing definitions of what constitutes a just and right relational balance between them, but without addressing, or adjusting to, these changes, until they wind up at completely opposite ends of the spectrum. In these cases, both adult and adolescent wind up feeling angry as a result of their respective beliefs that they've given more than they've gotten, and each institutes his or her reflexive, time-honored methods of evening things out.

So if these mutually perceived inequities in our relationship with our teen are inevitable, which they are, how do we ensure that we at least respond to them in ways that are constructive rather than destructive? The answer lies in forgiveness, the interpersonal salve that, when applied, helps to raise the likelihood that we'll manage our feelings of resentment, disappointment, and betrayal in ways that actually heal and build, rather than harm and corrode, our bonds with others.

Because forgiveness can mean so many different things to so many different people, it's important to define it clearly. While most of us don't have a clear idea of how to forgive, or what forgiveness even means, all of us have had experiences that have aroused in us a wish to either have forgiven or to have been forgiven. And of course most of us have also been fortunate enough to have actually been on the giving or receiving end of forgiveness.

To begin, let's try to understand forgiveness through what it is not. Forgiveness, in the context of the parent-teen relationship, does not mean tolerating behaviors that should not be tolerated or choosing to toss in the towel and become passive and powerless rather than taking a stand. It should not be equated with acquiescing or capitulating when our adolescent is trying to intimidate or outmaneuver us, nor does it involve taking responsibility for a teen's behavior.

Forgiveness is not the same thing as indulging or coddling, trying to avoid conflict and "make nice" or "be friends" while refusing to hold teens accountable for their behavior. Healthy forgiveness should also not be confused with forgetting, either— it's possible (and important) to forgive without forgetting what our teenager needs to be forgiven for. As psychiatrist Thomas Szasz wrote, "The stupid neither forgive nor forget, the naïve forgive and forget, the wise forgive, but they do not forget."

Most importantly, treading the paths of parental forgiveness does not mean that we will never again feel betrayed by, worried about, or angry with our teenager. In fact, one of the most beneficial outcomes of forgiveness is that we'll ultimately find ourselves better able to express our feelings of betrayal or worry or anger in more straightforward and fathomable ways than ever before. Instead of burying or misdirecting these feelings, we'll be able to reveal them in ways that assist us in resolving conflicts, rather than inflaming them.

The most useful definition of forgiveness during the adolescent years is that it is the individual process that releases us from the grip of our anger and disappointment in our teenagers such that we can continue to love, accept, and be proud of them despite their growing up in ways that we do not wholly approve of or feel comfortable with.

It is only through forgiving our teens that we can respond constructively—with empathy, insight, and compassion—when they don't provide us with what we insist we deserve from them, and that we can allow ourselves to see them, and allow them to see themselves, as good enough. Forgiveness gives our children quittance and frees them from owing us—and through doing so, it frees us from the wearisome burden of constantly being owed.

In my experience, the process of parental forgiveness can unfold in one or more ways. Sometimes it takes a *spiritual* form. Because forgiveness is such a core element of just about every religious tradition, for example, approaching it through spiritual practice (prayer, meditation, reflection, or ritual) seems to make the most sense. Sometimes it takes an *emotional* form. We so want to relieve ourselves of the saddle of excessive resentment that we do whatever we can and must to take the edge off these feelings. Sometimes it takes a *cognitive* form. We become increasingly aware that we, and our families, would be better off forgiving and actively try to create and establish a forgiving state of mind. More typically, our capacity to forgive is unique and involves some combination of all of these forms.

But one thing that I have seen over and over again is that simply *acknowledging* that forgiving might be of some help and have some relevance automatically sets the healing wheels into motion and moves us in the direction of acceptance and compassion. Envisioning oneself as having forgiven, rather than any one specific act of forgiveness, seems to be the surest way to forgive. Forgiveness expresses itself as a process, rather than as a discrete event, and reveals itself as much through openness as effort.

Another characteristic of forgiving is that it works as both a catalyst for and a culmination of change between parent and child. Our desire to forgive not only helps get us unstuck from the rut of resentment but is simultaneously a sign that we've gotten unstuck.

In whatever ways in which it is pursued and embodied, however, forgiveness will always assist us in seeing our children as good enough and absolve us of the doomed and counterproductive hope that we can secure compensation for our faults, failings, and losses through their achievements, accomplishments, and gains.

Let's examine a family in which the parents' willingness to find forgiveness enabled them to let go of unreasonable expectations and transformed their teenager from disappointing and disillusioning to good enough.

For more than a year, 17-year-old Darren's parents, Denise and Steve, felt that he had been depressed. He was increasingly difficult to talk to, had gotten into the habit of sleeping until dinner after school and past noon on the weekends, and had grown nonchalant about his academic work and his weight lifting, two activities which, up until recently, he had been quite attentive to. It was their concerns about his apathy that led them to give me a call and set up an appointment.

In our third session, after I'd had the chance to get to know Darren and his family a bit, I was in the midst of some time alone with him, and as we moved into a discussion of his social life, I noticed some squirminess. He began shifting restlessly in his seat, and the easy, direct eye contact that had characterized most of our time together quickly disappeared. Being that he was a junior, I got around to asking him at one point if he was planning on going to his high school prom this spring.

"No, probably not," he said, stoically.

"Have you been to a prom or homecoming before?"

"Nah—they're not for me."

"Do many of your friends go?"

"Not really."

"Do you have much of an interest in dating at this point in your life?"

"Uh-uh."

"Do you feel much of a sexual interest in girls?"

"Sort of—a little."

"Have you ever had any sexual feelings toward a guy?"

Silence. He looked down while folding and unfolding his hands.

"I don't know what's going on inside of you right now," I said carefully, "but I want you to know that just about all of us have, at one point or another, felt attracted to someone of the same sex."

Silence. More folding and unfolding of hands.

"My guess is that this is something that's been on your mind and that you haven't felt comfortable speaking with anyone about it. Am I on target at all?"

Silence. He sat on his hands.

"You wouldn't be the first or last person to feel some shame or embarrassment about his sexual fantasies or desires. Everyone has had that sense at one time or another."

He finally looked up, his eyes filled with tears. "I think I'm gay. Actually, I think I *know* I'm gay. Well, I'm not sure I am, but I *think* I am. And the problem is, if my parents find out, they'll kill me. But if I keep it a secret anymore, I feel like I'll go out of my fucking mind. *There*. Now you know." He bowed his head again, as if afraid of my response.

"First of all, I'm impressed that you have as much self-awareness as you do, and that you've been paying attention to your sexual identity as well as you have. It's an awfully important part of your life right now, and well worth exploring and understanding."

Darren sighed and seemed to relax. A first hurdle had been cleared.

"Second of all, it does sound like you'd feel better if you didn't have to keep this issue under wraps, and if you could talk about it with certain people, including your parents."

"Yeah, but I could *never* talk with them about it. I don't think they'd understand. I don't think they'd ever forgive me."

"What do you know about their attitudes toward homosexuality?"

"Look, it's not like they're majorly anti-gay or anything. They're your basic middle-class suburban couple—my mom's even a Democrat! It's just that I can't imagine them dealing with it very well, especially my dad. He's just dying for me to begin dating, constantly wondering when I'm going to start asking girls out. Little does he know that I actually *have* thought of asking someone out, but it's a guy. He likes to joke that I only go to the gym so much because I like to look at the girls, but, to be honest, it's really not the girls that I'm looking at.

"And my mom, she'd probably take it better than my dad, but I just can't see her being very happy with it. Her cousin is gay, and she's sort of okay with it, but when she talks about him she kind of pities him, like he's got cancer or something. 'Oh, I feel so sorry for him,' or 'Oh, I hope he doesn't get AIDS,' or, 'Oh, I *still* hope he meets a good woman some day.' That's what she has to say about him. So she's not exactly going to turn cartwheels about the news, either."

It was interesting for me to note that in just the couple of minutes since we had opened up this subject, Darren seemed to have come alive. He was animated, speaking in full paragraphs, and a sense of humor was beginning to poke through his previously laconic exterior. It was clearly a relief for him to be able to talk about this matter openly.

"Well, maybe you and I can work together to help prepare them. I'm not saying it's going to be easy for any of you, but there are better and worse ways to bring it up, and I'd rather we go after the former than the latter. For now, I'd like you to give some thought to how you might want to bring it up with them, and whether you would want to do it on your own at home or here in my office."

Darren seemed grateful to have my support, but, as adolescents usually do, he went about things his own way. Several days after having met with him, I received an agitated phone call from Denise, who reported to me that the night before her husband had turned on the TV and punched in what he thought was a video-cassette recording of his favorite show. What had shown up on the screen instead, to his horror, was a pornographic scene of two men making love. Apparently, Darren had "accidentally" left it in the VCR.

"Steve was sick to his stomach, and so was I, we couldn't even watch it. And so we really want to know, is Darren gay?"

"I think that that's something that deserves to be talked about with Darren," I replied.

"Well, we haven't mentioned to him that we saw the video, we haven't said *anything* about it. But we're just so distraught about this, we don't know what to do. Please help us figure this out."

"I know that it was upsetting to discover the tape by surprise, and your reactions to it are understandable ones. If you're comfortable doing so and would like to bring it up with Darren at home, I think that would be okay, but only if you are prepared to hear what he has to say in an open-minded way, without judging, refuting, or rejecting him. If you're not sure that's possible, it'd probably be better to wait until our next session."

"Oh, I don't know, I just don't know," she said, her voice on the edge of despair. "I mean, really, it wouldn't be a surprise to me to learn that he's gay. I've kind of been wondering more and more why he never has dated, why he shows no interest in girls. But my husband—I mean, I don't know *how* he'll react, he doesn't seem to have a clue. One time I brought it up with him, asked him if he thought Darren might be gay, and he just laughed at me and said, 'How could he be gay? The girls love him, and he's a hunk from all that weight lifting.' He thinks because Darren's not effeminate at all that Darren isn't gay. I have a cousin who's gay and he really *acts* gay, the lisp and the walk and being into fashion and everything. But *Darren*?"

"Well, it's up to you, but one way or another, it sounds like it's time for the two of you to have a discussion with Darren about his sexual identity, whether it's at your place or mine."

Denise decided, with great ambivalence, that it would be best for the three of them to broach the subject at home, knowing that we had our follow-up session to, in her pessimistic words, "pick up the pieces." As it turns out, there were plenty of pieces to pick up, as Darren straightforwardly acknowledged that the tape was his and then went ahead and announced to them that he was gay. Denise and Steve, in a state of shock, asked if they might come for the next session without Darren, which I agreed to.

"First of all," Steve began, "I don't know what my wife has already told you about me, but I want you to understand that I don't think there's anything wrong with being gay. I don't believe it's a disease, I don't believe it's a perversion, and I understand that about 10 percent of each gender is homosexual. So you don't need to give me any lectures or sermons."

"I'm glad to hear that you've educated yourself on the topic, Steve," I replied.

"However," he continued, "what I've also learned is that you really can't be sure that you're gay if you're only a teenager, and that lots of kids mistakenly believe they're gay simply because they're shy around the opposite sex or because they've had some sexual fantasies about the same sex."

"I would agree with that as well."

"So with that in mind, I don't think that we should be spending our time in here *accepting* Darren's being gay, I think we should be spending our time helping him to figure out *if* he's gay."

"That sounds like a good plan to me, too, Steve. Sexual identity is complicated and multidetermined, and, particularly during adolescence, constantly in flux. At one time or another, just about all teenagers have wondered if they're gay, and many have had some sexual daydreams of, or contact with, someone of the same gender that makes them think that they're gay.

"On the other hand, by the time adolescents reach sixteen, you do have to realize that their sexual orientation is beginning to crystallize, and that their feelings about themselves and their identity are not necessarily transient ones. Most of the gay adults that I've worked with or gotten to know over the years recall that by the time they were in their early teens, they were starting to sense that they might be gay, and that by their late teens, they were beginning to feel more or less certain that this was the case. That may not be true for everyone, but we have to keep it in mind as a possibility."

"You mean, he *could* be gay?" Denise asked, worriedly.

"Sure he could," Steve interrupted, anxiously. "But what we're saying, honey, is that he still could be straight. Don't you see, this business of being gay could be just a phase." He wasn't sounding quite as calm and matter-of-fact as he had initially.

Denise turned to me. "What do you think we ought to do?"

"I think Steve is on target, that our focus should be on helping him to discover and become comfortable with his sexual orientation, whatever it is. But to do that, we have to start out where he is now, and where he is now is that he believes that he's gay."

"But if we start there, like you say, don't we run the risk of reinforcing his being homosexual? If we agree that he *might* be, won't that make it more likely that he *will* be?" Steve said.

"I've never seen that happen," I commented. "I really don't believe that there's a whole lot that parents can do that will significantly affect their child's sexual preference in the long run. They can have a great deal of influence on how well their son or daughter adjusts to the reality of his or her ultimate orientation, but not on that orientation itself."

"But what about this Hollywood-saturated culture that we live in, where it's almost cool to be gay? Doesn't that make it more likely that kids will want to be gay, that they'll think it's okay to be gay?" Steve persisted.

"No matter what goes on in the entertainment world, I still think we would have to unfortunately agree that gays remain the brunt of a great deal of prejudice and negative stereotyping. Also, just as there's a limit to the extent to which parents can influence a child's sexual preference, there's a limit to the extent to which our culture can. We don't really know what accounts for a person being gay or straight—whether it's encoded in our brain, or our endocrine system, or our genes, or elsewhere—but we *do* know that it doesn't appear to be a matter of choice, and that no one has ever proven that it's the direct result of a parent's behavior, or the influence of the media, or casual fantasy or experimentation, or some critical event. So I think we have to start with the assumption that there's something to Darren's belief that he's gay and take it from there."

"What does that mean we should do?" Denise asked.

"It means you'll have to tell yourself some important things, and you'll have to tell Darren some important things. You'll have to tell yourself that if he is gay, it's not the end of the world, and it doesn't mean he's doomed to a life as a sexual freak or a social outcast. You'll have to tell yourself that this is just one aspect of his identity, and it doesn't mean he's suddenly become a stranger, an alien, to you or your family. You'll have to tell yourself that you haven't done anything 'wrong' or caused this in any way. And you'll have to tell yourself that you're entitled to a mixture of feelings—grief, sorrow, fear, shock, confusion—but that over time these feelings will pass."

"What do we tell him?"

"You should tell him that he'll be loved, valued, and accepted by the family no matter what his sexual preference turns out to be. You should tell him that you're pleased that he has trusted you enough to tell you—because most gay teenagers *don't* tell their parents—and that now that this has come to the surface he doesn't have to feel so isolated and alone anymore. And you should tell him that you'll help him in any way that he would like you to when it comes to sorting things out, whether he's gay or straight or somewhere in between."

"I don't know," Steve said, "I think that's sounding a little too much like we've surrendered, like we're just going to assume that he's gay and that's that, case closed."

"This isn't a war in which you can choose to fight or surrender, Steve. As Darren's parents, you are entrusted with helping him to develop a self-aware, satisfying, and safe sex life, whether he's gay or straight. You cannot assume responsibility for the direction his sexual preference ultimately takes—nothing you can do will 'cure' him of being gay. But you *do* have to take some responsibility for helping him to come to terms with his preference and finding fulfilling and healthy intimacy with whoever he is with."

"So we're just supposed to look the other way?" Steve asked, sounding increasingly annoyed. "We're supposed to let him watch his gay pornography and let him date guys and let him put himself at risk for AIDS and screw up his whole life? Is that what you're advising?"

"Steve, I don't think that's what Dr. Sachs has in mind here," Denise interjected. "I think he's saying that it's really our duty to be there for Darren, and that there's not a whole lot we can do to change things when it comes to his sexuality."

"Well, I'm not going to sit back and let him live a gay lifestyle just because he's a late bloomer, or because he's not into girls yet. I think that would be a big mistake, like we'd be letting him down. What if he takes that path and then finds that he's really

not gay, that he's nineteen or twenty-one and starting to get interested in the opposite sex?"

"I can hear how concerned you are, and I can't imagine a caring parent feeling otherwise. But if it's the case that, down the
road, his sexual orientation starts to shift back from gay to
straight, then he, like many young adults, will probably make the
adjustment and find himself looking back on this as an ex-
ploratory or experimental stage that helped him to further define
and understand himself. It's not like it's irreversible."

Steve sat without saying a word, folding and unfolding his
hands, just like Darren had done when we had reached a tense
moment during our initial session—like father, like son. Denise
stared at me helplessly.

"You know," I suggested, "you might consider forgiving Darren, and yourselves as well."

"What would that mean?" Denise asked. Steve remained
stonily silent.

"Parents generally don't start a family assuming that their
child will be gay. No matter how loving, well-informed, or well-
intentioned they may be, it's impossible for mothers or fathers to
be fully prepared for this eventuality. So whether your reaction is
anger or hurt or confusion or disappointment—and it's probably
some combination of all of these—it's important to be able to forgive your child for being someone who you didn't imagine he
would be, and, if it were up to you, someone you wouldn't want
him to be."

Denise began to cry. "I just don't know what to think. He's
still Darren, he's still my firstborn, he's still my only son, and I
love him, he's such a fine boy. But since we've begun talking
about this, all I can think of is, how he's never going to lead a
normal life, how he'll be at risk for AIDS, how he'll never be a father. I mentioned that I have a cousin who's gay, and he has had
such a hard life. He's been promiscuous, he's very bright and talented but has never gotten on track professionally, and mostly he
leads this desperately lonely life."

"But one of the reasons your cousin may have struggled, and
may continue to struggle, is not so much because he's gay but
because no one ever helped him to come to terms with being gay.
He probably has remained susceptible to the self-loathing, self-

punitiveness, and self-denial that all individuals are prone to when they can't accept themselves for who they are. You have a chance to create a different future for Darren if you can do a better job than your cousin's parents did."

"Well, I don't think there's any question that things were much harder for my cousin. He had to keep it a secret from everyone for years and years. He really didn't come out until he was in his thirties, although some of us suspected it by then. And amazingly enough, he still hasn't actually told his parents, my aunt and uncle, and they act as if they still don't know—and, who knows, maybe they don't. It's like this deep, dark secret that everyone has to pretend to keep."

"So, in my estimation, Darren is already ahead of the game because he's been able to tell his parents, which is often the beginning of the process of self-acceptance, particularly if the two of you can hang in there with him."

Steve finally spoke up again. "So let's get back to this forgiveness business. How are we supposed to do it?"

"In this case, I think forgiveness has to cut in a couple of different directions. First of all, you'll have to forgive Darren for not being the child of your dreams right now, for turning out differently than you thought he might at this stage in his life. As I said earlier, few parents anticipate or hope that their child will be gay, and it's natural to have a mixture of disconcerting feelings about this possibility.

"Second, you'll have to forgive *yourselves* as parents, because blaming yourselves or each other, tempting as it may be, will do nothing but increase everyone's feelings of resentment and disappointment and interfere with the entire family's ability to address this issue thoughtfully and sensitively."

"But how, specifically, are we to become more forgiving?" Denise wondered.

"I'd like you to do a couple of exercises that might move the process along. In terms of forgiving Darren, I'd like each of you to make two lists. The first is a list of the dreams or wishes that you had for Darren that are rooted in the assumption that he would be straight. The second is a list of the fears or worries that you have for Darren that are rooted in the assumption that he'll be gay."

"What are we supposed to do with the lists?" Denise inquired.

"Once you've completed them individually, I'd like you to read them to each other. And once you have read them to each other, I'd like you to burn each list in your fireplace and say, out loud or to yourself, the words: 'We forgive Darren for being who he is, rather than who we want him to be.' "

"What's the point?" Steve asked, skeptically.

"The point is that while all parents have dreams and wishes and fears and worries when it comes to their children, most of these have more to do with *us* than with our child. In completing this ritual and saying these words of forgiveness, you'll begin the process of releasing Darren from the burden of your expectations, loving as they may be, and releasing yourselves as well."

"What about the part about forgiving ourselves, too?"

"When it comes to self-forgiveness, and forgiveness within your marriage, I'd like you to do a little additional research into current understandings of the origin of homosexuality, so that you're as clear as you can be when it comes to this matter. And I'd also like you to go to a local PFLAG meeting—Parents and Friends of Lesbians and Gays—just to see what other parents who may be in similar situations have to say."

"Does it have to be a *local* meeting?" Steve asked with a slight smile.

"If you're concerned that you'll run into people that you may know, you could look for a meeting that's not close to your home. But remember that the parents who are there are probably there for some of the same reasons that you are."

Denise and Steve returned for their follow-up meeting with much to share.

"When you first asked us to do the ritual, I didn't think that we would really go ahead and follow through," Denise admitted, "because it seemed sort of pagan-like, what with the burning and all. But we went ahead and made our lists and shared them with each other, and it was reassuring to see that we each had similar dreams for Darren, and similar fears—like wishing that he would get married or have children or being afraid he'll get AIDS.

"And then when we burned them, I felt this tremendous sadness—like all of our dreams for him were literally going up in smoke. But afterward, I also felt some relief, and I realized that it's not the end of the world, that he can still lead a good life, that he can still be a father if he wants. Of course, I still secretly prayed, as I watched the flames, that maybe, just maybe, he'll meet the right girl one day and turn out to be straight. I just can't give up on that yet."

"I don't think that you have to give up on that. It'd be a mistake to presume that we know what Darren's destiny will be in any respect, whether it's sexually or personally or professionally. But we can make it much easier on him by being as understanding and supportive as possible while he's trying to figure things out, and forgiving him for whatever his tendencies are at this point will help him through this process immeasurably. How did things go for you, Steve?"

"I have to say that I thought it was a pretty weird assignment, too. But I went ahead with it and, in making the lists, I realized how upset I was about all that Darren might have to give up if he's gay, and how hard his life may be as a result. And I'd be lying if I didn't also think about how hard *my* life will be as a result, because there's still a lot of explaining to do to others if it turns out that he's gay, like with my parents and our friends and all. And of course, he's my only son. Who will carry forth the family name for me if he doesn't have children one day?

"But I thought a lot about what you were saying about Denise's cousin, that his life may have been hard not because he's gay but because nobody was there for him, and how awful it must be to have to live in shame, in hiding, for so much of your whole life, particularly with your own parents. So when we said the little prayer, I made the decision that I was going to love Darren no matter what his sexual preference was—he's my son and I'm going to love him and show him that I love him and hope that my love helps. Of course," he said, slyly, "if my love somehow helps him love a woman one day, that wouldn't be such a terrible thing."

"No parent ever entirely lets go of their wishes and hopes for their child, Steve," I acknowledged. "But I don't think there's any question that your finding a way to convey your love for Darren during this difficult time will increase the odds that he'll find a way to fulfill his own wishes and hopes, whatever they may be. And that's really the key to his happiness."

Denise and Steve also filled me in on the PFLAG meeting that they attended, one that was held more than an hour from where they lived. But they had found it heartening to speak with the other parents in attendance, some of whom were in the same boat that they were, with sons or daughters who were still developing their sexual identity but displaying distinct leanings toward homosexuality. And in reading over some of the literature that they picked up at the meeting, they were better able to understand that while being gay had no known, definitive cause, there still wasn't a tremendous amount that they had done, or could do, to cause a particular sexual preference to come about.

With Denise and Steve in a more forgiving and compassionate place, I invited Darren into our next session so that they might have the opportunity to discuss sexual matters more openly. One thing that they made clear to him was that they didn't want any pornography in the house, whether on videotape, in print, or through the Internet, particularly with Darren having two younger sisters who might be exposed to it.

I supported them in this limit being set, but also brought up the issue of how Darren was to get to know other guys that he might want to become more intimate with. Steve and Denise cringed, but I said that they could either make it safe and acceptable for Darren to begin dating guys or put him in the position of having to do it sneakily, and possibly dangerously.

"He's going to want to begin to seek out intimate relationships, just like anyone his age should do. If you don't sanction this, then he has no choice but to go 'underground' with it, and that can present problems."

"Like what?" Steve said.

"Like becoming vulnerable to individuals who might take advantage of his desperation. Or like being exploited by the objectionable guy or group of guys he'd have to hook up with to have some of his social or sexual needs met."

"That sounds like my cousin's life, right there," Denise commented.

After some further discussion, it was agreed that Darren would be allowed to use the computer to visit websites and chat rooms designed for gay teenagers, with the understanding that these would be evaluated and approved by his parents ahead of time and from time to time. I also encouraged Darren to look into the fledgling Gay/Lesbian Student Alliance (GLSA) that had recently been formed in the county school system as a way for teens to meet and interact with other gay and bisexual peers.

Denise and Steve continued to insist, both with me and with Darren, that they were not prepared to conclude that he was definitely gay. This remained a source of frustration for Darren. "When are they going to finally *get* it?" he repeatedly pleaded. I tried to help him understand how complicated this was for them, but also asked him to observe his feelings and desires carefully as he began to develop more intimacy with other gays so that he might develop more clarity about his sexuality.

After several months of working together, Darren announced in a family session that there was a guy that he had met through the GLSA that he was interested in and he wanted to go out with. This was an event that Denise and Steve had great trepidation about, and it took some time to prepare themselves for the prospect that Darren's being gay was less speculative and theoretical than they had hoped.

Because Darren's request made the reality of his sexual orientation more concrete than ever before, we had to revisit some of the themes that we had discussed when we first met—the need to forgive Darren for his homosexual interests; the need to see gay intimacy as a different, rather than as a deviant, form of love, a preference rather than a perversion; and the need to be supportive of any safe and positive efforts on his part to explore and define his sexual identity.

To their credit, Denise and Steve were eventually able to surmount their understandably mixed feelings and welcomed Darren's friend, Chris, into their home. The experience turned out to be a relief, in fact.

"I have to say, I'd never know that Chris was gay, he's not flamboyant or anything like that," Denise commented. "Plus, he's a straight A student and very polite. Actually, he's the kind of guy I'd like our daughters to date one day—except for the fact that he's gay," she laughed.

"It was harder for me than for Denise," Steve admitted. "I mean, he's a nice guy and all, but it's not quite what I had in mind when I dreamed about my son's first date. And of course, I don't even want to *think* about them being physical with each other."

"Just remember that whatever sexual interaction they engage

in is only going to be a part of their relationship," I suggested. "As with a straight couple, their intimacy, if it develops, will grow to consist of all of their communication and contact with each other, not just that which is physical. Chris is someone who Darren feels good about. If you can continue to create room for him to share that good feeling with you, despite your ambivalence, he'll be very grateful."

In the ensuing months, Darren's relationship with Chris continued to develop. More importantly, and not surprisingly, the signs of depression that had first led them to contact me had evaporated. His grades were back on the rise, he had returned to his regular weight-lifting routine, and he had found his involvement in the GLSA to be a great source of intellectual stimulation and social support.

Denise and Steve did not feel the need or desire to continue attending PFLAG meetings for now, and continued to quietly hope and pray that this might turn out to be nothing more than an experimental interlude in their son's life. But their ability to forgive Darren for not being the teenaged son that they dreamed of having, and to forgive themselves as well in the process, was all that was necessary for him to begin to approach the issue of his sexual identity with thought, care, and a healthy open-mindedness.

EXERCISE 4

Forgiveness is essentially a private, interior experience, one that does not require the participation of the individual that we may be trying to forgive. I have found that exercises that use trance work, music, or guided imagery can often help to promote the forgiveness process, because these slow down our thoughts and allow our more empathic, compassionate qualities to surface.

Try having someone you trust read the following text. Or make a tape recording of it yourself and listen to it. After you have finished, observe yourself; and see if your feelings about your teen have changed as a result.

Find a comfortable position, close your eyes, and take some deep breaths, in through your nose and out through your mouth. Keep breathing in this way until you find yourself in a slow, peaceful, effortless rhythm. (Pause for a moment.)

In your mind, place yourself in a setting that feels very safe and very comfortable. It may be real or imaginary, from your past, your present, or perhaps in your future. (Pause for a moment.)

Once you have located yourself there, invite your teen to join you. As the image of your child forms in your mind, gaze at him with as much love as you can summon, gently putting aside any angry, annoyed, or negative thoughts or feelings you have been having about him. (Pause for a moment.)

And as you are gazing, imagine that he is now able to talk to you about all of the things that he has never spoken to you about before—his pain, his fears, his concerns, his vulnerability, his sorrow, his grief, his longings, his struggles.

Imagine as he speaks that you are able, without any effort at all, to open your heart up to him, to listen plainly, quietly, lovingly, attentively. And imagine that in the process of listening, you naturally begin to feel within you a very deep and profound bond with your child, a bond filled with mercy, understanding, and kindness. (Pause for a moment.)

Now, tell your child that you forgive him for all his flaws, defects, failures, and imperfections, for all the ways in which he has disappointed, angered, hurt, and disillusioned you.

And, in your mind, extend your arms to your teen and bring him toward you, and feel him melt and give in to your warm embrace. Feel yourself melting, too, aware of the pain that each of you bear, and letting that pain bring you closer to each other. Feel the reassuring grace that comes with inviting him into your loving arms and the joyous freedom that comes with forgiveness. (Pause for a moment.)

Release him from your embrace and thank him for having met you here, for having unburdened himself to you, and, in so doing, helping you to unburden yourself as well.

Allow him to leave and watch him depart with new eyes,

seeing him bound to you, part of you, yet his own person, radiating a unique, indescribable beauty as he moves away from you and forward into the world.

Continue breathing deeply and quietly for a few minutes, cherishing the feelings of forgiveness that you have begun to discover and invite into your life. Promise to hold these feelings close to you as you awaken and move through the rest of your day.

EXERCISE 5

Forgiveness can also be a very rational, concrete, conscious process. Take some time to reflect upon the questions that follow, and see how your feelings about your teen may be transfigured through having done so.

1. In what ways does your relationship with your teen feel unbalanced or unjust?

2. Are you tending to feel *anger* (giving more than you're getting) or *guilt* (getting more than you're giving)?

3. Do you think that you are responding to this imbalance constructively or destructively?

4. What do you *hope* will happen if you are able to forgive your teen for not being who you want her to be?

5. What do you *fear* will happen if you are able to forgive your teen for not being who you want her to be?

6. What do you fear will happen if you are unable to forgive your teen for not being who you want her to be?

7. Can you think of a ritual, actual or symbolic, that you might create or perform that would help to put your disappointment to rest and better enable you and your teen to move forward?

8. What else in your life would change for the better if you could forgive your teen?

Noel came to me filled with rage and despair about his daughter, Tanya's, two-year heroin addiction. The horrifying roller-coaster ride that her chemical dependency had been taking the family on was "worse than anything I've ever been through, and I've been through plenty," and it apparently wasn't ending just yet.

Here are Noel's answers to this exercise.

1. *There's no question that my relationship with her feels completely unfair, because she's taking up all of our time, the whole family's time, with her addiction.*

2. *There's also no question that I feel like I've been giving more than I've been getting, so I feel angry.*

3. *I've probably done some of both, some constructive and some destructive. Constructively, I've tried to get her the help she needs, and tried so hard to be supportive and understanding over the years. Destructively, I've lashed out at her, I've blamed her mother, I've blamed myself, and at times I've just given up altogether and felt like it wasn't worth it—if she wants to use, let her use, if she's going to kill herself, let her kill herself—terrible thoughts for a parent to have, and I'm ashamed of myself, but that's how hopeless I feel sometimes.*

4. *If I could forgive her for her addiction, I'd be able to stop lashing out at her, I'd stop blaming myself and my wife, I'd feel less sorry for myself, and I'd be less likely to raise the white flag and give up.*

5. *If I could forgive her for her addiction, I'm afraid I'd just stop caring—somehow forgiveness feels like it would be a step away from her.*

6. *If I don't find a way to forgive her, I'm afraid I'll lose her entirely. She'll gradually succumb to the lure of the drug, or she won't, but there won't be any relationship with me in place anymore.*

7. *I've thought of giving up cigarettes as a way to join with her in giving up heroin. And I've thought of having a funeral for her addiction, ask-*

ing her to take whatever drugs and paraphernalia she still has and
making a gravesite for it all, so that we can finally bury it and put it
in the past.

8. I know that my relationship with my wife, Mia, would improve if I
could get past the blame and the resentment about Tanya. I know
that I keep Mia at arm's length whenever we're in these drug crises,
and I know that it would be better for everyone if we could forgive
ourselves, as well as Tanya.

Noel and I spent a subsequent session going over his answers
to these questions, questions that prompted him to spend more
time trying to understand Tanya and less time sitting in judgment
of her and himself. I encouraged him to follow through on the rituals that he had suggested, and he found both of them to embody
some healing properties.

A turning point came, during the mock funeral, when he had
the realization that only through forgiving Tanya would he truly
be able to love her again—his bitterness and helplessness had
squeezed out his loving feelings so completely that they no longer
felt like a part of the currency that he exchanged with his daughter. He also realized at this time that he needed to forgive himself,
to finally be shriven of the self-blame that had been afflicting him
for years before his daughter was even born. This had its roots in
the survivor's guilt he had contracted when he and his brother
were in a bad car accident as children, and his brother wound up
with debilitating injuries and the loss of an arm while Noel
emerged with only cuts and bruises.

It was still quite a while before Tanya eventually broke free of
her addiction, but the ability to re-experience love through the
process of forgiveness enabled this father and daughter to stay
connected through a nightmarish time.

SIX

CHANGING

One of the Just Ones came to Sodom, determined to save its inhabitants from sin and punishment. Night and day the Just One walked the streets and markets preaching against greed and theft, falsehood and indifference. In the beginning, people listened and smiled ironically. Then they stopped listening: they were no longer amused. The killers went on killing, the wise kept silent, as if there were no Just One in their midst.

One day a child, moved by compassion, approached the unfortunate preacher with these words. "Poor stranger. You shout, you expend your body and soul; don't you see that it is hopeless?"

"Yes, I see," answered the Just One.

"Then why do you go on?"

"I'll tell you why. In the beginning, I thought I could change humankind. Today, I know I cannot. If I still shout today, if I still scream, it is to prevent humankind from ultimately changing me."

—Elie Wiesel

My experience as a clinician has shown me that when parents actively embark on an exploration of the themes discussed in the previous four chapters—uncovering, acknowledging, understanding, and forgiving—positive changes in family life will quite naturally and spontaneously ensue. Under most circumstances, families are very resilient and display a tremendous capacity for self-correction and realignment.

However, the family transformation that occurs when children become adolescents is such a complex one that families will inevitably find themselves getting stuck at times, unable to adapt and create a new, more functional climate. Knowing more about how, where, and why these points are likely to occur goes a long way toward helping us to get unstuck.

With this in mind, let's begin by examining the status and nature of the family system at this very convoluted and contradictory developmental stage.

Every family is balanced by competing tendencies toward equilibrium and growth. The former is crucial to family members developing a sense of tradition, trust, and stability, while the latter is crucial to family members developing a sense of creativity, initiative, and self-reliance. The energy for healthy, manageable growth results from this eternal dialectic between engagement and differentiation, continuity and growth, intimacy and individuation.

During adolescence, a *renegotiation* of the family's previous equilibrium needs to take place. In response to the pressures exerted by developing teens and their drive for autonomy, the status quo is slowly or rudely disrupted, and the family is challenged to evolve. Sometimes the family system responds to these pressures by creatively adapting, gradually adjusting their expectations of and interactions with their rapidly changing teen, regenerating and refining the rules under which they all operate, and allowing new and more mature behaviors on every member's part to take root and flower. Sometimes, however, the forces that have kept the family in its steady state, for better or for worse, remain so effectively at work that the family system becomes rigid. Unable to depart in enduring or useful ways from the original status quo despite circumstances that seem to necessitate adaptation, parents remain tethered to their previous approaches to parenting even in the face of abundant evidence that these are no longer effective.

Instead of taking the risk of trying to create innovative ways of connecting, everyone desperately tries to recreate and reimpose the traditional ways of connecting, often with even more intensity and insistence than before. This leaves the family staunchly imprisoned in its accustomed patterns of interaction, no matter how unproductive and irrelevant these patterns have become. The system and its members stagnate.

To give an example, a parent and a 5-day-old son or daughter who are basically inseparable could be described as appropriately engaged with each other. But a parent and a 5-year-old son or daughter who are inseparable are inappropriately engaged with each other. And a parent and a 15-year-old son or daughter who are inseparable would be considered pathologically engaged. In this case, what was functional and growth-promoting at one stage can quite clearly be described as dysfunctional and growth-inhibiting at subsequent stages. A healthy adjustment has not taken place.

It is when families rigidly resist growth that psychological, behavioral, or medical symptoms begin to emerge—symptoms that point to the family's hitherto unsuccessful struggle to make modifications and create a new equilibrium. Further difficulties ensue when the parents—as most parents will do—begin to focus on the symptoms, rather than on the collective developmental obstinacy. We do this because the symptoms—which could be anything from underachievement to perfectionism, over-compliance to over-defiance, alcohol abuse to school refusal, irritability to anxiety—provide us with a consuming, convenient distraction from our inability to open up to a more advanced level of functioning. As a 14-year-old anorexic patient of mine once ruefully but insightfully commented: "All I have to do is skip a meal, and it's like my entire family drops everything and starts asking me when I'm going to eat."

Family systems, when they reach this point, are essentially in psychological quicksand. The more everyone thrashes about trying to address the symptom and clamber back up to dry land, the farther down everyone sinks, the worse the symptom gets, and the more hopeless the situation seems to become.

That is one of the main dangers of our tendency to so rapidly label teens with disorders and diagnoses. The problems that they display do not reside within them, but within the family system, and it's only through changing the system in which they exist that their behavior will ultimately change and growth resume. Instead of spending so much time and energy sticking adolescents with whatever is the diagnosis *du jour*—depression, ADHD, ODD, bipolar disorder—we should attempt to diagnose and reconfigure the troubling circumstances that surround our adolescents and actually engender, nourish, and sustain their most worrisome problems.

Through my clinical work, I have come to believe strongly that what is by far the most common source of difficulties when it comes to raising adolescents is not peer pressure or raging hormones or chemical imbalances or consumerism or the media but these very imbalances in the family system. And just about all of the imbalances that I encounter in my practice, the ones that account, whether families know it or not, for the problems that lead families to consult with me in the first place, can be classified in one of three categories:

- Power Imbalances
- Responsibility Imbalances
- Relational Imbalances

Let's spend some time focusing on the imbalances in each of these categories to see how they typically express themselves:

POWER IMBALANCES

Teens are hungry for power—to my way of thinking, it's more basic, more appealing, and more addictive than any substance or chemical that they will ever come across. Because of this, adolescents will typically fight like hell to claim power or hold onto the power that they already have, but when they wind up with too much power for their own good, it makes them feel extremely fearful, anxious, and uncomfortable. In a way, it's like giving an inexperienced driver a very powerful hot rod—there's some thrill and excitement, for sure, but there's great danger, as well, and a hazardous crackup is likely to be the end result.

The labyrinthian challenge for parents during adolescence is to continue to lead the family but to gradually begin to *share* their leadership with their teenager in subtle but noticeable ways.

This is more art than science, and it is impossible to avoid erring in one direction or another—in other words, either giving up too much or giving up too little power. However, if we keep our destination in mind, remain flexible, and make the appropriate adjustments in response to our teen's progress or lack thereof, we'll generally find that we get where we want to go.

Some parents find that they cede too much authority too soon. Or perhaps they never established sufficient authority in the first place, before their children even made it to adolescence. The family seems to have been built upside down, with the adolescent running the show and the parents serving as mere functionaries in their son's or daughter's Napoleonic court. Just as nature abhors a vacuum, so do adolescents, and when they sense a power vacuum in the family they'll often be the first to rush in and fill it.

Teenagers in these families demand, provoke, confront, and demean, and their parents appear helpless in the face of the onslaught, eager to do anything that will please their ravenous offspring just to calm them down, even momentarily. Of course, the only thing that would truly calm them down is a restoration of the appropriate order. But power, being extremely habit-forming for adolescents, is very difficult to pry away despite how nervous it makes them, and they somehow retain an Orphic capacity to entrance their parents and dissuade them from effectively fighting back.

Parents of adolescents may have many reasons for disavowing their parental duties and abdicating power, but usually it has something to do with their fear of their teen's rebellious reaction. The reality is, however, that what accounts for the most extreme teenaged behavior—violence, delinquency, running away, drug abuse, promiscuity—generally results from the *absence* of firm authority rather than its presence. But sometimes our frightful scenarios prevent us from taking decisive action and render us as ineffective, disempowered leaders—figureheads without any meaningful influence.

Often, the most therapeutic aspect of my work with families lies in my effort to reestablish an effective parental hierarchy in the presence of the teenager, who can then experience the secret relief of seeing his parents back in charge and return to the more necessary and achievable job of controlling his own life rather than everyone else's.

In one initial session, 16-year-old Jonathan, who had run away from home several times and was now court-ordered into treatment, constantly referred to his beleaguered father, Rich, as an "asshole" during our opening session. I tried to use this inter-action as a fulcrum with which to prop Rich back up into assum-ing the role of a strong, capable caregiver. Jonathan was in the midst of disdainfully listing his parents' insufficiencies while they sat passively and listened. I turned away from Jonathan and com-mented to his father:

"I have to interrupt here for a moment. Your son just called you an 'asshole' for about the fourth or fifth time in the last ten minutes. Is that all right with you?"

"Well, no . . ."

"Well then, I'm confused—you didn't say anything in re-sponse that made it clear to him that this was *not* alright with you."

"I just try to ignore him when he gets like that."

"Does that seem to work? Because he seems to use that word quite frequently. Does he do so outside of here as well, like at home?"

"I guess so."

"I have to ask you something. Do you *like* being called an asshole?"

"Of course not!"

"Well, then, why do you put up with it?"

"I guess I want him to get it out of his system."

"So he's entitled to say or do whatever he wants to as long as he's 'getting it out of his system?' "

"Not exactly."

"So you would rather he *not* call you an asshole?"

"Yes, that's right. But it's not that big a deal. I can live with it."

"I'm sure you can live with it—it looks like you're already do-ing so. But do you think that you *deserve* to be called an asshole by your sixteen-year-old son?"

"Not really."

"Not really? I mean, what exactly has he done with his life that leads him to think that he can call *you* an asshole? You, who have raised him, who work hard to make a good home and provide for him and his siblings. After all, he's still a kid—he has no job, he's earned no degree, he owns no home."

"Yes, you're right."

"You changed his diapers when he was a baby. You taught him how to use a toilet. You took care of him when he was sick. You cleaned his vomit. You helped him learn to walk and talk. You fed and clothed and sheltered him. Where exactly does he get off calling you an asshole?"

"I see what you're saying, Doc. I don't deserve that at all."

As I expected, Jonathan did not remain silent and chimed in at this point: "He's an asshole because he thinks he can tell me what to do and he doesn't know what he's talking about."

Rich sat frozen and said nothing. I stepped in again, this time with Jonathan directly.

"I don't agree with you. He's your father. You may not like him, you may not love him, you may not even *care* for him, but he doesn't deserve to be called an asshole."

Jonathan reddened and glared at me. It appeared to be the first time that anyone had ever told him that this was not acceptable behavior.

At this point, interestingly, Jonathan's mother, Chloe, stepped in to defend her son and protect him from my confrontation.

"I don't think you're getting the full picture of Jonathan. He's not some punk, some disrespectful thug, you know. This is a young man who was elected cocaptain of the lacrosse team. This is a young man who has a 3.0 GPA in high school. He's got a *lot* of strengths." She supplied him with a fond, indulgent smile.

"I'm sorry," I cut her off, "I'm sure he's a bright and talented young man, and I'd certainly be interested in learning more about his achievements, but not until he can learn to speak appropriately to his father."

"His father hasn't been such a great father, you know," Chloe replied, revealing an alliance between her and her son that was probably both cause and effect of this young man's difficulties.

"I'm sure he hasn't been perfect, and I'm not saying anybody should be let completely off the hook here," I responded. "Every one of you has some growing and changing to do. But I still don't believe that he has the right to call his father an asshole, and I'd be *very* surprised if, in your heart of hearts, you didn't agree with me." Chloe fell silent.

I turned to Rich: "What do you think?"

"I think you're right. I *don't* deserve to be called an asshole."

"Then you need to tell your son that. Tell him that right now."

"Jonathan, I don't want to be called an asshole anymore."

"Even if you are one?" Jonathan taunted.

Rich looked at me. "Tell him what you think," I urged.

"I'm not an asshole. I won't tolerate being called an asshole. You're not to call me an asshole anymore."

"Asshole," muttered Jonathan, but a little softer than before.

"He's testing you," I insisted. "Make it clear to him that this will not do. Make it clear to him that you don't want to be referred to in that way ever again."

"That's enough from you, Jonathan. From now on, you need to speak to me with respect."

"But I don't *have* any respect for you, Dad."

This was a notable comment because it was the first time that I had heard Jonathan refer to his father as "Dad," a sign that progress was being made, and that a necessary discussion about the basis of their lack of respect for each other was ready to be broached. Calling him by his appropriate parental moniker was, to my way of thinking, a begrudging acknowledgement on Jonathan's part that his father might again become a force to be reckoned with, and a step in the direction of reestablishing a healthier hierarchy.

Other families display the opposite imbalance—the parents have no difficulty owning power but are unable to gradually begin sharing the power in a way that recognizes their teenager's growing competence and need for autonomy. Differences of opinion are viewed as battles to be won or lost, and the concepts of compromising, accommodating, capitulating, or even just "going with the flow" are seen as tantamount to humiliating surrenders or irresponsible abdications of parental authority.

Usually, the need to maintain absolute, dictatorial control does nothing more than strengthen teens' already formidable resolve, encouraging them to dig their heels in and strenuously resist our efforts to get them to comply, cooperate, or modify their behavior in any way, even if such resistance clearly works to their disadvantage.

In the following excerpt from a session, 16-year-old Kendra is fighting for a later curfew, and her mother, Fran, is refusing to negotiate, based on Kendra's history of consistently coming home past curfew.

"I just don't see why I have to be in by eleven on a Saturday night."

"Eleven is late enough, young lady. I don't know what it is that you find so necessary to do that can't be done before eleven o'clock. You're allowed to leave the house as early as you'd like. That gives you plenty of time to have fun with your friends."

"I *can't* leave the house as early as I'd like, because you insist that we have dinner together as a family before I go out."

"Well, I think that's a reasonable thing. Saturday is one of the only evenings when we can all be together. I think it's nice for us to have a family dinner."

"But all of my friends are allowed to stay out later. It's *embarrassing* to have to be home by eleven."

"Since when are you home by eleven anyway? That's the problem, that's why we're here, you constantly come home *past* your curfew."

"Listen, Mom, I wouldn't come home past curfew if I had a reasonable curfew."

"What feels like a reasonable curfew to you?" I wondered.

"Midnight. Most of my friends have provisional licenses, so they can't be on the road past midnight, anyway. Midnight would work fine for me."

"Does midnight feel too late for you, Fran?" I asked.

"Absolutely. There's no way I'm going to allow her to be out until midnight. Not at the age of sixteen. Not when she's not even making her eleven o'clock curfew. If I made her curfew midnight, she'd probably come home at one in the morning."

"Mom, you're being ridiculous. If my curfew was like my friends' curfew, I'd be home *on time*! You don't know how hard it is to stop everything at eleven and say, 'Sorry, everybody, my mommy wants me to come home now.'"

"I don't care whether it's hard or not. Eleven is late enough."

"How many times would Kendra have to come home by eleven for you to feel trusting enough to consider extending her curfew?" I tried.

"I don't know. She's not even doing it now."

"I know she's not doing it now. But perhaps if she had some hope that there might be flexibility when it came to resetting her curfew, she'd be more motivated to meet her *current* curfew."

"This is not negotiable. I'm not budging."

"Fine, then I'll just continue to come home when I feel like it," Kendra interjected.

"Then you'll be grounded and won't go out at all."

"Then I'll sneak out."

"Then I'll lock you in your room."

Clearly, the harder that Fran was going to work to show Kendra who was the boss, the harder that Kendra was going to work to show Fran that she wasn't. This battle of wills was going to get them nowhere but more alienated and entrenched. I had the sense that Kendra just needed to see *some* sign that her mother would soften a bit, and then she might become a little more agreeable.

"Has Kendra been getting into any kind of trouble when she's out with her friends on the weekend?" I inquired of Fran.

"No, thankfully. They mostly just go out to a movie, get something to eat, or go over to someone's house. But just because she's not getting into trouble doesn't mean that she's allowed to stay out until all hours of the night."

"Well, we're not talking about her being out until 'all hours of the night.' We're talking about her being allowed to stay out a little later than she's currently allowed to."

"Nonetheless, it's not negotiable."

"What are you trying to accomplish by having her in by eleven?"

"I'm trying to keep my daughter safe. I know that *you* have a daughter, Dr. Sachs. I'm sure you can understand this."

"I certainly do, and I'm a big proponent of safety. But what is it that you're afraid she'll do between eleven and midnight that she couldn't do between seven and eleven?"

Fran didn't answer.

Sensing an opening, I continued. "You're right to impose a curfew, you're right to try to ensure her well-being, and you're right to expect her to abide by whatever curfew you set. But if Kendra were good about meeting her eleven o'clock curfew for four consecutive weeks, would you consider extending her curfew until eleven-thirty?"

"No way."

"Eleven-fifteen?"

"Well . . . I'll consider it. But she's got to keep her cell phone on so I can reach her, so I know where she is and if she's safe."

"Have you not been doing that?" I asked Kendra.

"If I leave my phone on, my mom will call me all the time. Who wants to be bugged by their mom when they're out with their friends?"

"No one that I know," I admitted. "But your mom would probably feel better knowing where you were and that you were okay. Most parents of young adults feel that way."

"So I've got to do things her way for a whole month just to get a lousy fifteen minutes on a Saturday night? Screw *that*!" (You might think that Kendra is being unreasonable here, but try to think back to how long a month felt when you were 16!)

"Don't screw it just yet, Kendra. You have the right to ask for a later curfew, and your mom has the right to give it some thought and make the final decision. But you might get things off on the right foot if you showed her that you can meet your *current* curfew and were available by phone should she need to reach you. Perhaps then she might be more willing to extend it."

"Well, I'll agree if she doesn't call me all the time."

"What feels reasonable, Fran?" I asked.

"I actually wouldn't call her at all if she would just call me. Maybe she could just promise to call me when she's leaving to come home or if there's a change in plans."

"How does that sound to you, Kendra?"

"Fine," she grumbled.

With some further "gentle persuasion" on my part, Kendra eventually agreed to be home on time at eleven for a month, and to keep her cell phone on and call her mother when she was heading home. Fran agreed to not call her more than one time unless there was an emergency and, if these conditions were met, to extend her curfew to eleven-thirty for a trial period. Assuming that Kendra was coming home promptly at eleven-thirty for another two months, a midnight curfew would be established for a trial period. It was also decided that any blown curfews would result in having to start the process over again. Fran's willingness to take the risk of negotiation made the system more malleable and helped to resolve a previously intractable conflict in a consensual way.

There's a third group of families I see who struggle with power imbalances as well. These are families in which the parents vary between giving up too much power and too little power, and in their unpredictable oscillations they confuse and enrage their children. Lacking an effective midrange, they career haphazardly between rigid toughness and extreme indulgence. Teens react with anger and bewilderment to this kind of instability because they don't know which parent is going to "show up"—the unyielding enforcer or the overly benevolent nurturer—and because the maddening alternation between giving permission and taking it back leaves them constantly feeling like they're being betrayed.

Sometimes the discrepancy resides between the two parents—one parent playing the role of "softie" while the other one plays the role of "tough one"—and sometimes both parents flip-flop between the two extremes. Either way, chaos is the eventual result.

Most often, parental guilt is at the root of these fluctuations. Feeling like they have been too busy, too distracted, too distant, or too irritable, these parents coddle or pamper or grant unearned privileges as a way of doing penance and assuaging their pervasive guilty feelings. When they don't receive the kind of grateful, appreciative, or cooperative response that they would like from their children, they "see red" and become harshly punitive. Then, feeling guilty again about their draconian response, they shift back into a state of big-hearted bounteousness, which of course elicits more of the very same selfishness or antipathy that so aggravated them in the first place.

It is no surprise that no meaningful improvements are ever forthcoming from the teenager in these families: the parents are so busy changing back and forth that there isn't ever a chance for their child to make changes and sustain them in one way or another.

Fifteen-year-old Trevor came home with three C's and three E's on his report card. His father, Duncan, the first recipient of this bad news, hit the ceiling and told Trevor that he was grounded indefinitely—no phone, no TV, no computer, no friends, no *nothing*. His mother, Siobhan, hit the ceiling when she heard about this consequence, lambasting Duncan for implementing an overly severe punishment without having consulted with her first. She also pointed out that she'd be the one who would have to implement the consequence, since Duncan usually didn't get home from work until late. She didn't want to have to be in the position of following Trevor around the house from the time he got home from school until bedtime making sure he didn't sneak onto one of their computers, TVs, or videogames or dealing with a grumpy teenager who'd been cut off from his friends.

Duncan relented, and they agreed to a one-week grounding. However, Siobhan reminded Duncan that Trevor had agreed to go to a friend's birthday party that weekend, and that it was too late to back out because the parents had already purchased tickets for a professional basketball game, tickets that could no longer be returned. Duncan agreed, and Trevor was not only allowed to go to the game but also allowed to sleep over at his friend's house.

The next week, Siobhan was home when Trevor's math teacher called, saying that he had bombed on the most recent test and had also not turned in the last three homework assignments. This time Siobhan was the parent who lowered the boom. "That's it," she told him, barging into his room while he lay on his bed with his headphones on, staring absentmindedly at the ceiling. "Your dad was right—you're grounded indefinitely."

When Duncan came home and found out about this, he was pleased to hear that Siobhan had finally "seen the light" and instituted the consequence that he had pushed for initially. However, the next week his boss gave him four free tickets for front-row seats to a professional basketball game that weekend. "These are unbelievable seats," he enthusiastically told Siobhan. "I'd love to take Trevor and a couple of his friends—he'll go out of his mind."

"What about the grounding?" she reminded him.

"Well, it's not like he's going to be doing homework on Saturday night," Duncan pointed out.

This time it was Siobhan who relented, and Duncan took Trevor and two of his best buddies to the game, with the understanding that Trevor would finish all of his homework the next day.

The following week it was Duncan who picked up the phone one evening when a call came from the school. This time it was the assistant principal, informing him that Trevor had cut two classes that morning and was now suspended for three days as a result.

"That's *it!*" Duncan shouted. "You're grounded, no if's, and's, or but's. You've pulled the wool over our eyes for the last time." Siobhan and Duncan agreed to hold tight with the grounding until the next report card, which was six weeks away.

However, Trevor came down with a bad cold the last day of his suspension. Bored and restless and unable to find a place for himself, he finally convinced his mother, after hours of whining, to let him watch some television. Duncan came home to find Trevor on the couch, feet propped up and a bottle of soda next to him, watching Cartoon Network.

"I thought we had an understanding!" he yelled at Siobhan.

"Do *you* want to stay home all day with a sick son who feels lousy and has nothing to do?" Siobhan retorted.

"Nothing to do?!? He's behind in just about every subject, he's missing homework, he's cutting classes. He should be doing schoolwork, not watching goddamn cartoons!"

"He's supposed to do schoolwork all *day*? You're being ridiculous, Duncan. He's done everything he's supposed to do. He showed me the work he completed."

"But that doesn't mean he should be allowed to watch TV!"

"That's what *you* do when you're not feeling well!"

"That's not the point, Siobhan—he's grounded and I'm not!"

"The point is that watching a couple of hours of TV is not going to kill him."

"The point is that he's manipulating you, and you're falling for it."

"*You're* the one who wanted to take him to the basketball game!"

"Well, *you're* the one who wanted him to go to his friend's birthday party!"

While Duncan and Siobhan continued to go at each other, Trevor contentedly sipped his soda and continued watching *Scooby-Doo.*

In this family, the parents' inability to unify and chart an even course precluded the possibility that their son would feel enough pressure to consider change. With parents who constantly found ways to cancel out each other's power, Trevor found himself in the position of power and didn't hesitate to exploit it.

Through these examples, we can see that a healthy balance of power in the family is crucial to creating the possibility of change. Parents need to remain in or establish an executive position that is clearly on top of the family hierarchy, but at the same time present carefully calibrated possibilities for their teenagers, possibilities that allow them to begin to feel comfortable with their own burgeoning power. It's not a simple matter of "getting tough" or "giving in," but of finding a middle ground that allows for authority without rigidity, leadership without tyranny, and involvement without intrusiveness. When parents can comfortably set up camp in such a middle ground during adolescence, the odds are greatly heightened that positive change will come about.

RESPONSIBILITY IMBALANCES

As is the case with imbalances in power, parents can find themselves bestowing too much or too little responsibility on their teens. In the case of the former, adolescents are burdened with responsibilities that far exceed their capacity to manage them, resulting in feelings of stress, futility, depression, and anxiety. In the case of the latter, adolescents are granted amnesty from responsibility to such a large extent that they feel no obligation to perform duties that benefit anyone other than themselves and experience no compunction about their lack of accountability. Let's visit families from each side of the spectrum.

Fourteen-year-old Yonita and her parents came to see me at the behest of the school system, because of Yonita's poor attendance. Absent three days a week on average, and often coming late on the days that she did show up, she was clearly in danger of losing credit for her entire freshman year and having to start over again the following fall.

Yonita's initial explanation, when I asked her why her attendance record was so spotty, was that "I have a hard time getting up in the morning, and by the time I'm ready to get moving, the day's half-done anyway, so why bother going?"

Her father, Avram, a retail store manager, said that he left for work at 5:30 in the morning, so he wasn't available to help Yonita get moving. "She doesn't want me waking her at five-thirty, and there's really no point to her being up that early. And, being the manager, I've got to be at the store by six o'clock, so it's not like I can hang around all morning waiting for her to awaken."

Her mother, Shefa, told me that she used to try to get Yonita up, but "there's no way to awaken her. She has two alarm clocks, and I come in and shake her, but she always falls back asleep."

"What do you do at that point?" I wondered.

"There's not much I *can* do," she admitted. "What, am I supposed to pick her up and carry her to school in her pajamas?"

A little surprised at the lack of effort that had been exerted on either parent's part to do whatever it took to get Sleeping Beauty out of her morning stupor, I obtained some history in an effort to figure things out.

I learned that Yonita had been a fine student in elementary and middle school, so it was unlikely that she was academically overmatched, even though it was her first year of high school. I also learned that Yonita had a fairly extensive network of friends at school, which diminished the likelihood that she was staying home to avoid social difficulties.

What did seem relevant, however, was that the younger of Yonita's two older sisters had left for college in the fall, which meant that Yonita was now the only child remaining at home. When I asked the parents what that was like for them, the answers I received were vague and superficial.

"Well, we've got more room, that's for sure," Avram joked, in a somewhat forced way. "And it's certainly quieter with just Yoni around—not as much commotion."

"We're kind of used to this, because our oldest daughter left for college four years ago. She's a senior now," Shefa observed.

"How about for you, Yonita. What's it like being the only one left?"

Yonita chewed her lip and stared out the window for a while before answering. "It's sort of weird, really. I mean, I was close to both of my sisters, but Mara, the one who just left for college this fall, she and I were the closest. We did all kinds of things to-gether."

"Like what?"

"Oh, just stuff. Once she learned how to drive, she would take me to wherever I needed to go, or we'd go shopping together. Sometimes, she'd even take me out with her and her friends, which was fun—not a lot of big sisters do that sort of thing."

"Who does the driving now, with your sister away from home?"

"No one, really," Yonita said, darting a look at her mother.

"Have the two of you found that the loss of a driver means that you've had to pick up the slack again?" I asked the parents.

"I don't do too much of that," Avram began, "because I'm away at work from early until late."

"So I guess the carpooling falls on you, Shefa?"

The room fell silent. Yonita started to nervously tap her foot, Avram looked over at Shefa, and Shefa took her turn staring out the window.

"What's up?" I asked, finally.

After a long pause, Avram said, "My wife's kind of been going through a tough time."

"Did you want to fill me in, Shefa?" I inquired.

Her face instantly scrunched up, and she began to cry. "I don't know what's going on. I'm so lost. I'm so tired. I don't know, I just don't know, anymore."

Over the next few minutes, their story tumbled out. Shefa had gotten very depressed over the last few months, and she had missed so much work that she had been put on administrative leave. What also became evident was that, with her father work-ing such long hours and with both of her sisters away at college, Yoni had become her mother's mother—whether it was her vol-unteering to play this role, her being subtly or not so subtly asked to, or a combination of both, she was "on duty" 24 hours a day, keeping a close eye on her mother to make sure she didn't de-scend any further into listless despair.

When I asked for some time alone with Yoni to discuss this privately, it was now her tears that came forth. "You don't know how helpless I feel. I'm so scared that if I go to school, she'll just give up on everything and kill herself—she has said that she might, that she can't take it anymore. She's *such* a mess, and I'm so angry with her, and my dad's not there and I don't know if he even cares, they don't even sleep together anymore because Mom's always crashing on the couch at night. And I *don't* see my friends and I *don't* do my homework and I'm *so* far behind at school now it's not even funny. I'll never catch up. And even if I do make it to school, all I can think about is what I'm going to come home to, the police at the house, or her sitting in front of the TV with that glazed look. . . . I don't know what to do, I *fucking* don't know what to do."

In this family, Yonita had been given so much inappropriate responsibility that she was unable to take on the more age-appropriate responsibilities of getting to school and developing her friendships. Without the maturity of judgment to know that it really wasn't her job to stay home and take on the role of being her mother's nursemaid, and with there being some understandable eagerness on her father's and sisters' parts for her to be recruited into this role so that they would remain free to attend to their own matters, this young woman had become overburdened, sacrificing her own life to care for and protect her mother's.

In the subsequent weeks we worked to redistribute the responsibility for Shefa's care, to reassure Yoni that her parents could better tackle these "adult issues" on their own and with professional help, rather than with hers, and to "fire" her from her role of mothering her mother. As a result she rapidly returned to regular school attendance and recommenced her connections with her peers.

In Yoni's family, her lack of responsibility, as evidenced by her not getting to school, was actually the result of too much being expected of her. In other families, teens' inadequate responsibility level is the result of too *little* being expected of them.

In these situations, the parents have been, and remain, so super-responsible that there is no room or need for the child to develop a sense of any real responsibility. There are many reasons why we may fall into this pattern. Sometimes it's a reaction to how much responsibility we had when we were children. One mother told me that she was so overwhelmed with chores growing up, to the extent that there was no time left over to go out with friends or participate in school activities, that she vowed never to ask her children to do anything around the house as a way of evening out the scales.

Sometimes our desire to rescue our children from responsibility is rooted in our guilt. Because we went through a divorce, because we work too-long hours, because we are impatient or cranky or self-absorbed, we try to compensate by smoothing their path and making things as easy as possible for them. Similarly, our expecting too little of them may reside in our feeling sorry for them, or pitying them. Because they're depressed, or overweight, or learning disabled, or lonely, we try to help them out by not *asking* them to help out.

Sometimes we protect them from being responsible because we've gotten in the habit of doing so from years of living at a frantic pace. After all, if we've got to get one child to her piano lesson, one child to her soccer practice, and a third child to a doctor's appointment all in the space of 30 minutes, it's difficult to be patient and insist that they all make sure their beds are made and their dishes are put away before we herd them out the door and head off down the road. Sometimes it's just quicker and easier to do it all ourselves so that we beat the clock, even though they're let off the hook once again.

We may even deprive our children of responsibility in a (sometimes unconscious) effort to maintain our importance to them, and to ourselves. In other words, as long as they're not fully autonomous and self-reliant, we're still indispensable to them, which may help us to stave off the feelings of irrelevance and mortality that begin to creep up behind us as they move ahead toward young adulthood.

And finally, despite how unpleasant it is for us to have to nag, and for our teens to have to *be* nagged, when they're not being responsible enough, the nagging does represent a bond between the generations. If we haven't found any better ways to connect during adolescence, we might find it preferable to at least have something to hector them about so that there's some reason to engage, frictional as this engagement may be.

For any and all of these reasons, families find it difficult to establish a new status quo during adolescence, and the parents' high level of responsibility virtually guarantees the teen's low level of responsibility.

In one family, 17-year-old Griffin, a standout athlete from the moment he began playing organized sports, didn't display the slightest bit of initiative when it came to being responsible in any arena other than athletic participation. Not only did he not wash any of his uniforms, but he wouldn't even take the time to ball them up and throw them into the hamper, simply leaving them on the floor of his room and expecting his mother to come in and lug them down to the laundry room and then fold and return the clean, dry clothing to his bed.

The family had purchased a third car for him to use so that he could get himself to his many games and practices, but he never took the time to fill any of the three cars with gas, instead just dashing out and jumping into whichever car had the most fuel. When his father tried to stop him, he'd insist that he was going to be late if he was forced to fill the tank on his way, a tactic that was always enough to earn him a "bye" from the gas station.

Not only was he was not expected to do *any* housework and yard work because of his hectic athletic schedule, he wasn't even expected to do the basics, like clean up after himself—plates and glasses that he had brought up to his room or down to the basement remained there until one of his parents eventually tired of the accumulation or started to notice bugs crawling around.

When they did try to intervene, he was somehow able to make things even worse for everyone. For example, their ill-fated effort to get him to do his own laundry backfired because he would simply remove any clothes that were already in the washer and shove them into a wet pile in the corner so that he could get his stuff started. Or, he'd leave his clothes in the dryer for days on end, meaning that anyone else who wanted to use it wound up having to empty it for him.

Because of the long-standing arrangement in which his parents had not demanded that some contribution to the functioning of the household was a priority, he had not yet developed a level of responsibility commensurate with his age. Griffin was, at this stage, nothing more than a huge, spoiled brat whose ace-in-the-hole was the athletic accomplishment that currently trumped every one of his mother's and father's cards.

In another family, the responsibility imbalance took the form of the parents shielding their daughter from normal challenges and disappointments, leading to greater, rather than lesser, feelings of vulnerability and inadequacy. Sixteen-year-old Chaundra was born with cystic fibrosis and had required a tremendous amount of medical attention over the years. She was referred to me because of recurring feelings of depression and some recent suicidal gestures involving pill swallowing and wrist slicing.

What I learned, however, was that her parents were allowing, if not encouraging, her to use her respiratory illness to avoid learning and attending to basic matters that were absolutely necessary to take on if she was ever going to have any hope of living independently. Even though she was a junior in high school, she was not expected to excel in school, despite being very bright; not expected to create a social life, despite having a pleasant personality; not expected to get a part-time job, despite her competence; and not expected to exercise, despite the obvious ways in which it would not only help her to look and feel better but also counter the process of her insidious disease.

Whether it was because of their guilt and helplessness, their desire to protect her from further harm and disappointment, their sense that she might not have long to live, or Chaundra's not-atypical desire to amplify her disabled state so as to excuse herself from the hard work of growth, it became clear to me that her parents had apparently decided, early on, to anticipate a diminished level of functioning from their daughter and staunchly refuse to challenge her to stretch, reach forth, and determine what she could truly accomplish in her life.

It appeared that Chaundra, seeing this reflection of herself in her parents' eyes, responded by diligently substantiating this shrunken image of her potential, and further diminishing her expectations for herself, setting into motion an almost insurmountably self-fulfilling prophecy. Her disabled respiratory system was serving to keep her and her family organized around the task of disabling her entire being, and a state of developmental stagnation had set in that was just as dangerous to her psychological development as the cystic fibrosis was to her physical development. No wonder she was depressed and saw suicide as her only way out.

In this family, it was my job not to focus on her depression, but to help to rebalance the level of responsibility in the system by encouraging the parents to see Chaundra as something more than disabled, to discover and amplify her competencies and focus on these to a greater extent than on her limitations, and to raise their expectations of her, as well as her expectations of herself. It was also important to determine the extent to which the parents had equated their self-worth with how well they "took care" of their daughter, to help them see that they could be good parents without having to coddle and pamper her, and to recognize that they were effectively dispossessing her of her selfhood if they continued to treat her so delicately and act so overprotectively.

In the subsequent months, as Chaundra's parents courageously learned how to carry less responsibility *for* her and to simultaneously assign more responsibility *to* her, her mood began to lift and she started to see some reason to go on living.

In the Salter family, a mirror image revealed the same dynamic. Forty-two-year-old Juliette, a single mother, was diagnosed with ovarian cancer when her daughter, Nekesha, was 14. Afraid that she would not survive, and not wanting whatever time she had left with Nekesha to be sullied in any way, she spent the subsequent months creating a Utopian wonderland for Nekesha, indulging her every wish and whim, excusing her from every imperative and duty. Fortunately, surgery and chemotherapy sent her cancer into remission, but because she continued to fear its return, as most cancer survivors do, she continued to ordain her daughter's Shangri-la existence. The result, two years later, was an immature 16-year-old who had become a demanding and intractable despot with almost no tolerance for the inevitable frustrations of daily living. Juliette had reacted to the fear that cancer would rob her of her life by inadvertently robbing her daughter of the chance to come of age.

But through our work together, she slowly came to see that the best way to prepare Nekesha for the independence that might one day be prematurely thrust on her was through promoting, rather than protecting her from, responsibility. With this new perspective having been soldered into place, she began shielding Nekesha less from stresses, disappointments, and challenges. In the process, she helped her to become much less brittle and vulnerable and much more capable and self-assured.

. . .

RELATIONAL IMBALANCES

Finding ways to navigate between too much closeness and too much separateness is one of the most knotty conundrums facing parents of teens, mostly because both generations experience tremendous, and perpetually shifting, ambivalence about how much involvement they want with each other.

A teenage girl will be sitting on her mother's lap one moment, and the next moment she'll roll her eyes and impatiently wriggle out of a hug. A teenage boy will suddenly pour his heart out to his father about his dismal love life and then withdraw entirely for days, without even the semblance of a two-way conversation taking place.

And of course it's not just the adolescents who are mixed up. We parents will at times sense the impending "end of an era," and want as much contact as we can have with our son or daughter before they begin to leave home. At other times we will grow weary of their sarcastic tirades or sullen retreats and actively fantasize about whether the leaving-home process could somehow be accelerated to warp-speed.

Relational imbalances, just like the power and responsibility imbalances that we have just examined, are unavoidable during adolescence, but the key to dealing with them remains the same—a gradual reorganization and renegotiation of generational boundaries that leaves room for both parents and teens to grow. The result is not simply a relational cutoff or amputation—complete independence as opposed to complete dependence—but a revamping of the system such that family members' cramped dependence *on* each other transfigures into a spacious interdependence *with* each other.

Some parents struggle too hard against their teens' demand for separateness, creating an atmosphere of toxic enmeshment that suffocates their offspring and precludes growth. Because there is so little room for the adolescent to carve out individual space, extreme, extraordinary, and sometimes even dangerous measures have to be invoked.

Fifteen-year-old Nicolai was referred to me because a local pharmacist had alertly noted that he was purchasing potent over-the-counter cold and cough syrups on a weekly basis. When we met for the first time, he forthrightly explained that he loved the feeling that came over him when he drank these elixirs, which was almost invariably when he was in his room after school: "It's like a total escape. I go into my own world, float away, and don't have to return for a long, long time. It makes things very interesting."

"What are you escaping from?" I wondered.

"Everything, really."

"Do you feel as if you're escaping from yourself?"

"Not really. I mean, I generally feel pretty good about things. I like being with myself."

"Do you feel as if you're escaping from school?"

"Nah—I do well in school, I don't mind it there."

"Do you feel as if you're escaping from your family?" I tried.

"If you were in my shoes, wouldn't you? I mean, my house is like a prison. My parents don't allow us to watch any TV, they won't let me go to movies with my friends, they won't even *consider* an Xbox or anything like that. I asked for a Discman for my birthday, and they bought me one, but they don't let me buy the CDs that I want to listen to. They're always worried that these things will get me into trouble."

"What *do* they allow you to do?"

"Not much," he complained. "They didn't even want me to go to the homecoming dance at our high school, until, luckily, my friend's dad called them and told them he'd be willing to take me and pick me up. And even then, they were so worried that something bad was going to happen to me."

"What are things like when you're at home?"

"It's like I'm in a fishbowl. I share a room with my little brother, and it's not a very big room. We have to have dinner together every night, and I mean *every* night. I wanted to go out for the school play, but they wouldn't allow that either, because some of the rehearsals are in the evening and I'd miss dinner. It's like there's no space for me—none at all."

I asked the parents for their perspective on Nicolai's harsh assessment of his home life. "We really believe that we have to shelter our children from the world," his mother, Manya, explained in heavily accented English. "We emigrated from Russia when Nicolai was only five, and when our younger two hadn't even been born yet. We don't want him to get himself into trouble like a lot of the kids we see. We know what happens at these school dances. We know how violent these movies and TV shows and video games are."

His father, Stanislav, agreed heartily: "We want Nicolai to fit in, that's for sure, but we don't want him to lose his heritage. He can be an American, all right, that's why we came here, after all, to escape Russia, to have more freedom—but we have to be careful because too much freedom can be a danger. That's why we keep such a close eye on him and his younger brother and sister."

It was interesting to note that the father used the same word that his son did. Just as Manya and Stanislav had bravely *escaped* what they had felt was an oppressive environment, Nicolai, too, in his own way, felt as if he was escaping oppression, albeit in a more hazardous manner. In their efforts to preserve their family's original culture and not lose their oldest son to what, for now, remained a foreign and threatening culture, these parents had created a climate that had yet to change shape to accommodate Nicolai's changing needs.

Our work together consisted of very slowly and delicately helping Manya and Stanislav to loosen their worried grip on Nicolai so that he could experience some healthy escapism without having to resort to drugs. I supported the parents in their efforts to not overexpose Nicolai to inappropriate media, for example, but also supported Nicolai in his efforts to participate more fully in his school and peer culture without it feeling like a threat to this immigrant family's identity.

A turning point came when they agreed to let Nicolai go on a three-day school-sponsored ski trip, which he agreed to pay for and from which he returned unharmed and overjoyed. On that trip he befriended a fellow child of eastern European émigrés. Marek, from the former Yugoslavia, and not only did Nicolai and Marek reinforce each other's respective efforts to balance their ethnic and American identities, but the two sets of parents connected with each other as well and supported each other's effort to assimilate in a satisfying way.

As Manya and Stanislav provided Nicolai with more room to grow, and saw that he could handle it without his or the family's integrity being threatened, there was less need for him to seek ephemeral freedom through pharmaceutical means.

The opposite situation can occur just as often, in which the parents are not overly involved with, but prematurely disengaged from, their child. This is especially likely to happen during adolescence for several reasons. Teens often mature physically more rapidly than they do emotionally, so that they *look* the part of a functional adult even if they're not yet willing or able to successfully *play* the part. Also, as we have learned, adolescents tend to experience their still urgently felt dependency needs as signs of weakness or failure, and work overtime in a desperate attempt to cover them up with pseudomaturity and autonomy. Behind this counterfeit confidence, however, lies a child who still requires attention, nurturance, supervision, and guidance, whether or not he knows, likes, and is willing to admit this.

Parents, too, play a role in this process, because we are often quite eager to see our teens as more separate, capable, and independent than they really are. Agreeing not to look behind their carefully cultivated façade of urbane sophistication and self-sufficiency serves many purposes, among them reassuring us, albeit falsely, that our teens are less vulnerable than they really are and liberating us from having to be as involved with and responsible for them as we still need to be.

While both parent and teen may appear to benefit from this premature disengagement in the short term, the long-term costs can be quite steep, with an adolescent ultimately feeling not emancipated but ejected, not liberated but exiled.

Fifteen-year-old Jenna's parents marveled at how grown-up she had always been. "Even as a little girl," her mother, Geri, explained to me, "she was always ahead of her peers and classmates, so independent, so articulate. Her first couple of years in elementary school, her teachers suggested that we consider having her skip a grade because she was so advanced. Her friends were always a year or two older than her, but she was always accepted as if she was their age. When she hit middle school, everybody thought that she was already a high school student."

Her father, Keith, added, "I guess it's because she had two

older brothers and an older sister, but whatever the reason, she's always been ahead of the curve, when it comes to her social life."

Despite the great pride that Geri and Keith clearly took in Jenna's precocity, they were not seeing the extent to which it had endangered her. In reality, the family had come to work with me because the guidance counselor at Jenna's high school had informed them that she had developed a reputation for being a "skank," and that she had been caught leaving school grounds with a variety of unsavory individuals, including one who had dropped out of high school and was probably close to 20 years old.

I learned that all three of Jenna's older siblings were now living away from home, one a sophomore in college, and two having already graduated from college, and that her parents had become increasingly busy with their careers. Keith had finally earned a management position in the company that he had been a salesman in for many years and he was devoting a tremendous amount of energy to his work in an effort to show his superiors that he was worthy of the long-deferred promotion.

Geri, an attorney, had finished law school the year before her oldest was born. Since that time, she had been working as a half-time employee of a law firm and resisting their efforts to encourage her to work full-time and become a full-fledged partner. When her third child had left for college the year before, she had finally agreed to their proposition and taken a full-time position, and, like her husband, had begun working very long hours in order to validate her partners' faith in her.

So it was not unusual for the very self-reliant Jenna to be left alone by her parents in the mornings to get herself to school, and not to have any adult at home until as late as 7:00 P.M., providing her with almost five hours of unsupervised time in the afternoon. Family activities that involved the three of them had basically ceased, with both parents happy to have Jenna occupied with her "friends" in the evenings and on weekends so that they could attend to professional matters. Even the family's annual ski trip on Presidents' Day had been mothballed once their third child left home, as if Jenna, like her siblings, was no longer living at home.

While Jenna never complained to her parents about the family's arrangement, and, to some extent, of course, even enjoyed and took advantage of it, it seemed evident from her promiscuous behavior that she needed more parenting than she was getting. But Keith and Geri were so enamored with her pseudo-independence, and with the freedom that they believed they had to more fully invest in their careers now that they had launched their first three children, that they were no longer attuned to Jenna's developmental requirements.

Once I helped Keith and Geri to understand that they still had to finish the job of raising their remaining child, despite their success at having gotten the others on their way and their eagerness to make up for lost time professionally, they were able to restructure their lives so that Jenna became more of a priority than an afterthought. And as Jenna was slowly, although not completely, pulled back into the family's orbit, she was better able to resist the pull of her peers and make better choices when it came to who she spent time with and what she did with them.

Knowing that all families are prone to these inevitable power, responsibility, and relational imbalances during adolescence, how do we realign the family system such that there's a more appropriate and constructive symmetry? In Chapter 7 I will be providing you with some specific, concrete strategies and recommendations that will help. But to heighten the effectiveness of those suggestions, here are some general axioms about the nature of family change that are worth keeping in mind.

1. True change only occurs in a loving relationship.

No strategy, no technique, no tip or tool or tactic will ever be a catalyst for growth unless it is implemented in the context of a close, supportive parent-teen relationship. In *The Good Enough Child,* I proposed the incongruent, counterintuitive theorem that children are more likely to change if they know that they'll be loved and accepted for staying the same, and the same truth applies to adolescents: only when we dare to embrace them as they are will they move beyond our embrace and become all that they are meant to be.

Taking this approach often creates great anxiety for parents of teens. "How can I accept him for who he is when who he is means his doing so many things that seem to work against his best interests?" But when adolescents understand that we have great tolerance for all of their mistakes, for all of their misjudgments, for all of their baffling, graceless blunders, and when they trust that they'll be cherished and appreciated nonetheless, they are much more likely to learn from their experiences and discover more positive ways to manage their lives and present themselves to others.

2. Adolescents don't change unless families change.

Mahatma Gandhi wisely wrote, "We must become the change we want to see." As we have already noted, adolescent problems do not occur in a vacuum, but instead gestate in an environment that simultaneously influences and is influenced by every family member. With this in mind, no positive, abiding change on a teen's part will ever last unless the system has changed as well.

The main reason that family therapy is such a powerful psychotherapeutic endeavor is because it is assumed from the start that, while no one family member is to blame for difficulties, *all family members are responsible for contributing to the conditions in which these difficulties reside.* I will often encounter resistance when I set up initial consultations with a teen and both of his or her parents, or invite siblings or grandparents or other significant family members into sessions. Typical responses are, "Why should I have to come? There's nothing wrong with me, it's my daughter who's failing in school!" or "Her brothers aren't a part of this—they're all good kids and doing fine," or "My husband's too busy at work, and, anyway, I'm the one who deals with the kids—he's never even around most of the time."

But not only does the presence of all family members provide me with invaluable information and numerous pieces of the family puzzle; it also sets a tone that this is a joint endeavor, one in which everyone has an important part. Trying to treat a distressed teenager as an individual who is not intricately connected with his family's ecology is like trying to treat a distressed organ system without looking at its intricate connection with the body's other organ systems.

In fact, not only does focusing on an individual adolescent in treatment tend to be unproductive, it is often *counter*productive, because it leaves everyone else in their world off the hook, reinforcing the erroneous belief that the problem is located "inside" the teen and thereby precluding the possibility that the entire family will rise to the occasion and rewrite their constitution so that everyone is invited to grow.

3. For change to come about, the *reasons* for changing may have to change, too.

We learned early on that one of an adolescent's main jobs is to differentiate from his parents, and begin to manage life in his own way, on his own terms. Because of this, trying to get teenagers to change only because we want them to change is unlikely to result in anything more than limited success, and more likely to result in a deleterious combination of intransigence, passivity, and resentment.

While parents always have to be prepared to do the hard work of setting limits and imposing positive or negative consequences, that is not their only job. They also have to find ways to put their children in charge of sorting out their dilemmas and beliefs and achieving their goals and objectives. Paradoxically, adolescents (as well as adults!) may be more likely to change not just when they are experiencing any external urgency or pressure to do so but when parents and other caring adults signal respect for the choices they have made up until now, empathize with how hard it is to make different choices, help them to examine why they haven't made these choices yet, and join them in clarifying what the advantages and disadvantages might be if they decide to embark on choosing differently. In other words, we have to be more compelling than controlling, more inspiring than insistent, more motivational than intrusive.

Under these conditions, teens feel more self-determination and become much more willing and better able to assess what is and is not working in their lives and make the necessary alterations that would lead to improvement. Parents should generally take on less responsibility when it comes to trying to change a teen and more responsibility for creating the conditions that invite a teen to change.

4. Change is difficult and always presents risk.

As we observed in Chapter 4, what adults designate as a teen's problem is likely to be a teen's *solution* to a problem. One of the main reasons that adolescents resist change is because they're aware of this, at some level, and fear that changing means they'll have to relinquish their hard-won "solution," which will perhaps result in even greater problems.

All adolescents are guided by certain beliefs that significantly influence their behavior, beliefs that have to be recognized and brought out into the open so that they can be examined and perhaps modified, particularly if they are inhibiting growth. Here are some typical examples.

"If I give in on this argument, I'll be seen as weak and never get my way, so I'll have to keep fighting, even if I no longer have faith in what I'm fighting for."

"If I soften even an iota of my carefully constructed bleak, tragic, moribund outlook on life, everyone will think I'm numb, dumb, and happy, just like they are."

"If I make a positive adjustment to this custody/visitation arrangement, my parents will conclude that I've gotten over their divorce, and that their decision to break up the family was okay."

"If I appear too independent and responsible, my mother will conclude that I no longer need her, and not fight so hard to survive breast cancer."

"If I stop using drugs in response to my parents grounding me, then they'll always ground me whenever I do something they don't want me to do. So I must not give in."

Of course, rare is the adolescent who can phrase his guiding principles as crisply as I have just done for the sake of this discussion. In fact, a good deal of my work with adolescents and their families is centered around the process of gently teasing these unconscious credos to the surface. But they exist nonetheless, even in an inarticulate, inchoate form, and demonstrate that while the changes we may ask our teens to make will sometimes work to their advantage as well as to our own, at other times these changes may seem like a terrific idea to us but present great risks to them.

What's also important to keep in mind is that change is scary because it leaves us unable to recognize ourselves for a period of time. This is particularly hard on adolescents, who are already having a difficult time recognizing themselves because of all the physical and emotional transformations that are hijacking their bodies and minds. In one case, a patient had been working with me on what it would be like to take her academics more seriously during the second half of high school than she had taken them during the first half, so we came up with a list of strategies that would help her to maintain her focus. During the next session, she confided that she had found it "scary" to discover herself "*really* studying and learning, rather than just *pretending* to study and learn, like I usually do—it's like I didn't know *who* I was or *where* I was—I was in my room, at my desk, like I usually am, but it felt like I was in another world."

No change is likely to come about without addressing the potential hazards, disruptions, and dislocations that change will tend to create.

5. Things can always change from bad to worse.

The doctrine of most helping professionals is, "First, do no harm." The same words could be applied to parenthood as well.

You may have very good reasons to want your teenager to change—to be more scholarly, more responsible, more social, more directed, more conscientious—but changes of any significance always emerge from the inside, not from the outside, and they don't always reveal themselves at the pace or rate that we might prefer. If you get perpetually locked into hopeless power struggles in an effort to legislate change on your terms, rather than your teen's terms, you'll always run the risk of making things worse, which may result in change, but change that moves in the wrong direction.

One set of parents that I was working with became so frustrated with their daughter's sluggish approach to her education that they rolled out every big gun they could summon: she wasn't allowed to get her license, to get a part-time job, to participate in any after-school activities, to go out with friends, or to use the Internet until she raised her grades from mostly C's to all A's and B's.

Not only did she *not* raise her grades, but, without the stimulation and challenge of activities like driving, holding a job, socializing, and being involved in extracurricular activities, her grades dropped even further, to D's and E's. *And* she started smoking cigarettes, "mostly because I'm bored, and because I don't want my parents to think that they're going to win this battle."

It was only when her parents were willing, for the time being, to tolerate her lackluster academic achievement and restore some reasonable rights and privileges, as long as she was not failing any classes that things began to improve—not to the point of her getting A's and B's, but at least back up to a C level.

6. Behaviors may change before attitudes do (and attitudes may *never* change).

I remember working with the parents of a teenager, Steven, who was quite underresponsible when it came to completing the household chores that had been assigned to him. We worked out a simple, straightforward program in which his use of any electronic "screen"—computer, television, videogame—was prohibited until his assigned chores had been taken care of to his parents' approval.

When the family returned a couple of weeks later, I asked Steven how he'd been handling his duties. "I've done everything that's been asked of me," he replied, without hesitation. When I checked in with his father, Randall, however, the assessment was somewhat less affirmative. "Well, he's sort of been doing okay, I guess."

"You don't sound very enthusiastic," I commented. "Has he been taking out the garbage and recycling?"

"Yes."

"Has he been keeping his room clean?"

"Reasonably well."

"Has he emptied the dishwasher?"

"Pretty much."

"So why aren't you more pleased with his progress in carrying out these missions?"

Randall thought for a moment, and then answered. "He's doing everything that we've asked him to—it's just that he doesn't seem very *happy* when he's doing it."

This was a poignant example of a parent who was having great difficulty seeing his son as good enough because he was focusing on changing attitude, not behavior. It was realistic for Randall to expect Steven to be more helpful around the house. But it was definitely *not* realistic for Randall to expect Steven to be merrily clicking his heels as he went from trashcan to recycle bin to dishwasher.

Many parents that I work with spend a great deal of energy trying to dictate their teen's personality or mood or disposition, an endeavor that is always doomed to fail. Better to stick with observable behavioral changes and let the "attitude"—be it ungrateful, sassy, impudent, or whatever—take care of itself. In fact, calling less attention to the latter often results in teens paying more attention to the former, since they then don't have to busy themselves with bolstering the pestilent posture that they enjoy seeing you so perturbed by.

7. Not every step will be a forward step, but all steps can eventually lead forward.

Change within families does not usually occur in a smooth, linear fashion. It's more of a rocky incline than a gentle slope. With this in mind, it should be anticipated that things will often get worse before they get better, and that there will generally be slips and backslides that occur on the road to change. It is best to view these setbacks not as disastrous or even disappointing events, but as additional opportunities to learn and as springboards for further change. In fact, it has been my experience that individuals who experience some slips and try to apply the lessons they've learned from these slips are far more likely to eventually enjoy substantial and lasting change than those who seem to turn things around instantly, without any observable difficulties.

Julia's mother had come to meet with me after it was discovered that Julia had been abusing drugs regularly—a police officer doing a raid at her school had confiscated a bag of pot, a jar of Ecstasy pills, and several aerosol cans and Visine bottles from her locker. After several months of hard work on everyone's part, Julia was able to get clean, and she and her mother cautiously rejoiced. Her next several weekly drug tests came up negative as well, but one night, almost three months after she had finally gotten on top of things, Julia came home glassy-eyed after curfew, and when confronted, she admitted that she had begun smoking pot again.

Her mom, Sonjora, was devastated: "Here I thought we were free and clear, really moving ahead, and now it's like we're back to square one, starting all over again. I can't believe it."

"It must be painful for you to feel that all the progress that has been made over this last year is for naught."

"It's *horrible*, that's what it is! Why would she go and do this when she'd worked so hard to get clean?"

"Is is possible for you to imagine that genuine progress really was made, but that Julia simply slipped?"

"How can you call this a slip? She said she's smoked up twice since last week. And if she says it's two times, it's probably more like six."

"It's not, Mom, it's been two times—I'm trying to be honest here. It's just been twice."

"Two times, three times, six times, what's the difference? All I know is you're back in the hole again."

"I'm *not* back in the hole, Mom. I just forgot some of the things I had learned to do. I forgot to be careful who I hang with. I forgot to bring along some soda so I wouldn't be tempted by drugs. I forgot to call Uncle Tomas when everyone started to pass around the bong, like I promised I would do, like I've *been* doing."

"You forgot because you *wanted* to forget, Julia!"

"*No*, Mom, I know I screwed up, but I'm learning that I can't mess around, no matter how many months I was clean."

"You screwed up because you're a screw-up, Julia. *That's* your problem—you're a screw-up!"

Sonjora was so frustrated and so frightened by her daughter's relapse that it was difficult for her to put it in perspective, to see it as a step back, rather than as a complete collapse of her resolve. Interestingly, Julia was, at this point, better able to turn this experience into a lesson, rather than a catastrophe, than her mother was. She was coming to the realization that she had begun taking her hard-earned sobriety for granted and was no longer being as vigilant about maintaining it as she had been at first.

Using this one-week flareup as a sign that it was time to tighten things up and re-commit to her game plan was all that was necessary for Julia to once again resist temptation and continue her forward progress. Slips did continue to occur every few months for the next couple of years, and each time, we tried to use these to determine where more work needed to be done on both of their parts and how each needed to stay on their toes. Sonjora was eventually able to understand that Julia's recovery did not have to be a perfect one to be a successful and meaningful one, and as she, too, began to look at things differently, her daughter's setbacks began to feel less cataclysmic and more instructive for both of them.

8. Change is not always visible.

When we think back upon the important changes that we have made in our lives, we will probably come to the retrospective realization that these changes rarely occurred "in a flash" or all of a sudden. Usually, there were preparatory, possibly invisible, stages that preceded the visible change, during which we were contemplating what it is that we wanted to do differently, mentally readying ourselves to do so, and trying out small versions or prototypes of these changes to see how they felt and what resulted. Like creative expression, or any endeavor that requires a ripening, change evolves at its own pace and cannot be rushed, no matter how quickly we'd like it to happen.

One of the many aspects of adolescent development that try parents' souls is the fact that much of their growth is occurring under the surface, concealed and undetectable. Just as a plant must send down invisible roots so that it can send out observable shoots, adolescents must complete a tremendous amount of interior work before it becomes manifest in their exterior lives. Because of this, teens are usually growing and developing under our very eyes, but without our being able to notice. What makes things even more difficult is the fact that they may be as unaware of these changes, and so as incapable of testifying to them as their parents are. Or, sometimes they are well aware of these changes but want to shield them from view so that they retain sole ownership of them.

A 17-year-old patient of mine, Neil, proudly began our session by telling his parents and me that he had finally gotten a job. What was most surprising to them was not that he had done so, as this was something that they had been wanting him to accomplish for months, but the extent to which he had been working at it all along, without their even knowing.

"You guys don't know this," he delightedly confided to them, "but I actually started picking up job applications and filling them out more than a month ago."

"But why didn't you tell us?" his dad exclaimed. "We wouldn't have kept bugging you about finding work if we knew that you had already put it into motion. All we wanted to see was your effort."

"I guess I just wanted to see what I could accomplish without the two of you being involved," Neil answered honestly. "If I had told you that I was applying for jobs, you would've gotten all happy and excited, which I can't stand, and then you would've started asking me where I was applying and giving me advice on how to fill out the application. It would've gotten so complicated, and we just would have fought about it, and I probably would've just given up. This way, I showed you that I could do it without your help."

Neil's insight that the job search had to be *his* search led to his decision to keep it under the radar, but just because it was under the radar didn't mean that it didn't exist at all. Only when he felt safe presenting the results of his search to his parents did it become evident to them that changes had been happening all along.

9. Talking about change is not the same as changing.

Over the years, I've seen enough in my home and office to conclude without reservation that actions always speak louder than words when it comes to making change come about. It is fine to foster discussions and conversations about important matters, and there is no question, as we will see in Chapter 7, that good verbal communication can provide part of the foundation necessary for changes to ultimately come about. But talking is never a substitute for doing.

So many times I've heard mothers and fathers optimistically tell me that they've "had a good talk" with their adolescent, and that he or she has readily agreed to (fill in the blank):

- Take homework more seriously
- Clean her room
- Be nicer to his siblings
- Stop drinking
- Finally complete his college applications
- Start exercising
- Etc.

Then, of course, there's that old, sinking feeling when these promises, no matter how well-intended, are broken once again.

But if parents want to see behavioral change in their teens, teens have to see behavioral change in their parents. Another way of conveying this is through the following theorem:

The more parents seem to *talk*, the less teens seem to *do*.

Somehow, in some way, our words have to be anchored with concrete measures for them to begin to take hold. These measures may consist of nothing more than imposing consequences, positive or negative, depending on whether family rules are adhered to or violated, but unless there is something beyond lectures, sermons, and diatribes, there is little motivation for adolescents who have run aground to contemplate change and again set sail.

In a similar vein, I'm less interested in adolescents talking or feeling differently and more interested in their handling and managing things differently. One small behavioral change in the right direction will convince me that we're in business more than session after session of insight and awareness unaccompanied by any difference in behavior. I've seen hundreds of teens and parents *talk* a good show, but unless there's something more, there's usually *nothing* to show.

10. Predicting change increases the chances of change.

Every thinking parent of an adolescent will at times fall prey to pessimism and despair, concluding that things won't get better and will only grow worse, that improvement will constantly lurk around a corner that we'll never turn. Of course, when adolescents sense that their parents have given up, they are much more likely to give up too, at which point the likelihood of growth shrinks to an infinitesimal level. There has been a great deal of research demonstrating quite convincingly that our outlook alters our reality and our beliefs influence our neurochemistry as much as the other way around. That is why parents must remain beacons of hope during the darker stages of adolescence and never lose sight of the possibility that change can take place. We must constantly be willing to take the risk of having more faith in our teens than they are likely to have in themselves.

When I work with families, I've learned to frame my questions very carefully so that this propitious perspective is always present in our discussion, and I encourage parents to learn to do the same.

For example, when I'm working with a depressed teenager, I ask *when* (not *if*) she believes she'll begin doing the things that have been proven to fight off depression, like exercise, prayer, service, creative expression, and journal writing. When I'm working with a chemically dependent adolescent, I'll ask him how long he imagines it will be before he starts connecting with friends who don't use drugs, a first step toward getting on top of his addiction, or what he'll be doing with all of the time, energy, and money that are currently sucked up by drugs and drug acquisition.

If I receive the (somewhat predictable) "I don't know," accompanied by the (just as predictable) languid shrug of the shoulders to these questions, I'll pursue them further: "A day? A week? A month? *Two* months?"

These queries, annoying as they may be, convey to teens and their families something important, which is that change *can* and *will* happen, a mindset that greatly serves to disperse their collective feelings of helplessness, getting them to focus instead on being on the lookout for the small shifts that signal the initial movement toward transformation.

11. You can promote change, but you can't choose the ramifications of change.

Wanting to see change come about means accepting the possibility that not all change will be welcome change. Just as working to clamp down on one end of an emotional spectrum, such as sadness, means that the other end, joy, is automatically clamped down, too, trying to precisely arrange only for those changes that we are comfortable with will limit a teen's overall capacity for change.

If we want our clingy teenager to be more independent, for example, we have to allow for her independence to lead her in certain directions that we may not approve of—otherwise, independence will be resisted. If we want our isolated teenager to be more social, we have to accept the fact that we may not be thrilled with everyone that he socializes with—otherwise, socializing will be resisted.

Likewise, change always catalyzes more change, which may create new challenges. The family of the teen who has elected to give up the award-winning scapegoat role that he had played for years will now have to contend with the pressure to find a substitute scapegoat or begin to deal with the uncomfortable issues that the scapegoat was helping them all to avoid. The parents of the teen who has chosen to forge ahead with her plans for departure after a couple of years of appearing to be stuck in reverse will now have to figure out what they're going to do about all of the unresolved marital disputes that have been simmering just below the surface for the past decade.

Parents have the right to push for change, but they must recognize the unpredictability of metamorphic powers and the mixture of rewards and risks that change always confers on us.

12. Expected change is easier to adjust to.

While change is always stressful, it need not be traumatic. The most stable families are not the ones that are the most rigid and unyielding when faced with change, but the ones that keep their knees flexed and maintain their pliancy. Short of the beginning of family life itself, nothing tests a family's mettle more than adolescence, and one of the best ways to remain as springy as possible during this stage is to anticipate and forecast changes, rather than trying to avoid, shun, or repeal them.

The parents who are prepared for a temporary loss of moorings will be the ones who are best able to make the necessary accommodations during periods of instability and eventually lead the family through transitions successfully, creatively changing the shape of the system so as to better meet the altered needs of its evolving members.

13. *Over*playing the necessity of change actually undermines the possibility of change.

Our tireless desire to perfect our children as they move through adolescence, to fine-tune them so that they're just so, the "very best that they can be," may paradoxically help to create one of the most insurmountable obstacles to change. Years of trying to nudge teens closer and closer to excellence or virtuosity or superiority through tutoring, medicating, therapy, coaching, specialized instruction, and the dozens of other supports and services available to us will, over time, serve to erode their sense of efficacy and self-confidence, the very qualities that they need to survive and triumph.

This is a complicated matter, because of course none of us want to deprive our children of opportunities that might heighten their chances for success. If everyone else's child is taking private classes to prepare for the SATs, for example, how do we justify not doing so? Won't it leave our son at a distinct disadvantage when it comes to test taking? If all of the other high school softball pitchers in the area have personal trainers, then shouldn't our daughter have one as well? Otherwise, isn't she going to be left in the dust? If all of our son's friends are being evaluated for ADHD and given medication to help them focus, shouldn't we push for the same diagnosis and intervention? Why should he be the only one who possibly suffers from an unaddressed handicap?

While it's important to learn when and how to ask for help, however, it's another thing to be convinced that we have to be dependent on outside help. The way in which teenagers will, over time, tend to interpret the expense and effort we invest in providing them with these external supports will generally not be, "My parents must really care about me," but instead, "I must not be good enough to make it on my own. I will always have to rely on others if I'm going to have a chance to succeed." This induces feelings of insecurity and a lack of self-trust and serves to undercut the likelihood that they'll summon their inner resources and respond to challenges independently.

Doing, or having others do, for our teens isn't always in their best interest. Change will ultimately, and more reliably, come about when they feel empowered by the experience of learning to do for themselves.

EXERCISE 6

In this chapter, we saw that the shifts that occur in the family during adolescence usually result in imbalances in three basic areas:

- Power Imbalances

- Responsibility Imbalances

- Relational Imbalances

Pick an imbalance that currently exists in your family, and decide which of these categories it best fits into.

Now, answer the following questions as a way of understanding more about the imbalance, and how to redress it.

1. When did you first notice this imbalance occurring, and how long has it been in place?

2. Is it stable, or does it tend to shift or vacillate? If the latter, is there a pattern?

3. What are you doing that is contributing to the maintenance of this imbalance?

4. What is your teen doing that is contributing to the maintenance of this imbalance?

5. Which of the following axioms of change that were examined in this chapter have some relevance when it comes to adjusting this imbalance?

- True change only occurs in a loving relationship.

- Adolescents don't change unless families change.

- For change to come about, the reasons for changing may have to change too.

- Change is difficult and always presents risk.

- Things can always change from bad to worse.

- Behaviors may change before attitudes do.

- Not every step will be a step forward, but all steps eventually can lead forward.

- Change is not always visible.

- Talking about change is not the same as changing.

- Predicting change increases the chances of change.

- You can promote change, but you can't choose the ramifications of change.

- Expected change is easier to adjust to.

- *Over*playing the necessity of change actually *under*mines the possibility of change.

6. What is one change that you could make, even a very small one, that would neutralize or diminish your contribution to this imbalance?

7. What is one change that your son or daughter could make, even a very small one, that would neutralize or diminish his or her contribution to this imbalance?

8. Were this imbalance to be more effectively balanced, what other imbalances might occur as a reaction or repercussion?

Meghan, the mother of Griffin, the underresponsible athlete mentioned earlier, came up with the following answers to these questions:

1. *I would have to say that we noticed this imbalance very early on. I guess we were always so busy with Griffin and his games and practices that we were constantly picking up after him. He's such an intense kid, and he did so well and took things so seriously that we wanted to support him in this. Plus, he was never that organized or neat to begin with, so that didn't help.*

2. *I'd say it's stable, all right, that's the problem. I mean, I just don't see any effort or motivation on his part to do things differently. So the "pattern" is "all the time."*

3. *Now that I'm thinking about this, I would have to say that our contribution to the maintenance of this imbalance is that we constantly cover for Griffin. The fact is, there's always a car that has gas in it, he's never missed a practice or game, or even been late, he's always got us making sure he's got his uniform ready, or his clothes to change into. In other words, there's nothing he needs that we don't do for him, and we've been doing it this way for years.*

4. *Griffin is contributing by not taking on any responsibility, although, as I said above, I'm starting to realize there's really no reason for him to take on any responsibility, since we're all responsible for him.*

5. *I think the axioms of change that have some relevance here are as follows:*

   • *Adolescents don't change unless families change*—because unless my husband and I make some changes, it's clear that *he's* not going to.

   • *Change is difficult and always presents risks*—because we're all used to this pattern now, and part of me doesn't think there's any point in trying to change things around when he's already seventeen.

   • *Things can always change from bad to worse*—because in many ways, he's a good kid, and we're proud of his accomplishments, so we don't want to start something up that riles him.

   • *Talking about change is not the same as changing*— because we've talked about this endlessly, but don't seem to do anything differently.

6. *One small change we could make is to pick out one thing that we do insist that Griffin be responsible for, and really vow not to pick it back up for him. Because the laundry plan didn't work out all that well, I'm thinking that we should not let him use any car but the third car, and make sure that we don't bail him out if he's out of gas sometime. Also, he should really be paying for that gas himself, not just bumming cash or our credit card off us. He makes pretty good money as a ref in a kids' basketball league, so he should be contributing more.*

7. *I guess the change that he could make would be to go along with our change.*

8. *I'd have to think about that, because I know that he's not above blackmailing us. I know that if we implement this plan, he's going to*

come to us in a panic and tell us that he needs to use one of the other cars because he's out of gas and doesn't have time to stop on the way. And if we don't give in, he can get pretty nasty. But I'm hoping that his desire to get to where he needs to go is enough to overcome his irresponsibility, and that he'll get the message if we refuse to rescue him.

As it turns out, the situation played out exactly as Meghan predicted it would. She and her husband told Griffin that he was only to drive the old sedan, and that he was responsible for keeping it filled with gas and changing the oil. One week later, on a Saturday morning, Griffin dashed down the stairs asking if he could borrow one of their cars because he was running late for football practice and "his car" was low on gas. First his mom, and then his dad, held their ground and reminded him of the agreement.

He hollered and cursed, telling them that they'd have to pick him up if he ran out of gas on the way to practice, and that it would be their fault if he stopped at the station and wound up going late to practice and having to run extra laps, but his parents didn't budge.

Several hours later, he returned home mad as a hornet, having indeed chosen to stop to get gas. As a result he had to endure an extra 10 minutes of "suicide" sprints at the end of practice while the rest of the team rested and watched.

However, from that time on he was more responsible when it came to the use of the car. Meghan and her husband were so pleased with the outcome that they successfully extended this very simple approach to a couple of other areas of Griffin's life, including laundry (assigning him two days when he could use the washer and dryer, and making them off-limits the rest of the week, as well as refraining from doing any laundry for him) and keeping his room clean (removing his bedroom door from its hinges, thus eliminating any hope of privacy, unless the room was, according to their standards, shipshape).

SEVEN

THE GOOD ENOUGH PARENT

Treat people as if they were what they ought to be, and you help them to become what they are capable of being.

—GOETHE

No matter how good a job we try to do as parents, all healthy teens will still present us with numerous, age-appropriate problems that bedevil and stymie us, even if we have given careful thought and reflection to the information presented in the previous chapters, completed all the exercises, and enhanced our awareness of the matrix of conscious and subconscious forces that influence our adolescent and shape the dynamic between us. So in this chapter, I would like to present you with a substantive set of tools and strategies that will also help you to go about laying the groundwork for positive, constructive change. Since it is unlikely that all of them will apply to your particular family situation, feel free to pick and choose those that seem to have the most relevance and put them into play to see what results.

PARENTAL LEADERSHIP

Just because our government is designed as a democracy doesn't mean that our family should be also. In well-functioning families, parents maintain sovereignty by displaying thoughtful, firm executive leadership, leadership that ultimately strengthens the children so that they can eventually lead their own lives and perhaps one day lead their own families, as well.

One aspect of parental leadership involves establishing rules. In flexible and adaptive families that are accommodating to the needs of their growing children, rules serve as stimulants and guidelines for growth. In families that are inflexible and stuck, rules serve solely to maintain an outmoded equilibrium. In my practice, I have observed that the main reason that adolescents don't follow the rules is because parents haven't given enough thought to the rules' role and purpose, and, as a result, they don't lay out the rules as clearly and specifically as they need to.

Here are some questions that you should be able to answer if you are going to establish a useful, growth-promoting rule. Some sample answers are provided in parentheses.

- What is the rule? *(No television, video games or Gameboys on school nights.)*

- What is the reason for the rule? *(Your grades have been dropping, and it appears that this is partially because you have been having a hard time breaking away from the TV, the Xbox, and the Gameboy to get to your homework.)*

- What problems could arise if the rule wasn't in place or was consistently broken? *(Your grades would continue to drop, and you would severely limit your options for your future after high school.)*

- When is the rule to be in place? *(Sunday night through Thursday night.)*

- Are there any exceptions? *(Not at this time.)*

- How long will the rule be in effect? *(Until you have maintained a 3.0 average in all of your classes for an entire marking period.)*

- How will the rule be monitored? *(We'll be supervising you when we're home. When we're not home, we will trust that you will abide by this rule. If we find that you have violated our trust, we will eliminate the privilege of television, Xbox, and Gameboy for at least one weekend as well.)*

- What will the rewards be for following this rule? *(Unsupervised use of television, Xbox, and Gameboy on weekends, with parental discretion if it appears to us to be getting out of hand.)*

- What are the consequences for breaking this rule? *(Loss of television and Xbox on weekends and vacations as well, and confiscation of Gameboy.)*

- How will we evaluate the ongoing relevance of the rule and determine when it is no longer necessary? *(When you have maintained a 3.0 average for two grading periods.)*

Another important component of effective leadership is finding ways to maintain that leadership. Here are some ways that parents, with or without their awareness, will tend to relinquish their leadership.

- Establishing unrealistic goals *(goals that set the bar too high or too low)*

- Coming up with irrelevant or impractical consequences for misconduct *(punishments that are harder for the parents to take than the teenager)*

- Lack of effort when it comes to implementing consequences *(not following through to make sure that a curfew is enforced)*

- Lack of cohesion *(one parent undermining or sabotaging the other)*

- Impulsivity *(administering an overly punitive punishment and then feeling guilty and having to remorsefully retract it)*

- Wanting, or expecting, to be popular with or liked by one's adolescent

- Rescuing adolescents from the natural consequences for their behavior *(paying their speeding ticket for them, or writing an absence note when they've stayed home from school to catch up on work that they could have finished on time)*

Here are some ways to establish leadership, or reclaim compromised leadership.

- Solicit input from your teen on important matters, without sacrificing your authority. *(I've already got some ideas on this, but I'm interested in yours. What do you think your allowance should be, and what should earning it be contingent upon?)*

- Be permeable to their influence without completely capitulating or relinquishing your standards. *(I suppose you're right, there's always been conflict between parents and teens about what kind of music should be listened to. So I'll let you hold onto those Parental Advisory CDs that I really don't approve of, but if I start to hear you using the kind of language that you're hearing on them, they'll be confiscated.)*

- Allow yourself to change your mind from time to time. *(I think I may have overdone it with that two-month grounding. I was so upset with the grades on your report card that I just went ballistic. So I'm going to give you a chance to earn it back to one-month by checking in with me on a weekly basis to show me that you're taking care of business in school.)*

- Respond at *your* pace, not your teen's. *(I'm not sure I can agree to your weekend plans just yet. You're going to have to put your friends on hold for an hour or two until I can make the time to think it over, and discuss it with your mom.)*

- Choose battles selectively. *(I can live with your room being a mess, but I won't tolerate your leaving piles of your stuff throughout the rest of the house for all of us to have to trip over.)*

- Establish a partnership with your teen when it comes to set- ting goals. *(We've been telling you for years what grades we think you're capable of achieving, but we're wondering, now that you're in high school, what grades you think you're capable of achieving, and how we can be of some support to you in achieving them.)*

- Distinguish between what is and isn't under your teen's control. *(I'm not expecting you to enjoy being with your little sister, but I am expecting you to keep your hands off her at all times.)*

When it comes to consequences, parents have always been well-advised to be as consistent as possible, and there are certainly many advantages to maintaining regularity in most of our dealings with our offspring. However, when we go from raising *children* to raising *teenagers*, consistency has to be cantilevered with creativity or we'll quickly lose what leverage we have. As I've learned (the hard way!) from many years of coaching soccer, trying to run the same play over and over again, no matter how good a play it is, will eventually result in failure once the other team catches on.

In one family I worked with, for example, every adolescent in- fraction was met with the same parental response: grounding. Grounding was imposed for missing homework assignments, for backtalk, for tormenting younger siblings, for porn sites popping up on the computer monitor. Not surprisingly, this warhorse of a consequence had become a tiresome, almost reflexive response to misbehavior, one that had long since been bled of relevance, meaning, and impact.

It wasn't even clear that it had any negative ramifications any- more. Sheena, the family member who was the most frequent re- cipient of "groundation," as she playfully referred to it, didn't seem to mind being grounded at all. "I basically just hang out in my room, listen to music, IM my friends, get stuff done. The other weekend I was grounded for getting a ride home from school with a friend who I wasn't supposed to be in the car with, and I used the time to finally clean my room. It looks really good, now." (It occurred to me at that point that if she was going to be sent to anyone's room, it should've been her parents' room, where there was much less enjoyable stimulation available to her.)

Parents lose capacity for leadership when they become too predictable, which is why surprising and innovative consequences often carry more weight. For example, instead of simply taking away privileges in response to problem behavior, you might consider insisting that a constructive task or an arduous ordeal be completed, such as stuffing envelopes at the church or synagogue office, painting your elderly neighbor's fence, cleaning the bathrooms in the house, or volunteering to read books to hospitalized children.

Likewise, as mentioned above, consider asking your teenager to come up with her *own* appropriate consequence for her transgression (without having to agree to it if it feels too light), rather than having to wrack your brain to come up with one on your own. Putting more pressure on her to come up with a way to "do penance" while putting less pressure on yourself to decide on and impose sanctions, and then to have to stay on top of them, can restore your superintendence and capture your teen's attention much more effectively.

Many parents surprise me by being surprised by their teen's reaction when consequences are imposed. Some parents even fall for their adolescent's "playing possum." It's not uncommon to hear parents express this kind of logic: "She said it really doesn't matter whether we take away the computer or not, she's not going to change anyway, so we just went ahead and gave it back to her. What's the point of the restriction if she says it doesn't bother her?"

Other parents relinquish their authority and give in to their adolescent's "bucking bronco" strategem—throwing household items, gashing holes in drywall, and other unruly behavior designed to intimidate parents into submission and shrivel their presence and command. In both cases, true leadership consists of calmly executing whatever maneuvers you have decided upon and trusting that the teen will gradually sense your solidity once he sees that you haven't budged, and begrudgingly settle in to do his time.

One final note about consequences. Never minimize the value of the most important positive consequence that exists, which is *time*. In our frenetic, sped-up world, the commodity of time has become so rare that it's just about priceless. You may think that offering uninterrupted time together—no distractions, no siblings, no pagers or cell phones—may seem more like a curse than a blessing to contemporary teens, something that would cramp their style and their social life. But most of the adolescents I've gotten to know miss their parents, are hungry for close contact with one or both of them, and suffer immeasurably for the lack of it. Before you leap into forking over monetary gifts for good grades, or videogame cartridges for completed chores, think about how much solid time you typically spend with you teen without there being any other agendas, and whether that might actually be the most generous gift of all.

Parents Unite

Another aspect of effective leadership is working in league with other leaders. For example, I'm always amazed at the gullibility of parents when it comes to what their teenagers have to say about their friends' parents. "Jill's mom says that it's all right for us to go to R-rated movies." "DeShawn's parents told him that he can always have friends over at their house, even without any adults around." "The Sheltons have been letting *their* kids have co-ed sleepovers since they were in tenth grade." "I'm the *only* one of my friends who has to be in by midnight. Everyone else gets to stay out until two A.M." I've actually had adolescent patients confess to me privately that they were shocked at how easy it was to snow their own parents when it came to convincing them what other parents' standards were.

Of course, teenagers are astute enough to sense our hesitancy to intrude on our fellow parents' lives, and are not at all reluctant to exploit this. That's what emboldens them to come up with such fanciful descriptions of the blissful lives that "all the other families" are lucky enough to lead.

I'm not sure what makes it difficult for parents to check in with other parents in an effort to communicate more effectively and parent more collaboratively, but I do know that when they choose to do so, it is not just their own family but the entire community that benefits.

The next time your son tries to convince you that his best friend doesn't have to do any chores at *his* house, express befuddlement as to how things are managed there and make a call to his mom or dad to see what the real story is. The next time your daughter attempts to persuade you that there will "definitely" be an adult at the party that she's going to, get the number, pick up the phone, and see what's what over there.

Even if you find out that your teen is actually telling you the truth, your willingness to stick your neck out will help keep him honest and force him to think twice before he tries to pull the wool over your eyes the next time.

Set the Tone and Stick with It

We saw in Chapter 3 how parents bring to childrearing a frame— a way of perceiving teens' behavior that, more than the behavior itself, influences how we experience them. We saw how a frame originates with our own experience during childhood and adolescence and becomes the filter through which we evaluate and interact with our child. Parents with an optimistic frame interpret the same behavior differently than parents with a negative frame. This has special relevance during the teenaged years, when adolescent behavior is confusing and complicated, subject to multiple and at times contradictory interpretations.

For example, a mother with an optimistic frame might experience her son's growing independence as a chance to add new dimensions to their relationship, while a mother with a negative frame might experience it as a loss, the "beginning of the end" of their relationship. A father with an optimistic frame might experience his daughter's argumentativeness as a testament to her growing self-confidence, her readiness to begin thinking and speaking up for herself, while a father with a negative frame might experience it as being "bitchy" and oppositional.

In reality, every one of our teenager's traits can be understood as a strength or a weakness, depending on the lens we are looking through—they can be described as lusty or greedy, exuberant or insensitive, discerning or hard-to-please, courageous or defiant, deliberate or slow, introspective or depressed, energetic or hyper, persistent or stubborn.

It becomes easy, then, to see how our frame can lead directly into a self-fulfilling prophecy. In other words, our readiness to perceive our teen's behavior as positive or negative leads us to define their behavior as positive or negative. We then react accordingly and reinforce whatever it is that we believe we have seen, eliciting even more of it. As a noted family therapist once observed, "All psychological disease is a failure of imagination."

As much as possible, then, it behooves us as family leaders to try to adopt a positive frame, even if our history, our temperament, or what we have heard or read would lead us to think more negatively. Sometimes, this shift takes conscious thought and practice, particularly if we are in the habit of being on the pessimistic side, but it's always worth it.

The diplomat Abba Eban once described a foreign leader he was frustrated with as an individual who "never missed an opportunity to miss an opportunity." When I'm working with parents who tend to view family life through a negative filter, I'll be sure not to allow them to miss too many opportunities by inviting them to take out an imaginary magnifying glass between sessions and focus on the positive moments or the "exceptions to the rule" that they might typically miss or gloss over because they are just not looking for them. Or I might assign them the task of finding three things about their teen that they had not known or noticed before.

I'll also try to find evidence in our sessions that challenges or confounds the pejorative reality that the parents may seem most comfortable clinging to. "You say that every time you try to talk to your son it turns into a terrible fight, and yet you've both been in here discussing many complicated matters for almost an hour now, and while the two of you haven't always agreed, there certainly has been no terrible fight. How often does *that* happen?"

I always try to keep in mind that what I hear from parents about their adolescent is a selective symposium that has its roots in the frame that they have brought to this stage of parenthood. A major part of my job is to help them to rewrite the symposium in a more buoyant and balanced way.

Shared Responsibility

Many organizational consultants would define effective leadership as the process of organizing, and benefiting from, an effective mechanism for the suitable distribution of responsibility. To be the parents of Good Enough teens, we need to very deliberately step back from being overly responsible and allow them to assume, by degrees, the burdens and rewards of their failures and successes.

For the current generation of parents, making this shift can feel downright revolutionary. After all, from childbirth on—even, in some cases, prenatally—we have been pushed to carefully engineer and orchestrate our children's lives: exposing them to the right educational toys; arranging playdates with the right peers; selecting the right schools, teachers, and tutors; signing up for the right activities, teams, groups, and lessons. Children these days, for various reasons, are almost *never* left to their own devices, and because of this they become convinced that our involvement is crucial to their growth, a belief that depletes their sense of self-assurance.

I believe that one of the reasons that the Harry Potter books (and other similar tales and myths) are so popular and compelling even with teenagers is because of the vicarious thrill associated with accompanying the "orphaned" Harry on his adventures— contemporary children who feel so cosseted and confined by their well-meaning but suffocating parents feel liberated by the antagonist's freedom to live without any direct parental supervision.

While offspring at any age will at times need our support, our correction, our praise, and our presence, at other times, particularly during adolescence, they need *space*. Sometimes they need the space in which to stagger around, to make mistakes, to feel sad, frustrated, anxious, and angry, to work their way out of their own bungles, to stumble into and figure out how to survive their repeated collision with the hard truths and painful realities that even the most protected and privileged lives will always offer up. Sometimes they need the space simply to discover who they are and what they want, to distinguish their goals from their parents' and everyone else's goals, to try to synthesize their inner self and their outer self and create their own future, just as we have learned to do.

While I'll never be the extraordinary baker that my dear father-in-law was when he was alive, I learned enough from his instruction to know that dough always needs a chance to aerate and rise on its own. If you're constantly kneading it, it'll never turn into good bread. Likewise, if we're constantly feeling the "need to knead" our children into the right shape and consistency by assuming too much responsibility for them and their lives, they'll never have a chance to rise and grow into their own person.

D. W. Winnicott, whose theories of child and family development form the foundation for much of what I've written, observed, "Inherited potential will be realized when the environmental provision is *adequate* (italics mine)." I interpret this to mean not just that good enough parenting will be all that's necessary to nurture our children into fruition, but that trying too hard to be *over*adequate will actually *under*cut the realization of a child's potential.

Turning responsibility over to our children doesn't mean abdicating our role as parents and excusing ourselves from any accountability. But it does mean getting them used to solving their own problems, managing their own risks, dealing with their own defeats, setting their own goals, assessing their own results, making their own compromises, and, most likely, celebrating their own triumphs—triumphs that, if we stay out of their way, will truly feel like theirs to celebrate.

This process is of particular importance during adolescence because teenagers have so many crucial decisions to make— whether to take calculus or become sexually active or try a drug or go away to college. The self-awareness that is the basis for making good choices can only result from their having been provided with gradually increasing levels of responsibility for conducting their lives. When parents of teens are doing all the work, parenting simply *won't* work.

One other important point to emphasize when it comes to teaching responsibility is that teens need to know that they have responsibilities for others besides themselves. If we bring our adolescents up in a culture that emphasizes acquisition and self-gratification over everything else, we have no right to complain if we notice that they're living by these same canons. If we have spent years single-mindedly devoting ourselves to granting their every wish and whim, then we have not fulfilled our responsibility as parents.

CHANGING COMMUNICATION AND COMMUNICATING CHANGE

If there's any sector in our relationship with teenagers that feels like it's a minefield, it's communication. After all, we're told that we need to communicate with them to have a good relationship with them, but they seem to work so hard to subvert and corrupt communication. If we ask him how his day was, we receive a grunt or a mumble, or are caustically condemned for not respecting his privacy. If we wonder what's bothering her after observing days of disconsolate moping, she bites our head off with a ruthless outburst, insisting that we'll never understand, so why bother telling us? If we inquire as to what he's doing with his friends that evening, and what time he'll be home, we elicit a ferocious tirade about how we don't trust him enough. If we remind her to clean her room and call her grandmother before heading downstairs to the computer, she contemptuously reminds us that we nag her much more than her friends' parents do. If we hold him accountable for misdeeds, he lashes back at us with a week of savage silence. Is it any surprise that parent-child communication suffers at the very point when it so needs to take place, that a satisfying *lingua franca* seems forever out of reach?

Fortunately, I have seen that there are some approaches that seem to work better than others. They may not ensure that you always have long, lovely conversations with your teenager about intimate matters, but they are likely to help you get your point across, promote mutual understanding between the generations, and make important changes more likely to come about.

Convey Empathy

As we saw in Chapter 6, talking about changing is not the same as changing. But how we talk about change to our teenagers often helps to set the stage for transformation. Adolescents quickly tire of and tune out grown-ups' "stump speeches"—the ones that repetitively attempt to sell their parents' point of view. Most teenagers already believe that they're making the most sensible choices available to them anyway, so vainly trying to "talk some sense into them" or muscle a point across is unlikely to be productive.

Instead, the basis for successful change-promoting communication is embedded in our capacity to empathize with our child's dilemma about change, the "guiding beliefs" that we discussed in Chapter 6 that convince them that change may not be a good thing, and that the solution that they've come up with for a problem is the best or only solution available to them. After all, they've usually spent at least months, and probably years, developing their precious worldview and hammering their identity into shape, so they're not going to surrender either very easily in a toe-to-toe battle.

Having their attitude or approach reflected back to them in a nonjudgmental way will not only build rapport and trust, it will also thaw out some of their rigidity, making them more permeable to our influence and allowing movement in other, more productive directions to become more feasible.

"I sometimes think that you'd like to start doing better in school, but feel like too much will be expected of you then, and that you'd inevitably wind up disappointing everyone."

"It's probably no picnic having such a perfect older sister who everybody seems so happy with all the time. Do you ever get sick of suffering by comparison and feel like just screwing the whole works?"

"When I was in your shoes, I didn't make the choices that you are making. On the other hand, a lot has changed since I was a teenager, and while we've got some similarities, we're also different, so maybe it's really not possible for me

to be in your shoes. Nonetheless, I'm wondering whether you'd want to hear what I would suggest doing."

"If you decided to give up drinking, which I strongly suspect you'd like to, and are ready to, do you think this would mean admitting you were wrong, and having to tolerate a lot of smug 'I-told-you-so's' and 'Don't-you-feel-better-now?'s' from your father and me?"

Adolescents become more willing to abandon their vestigial, growth-inhibiting ideologies if they know they won't have to feel ashamed for having had them in the first place, and if they believe that new and more relevant ideologies are their own idea, and in their own best interests. The more that we can present change in ways that preserves their sense of autonomy and honor, the more appealing and advantageous change will appear to be.

Be Honest

Nothing alienates teens more than bogus communication that is designed to obfuscate, shade, or alter the truth—communication that prohibits, rather than embodies, candor and contact. In many of the families that I work with, the Golden Rule of Communication seems to be, "Whatever you say, don't really say anything."

In reality, every adolescent benefits from hearing more about how she is being experienced, how she comes across, how she impacts on others, as well as hearing more about how we, as caring adults, are managing things. Refusing to articulate hitherto unvoiced realities due to our reluctance to hurt, anger, or disappoint our teen deprives her of important information that would enhance her ability to make necessary adjustments and alterations in her character. Of course, appropriate tact and timing help to soften the message. It won't take too many blistering observations or doomsday prophecies to turn off even the most solid young adult, but there is still no substitute for forthright feedback when it comes to establishing a trusting relationship:

"I'm realizing that I've got less and less influence over you, and it's scaring the hell out of me. I didn't even want to acknowledge this to you, because I was afraid that you'd start doing even more dangerous things upon hearing my admission, but I figured it was best to be straight with you."

"I'll always love you, and I know you'll always love me, but based on the horrible way we've been getting along over the last few months, I don't think I'll miss you very much when you go away to college, and I strongly suspect you won't miss me much, either."

"If I seem more irritable than usual, you're not imagining it, and I have to take responsibility for that and apologize. I haven't been feeling very well, I've got a lot on my mind, and while I wish that I could be more patient and pleasant, I just don't seem to be able to get there. Have you ever been in that kind of place?"

"I know that you're in a lot of pain right now, and I am sorry to say that I don't have any magic wand that will make it go away. Believe me, I wish I did. It's no fun feeling helpless when someone you love is hurting, but right now all I have to offer you is my love and support, unhelpful as they may feel to you right now."

Chances are, if you've been consistently thinking something about your teen, even if it's unfavorable or unpleasant, she deserves to hear about it. Rather than keeping it under wraps, do her, and yourself, a favor, and put it out there in as guileless and authentic a way as you can.

Less Is More

What I usually see in my office when parents are talking to their teens is that they're losing them in the delivery, coming on so strong and struggling so mightily to proselytize that they're actually not being heard at all. Whatever it is that you want to say, try to keep it short, if not sweet. As Fred Astaire once advised a young choreographer, "Get it 'til it's just right, then cut three minutes."

Also, don't lock yourself into verbal exchanges of information. Sharing your thoughts, ideas, or viewpoints in a personal letter often enables adolescents to better take in what you're offering, because they're then allowed to process it privately, at their own pace, without worrying about how they're coming across or how you're reacting. Rare is the teenager whose curiosity won't be piqued by an envelope with her name on it lying on her bed.

Finally, if arguments are ever beginning to cross the line and become threatening or abusive, end them immediately. Never feel that you need to function as an audience or sounding board when your teenager is saying or doing things that make you uncomfortable. Whether it's leaving the room or going for a walk or a drive, your decision to terminate a deteriorating encounter is ultimately reassuring for an adolescent, establishing unmistakable criteria for what is and is not acceptable, and making it clear that things are not going to be allowed to spiral out of control.

> *"I don't like the way this is going. I know you have strong feelings about this matter, but only when you can find a way to express yourself without losing your temper will I be available to listen to you. For now, I'll be in my bedroom and don't want to be bothered."*

Invite Contention but Search for Accord

Tiresome as they may be, our teens' arguments with us are best seen as reflections of their attachment to us, not as signs of disinterest or disaffection. After all, most of us don't make the time to contend with individuals whom we couldn't care less about. That is why a certain amount of parent-teenager disagreement should not only be supported, but even sanctioned, because, as a result of engaging in disagreement, adolescents are more likely to learn to articulate their viewpoint, advocate for themselves, and persist in the face of defeat, three of the most necessary ingredients for success. Generational disputes should be something to take pride in, not to feel embarrassed by.

On the other hand, despite their commitment to legalistic re-monstration, adolescents (and their parents) still feel uncomfort-able if a state of discord remains for very long. Finding the spaces, however small, where concord does exist, and searching for ways to end a discussion on a positive note, will all go a long way to-ward preventing a discussion from becoming hostile.

> *"We've been going at this for a while, now, and while we're not exactly seeing eye-to-eye, it does sound like we both agree that there should at least be some driving restrictions for having gotten your second speeding ticket this month. What say we take a break for a while, each give it some thought, and then check back in with each other on this later tonight?"*

> *"You've made your point very well, and I give you credit for that. I'm not going to change my mind in this matter, but I'm impressed with your capacity to state your case with such passion. That's a real strength, and one that I hope you can put to good use in other parts of your life as well."*

> *"I'm sure you're not surprised to hear how unhappy I am that you've been smoking pot, but I'm heartened by the fact that, for the first time, we've begun to talk about this. I hope that we can continue to find ways to strengthen our relationship."*

Sometimes reaching what my friend George facetiously refers to as a state of "violent agreement" is quite an achievement for a parent and a teen, and worth accepting as good enough.

Acknowledge Uncertainty, Engender Curiosity

Even though we might have a pretty good idea as to what makes our children tick, by the time that they reach adolescence, they need to begin figuring themselves out, rather than relying on their parents and others to do the job for them. Because of this, an essential component of good communication at this juncture is to promote their own inquisitiveness. We do this by humbly acknowledging the limits to our knowledge and insight (even if we're not feeling very humble), and encouraging them to enhance their own.

"I have to admit to being a little puzzled here. You had said you were going to bring your grades up this year, and yet the midterm progress report says that they're right where they were before. Got any idea what's going on here?"

"I've racked my brains trying to determine why you do some of the self-destructive things that you do, and I'm realizing that I'm just at a loss. That doesn't mean I'm tossing in the towel here, but I'm curious—do you ever find yourself as mystified by your behavior as I seem to be?"

Don't Overreact

I've seen many parents shoot themselves in the foot by responding to their adolescent with greater intensity than is warranted, creating the unintended and paradoxical effect of making things worse rather than better.

For example, gushing forth with praise and gratitude when teenagers have done something that we've been recommending or requesting will ensure that they don't do it again. This reaction makes them feel like the change that they have made is more for our benefit than their own. A simple, mild commendation is much better than an extravagant and unrestrained one:

"Good to see the dishes got put away, as I had asked," rather than *"Thank you so much for putting the dishes away. It makes my life so much easier. I'm so proud of you!"*

"I noticed a couple of A's on your report card—looks like some of your hard work is paying off," rather than *"Now doesn't it feel good to see those A's? We just knew you*

could do it. That's what everyone's been saying about you all along—how smart you really are!"

On the other hand, when there remain things to be worried about, becoming shrill, hysterical, patronizing and overbearing will not only diminish effective communication, but, worse, make it hard for them to create an exit strategy and save face without having to feel ashamed for their initial errors in judgment:

"I know that you're only smoking a few cigarettes a day now, but I'm sure you're aware that nicotine is a highly addictive drug, and that it's possible that, at some point, you'll wind up hooked despite your best efforts to not be," rather than "How dare you smoke, when both of your grandmothers died of lung cancer! Do you want to wind up in an early grave yourself? What could you possibly be thinking?"

Listen

Listening is the great parental nostrum, but one that never seems to be administered often enough. Parents will often complain to me that their teen doesn't listen to them, but quite often the teen is feeling just as unlistened to as the parent. Listening does not mean agreeing with what you're hearing, nor does it mean that you can't eventually respond. What it *does* mean is making it clear to your child that what she has to say is important and worth attending to without being dismissed, rebutted, or contradicted.

One exercise that I'll often give parents in an effort to create the space for more listening is to see if they can spend 15 minutes with their adolescent minus the usual distractions (phone calls, e-mail checks, television, etc.) and without doing any of the following:

- Asking questions
- Offering unsolicited feedback or advice
- Making a request
- Giving a directive

Difficult as this may be, it often results in the discovery of new steps that take you out of the conventional conversational dance.

SELF-DEVELOPMENT

To be more of a mother or father during your child's teenaged years, we have to be more than a mother or father. If we want our adolescents to feel free to pursue their own growth and development in unencumbered ways, we have to pursue ours as well. This can be a difficult undertaking if we choose to see our teens' proliferating independence as the beginning of the end of our own lives.

Instead, it is important to view their adolescence as an opportunity for us to blossom into more fully human, more fully evolved individuals, to rediscover talents and reclaim powers that have lain dormant, to experience an adult renaissance and find new ways to explore and synthesize the entire range of our capacities—intellectual, emotional, relational, physical, spiritual, and creative.

Keeping in mind that the person *of* the parent must, at this stage of life, be on par with the person *as* the parent, will enable us to accomplish several important goals.

- *It prevents us from falling prey to the unrealistic expectations that so incessantly corrode the parent-teen relationship.* We're less likely to focus on the ways in which our adolescent is disappointing us if we find some ways to alleviate whatever disappointment we carry within ourselves. Outside enterprises deposit self-respect and self-confidence into our emotional bank accounts at a point in our lives when we may be a little overdrawn, and these deposits will in turn pay handsome dividends as we draw on them to complete the job of successfully launching our offspring.

- *It provides important modeling for your teen.* In one family that I worked with, a father's decision, after much hemming and hawing, to go back to college and finish his undergraduate degree turned out to have a great deal more influence on his son's underachievement in school than all of the lectures and lamentations about the mistake he had made by not having done so. At this developmental juncture, *our* action will be what most saliently inspires *their* action.

- *It prevents us from inappropriately underwriting our teen's liberties as a result of not allowing ourselves to take any.* A single mother that I worked with, one who had not dated at all in the seven years since her divorce, seemed to take so much vicarious pleasure in her 16-year-old daughter's active social life that she was no longer setting reasonable limits for her. Any request to go out, no matter how late, no matter what night of the week, was met with her mother's smiling approval. The upshot was that this young lady wound up in serious academic trouble because she was, without being aware of it, busy gratifying her mother's unmet desires.

- *When we have other sources of satisfaction in our lives, we are less likely to experience our teens' growing independence as ingratitude, rejection, or abandonment, and more likely to see it as the beginning of a new stage in our lives, and in our relationship with them.* Investing in relationships, careers, and activities that provide us with an abiding sense of purpose and satisfaction helps to buffer us from the unrest caused by an adolescent's maturation. We're less prone to take their rudeness, criticism, self-absorption, and insensitivity seriously and better able to maintain our sense of humor and roll with the punches.

- *It focuses less attention on the symptomatic teen and, by definition, diminishes the power of the symptom.* There is always a "conservation of energy" within the family—members can only attend to so many matters at the same time. With this in mind, it follows that if parents' attention is happily diverted to their own meaningful activities in a balanced way, there is less attention available to be paid to the teen's symptoms, symptoms that require parental attention if they are going to stay alive.

- *It mitigates the self-absorption that all teens are predisposed to and helps them to see that other people have important lives too.* If we have spent years making sure that the mechanism of the family rotated on the axis of our children's ventures and accomplishments, it is important at this point to reconstruct that mechanism so that they don't grow up believing that this is how real life will proceed as well. Making it clear that *our* growth is now deserving of a significant place setting alongside theirs at the family table cuts down on the narcissism that we may have been feeding and leaves them better prepared for the transition from our protective greenhouse into the less-protected world at large.

- *It reassures teens that they needn't worry about us moving on with our lives without them.* Teens who worry about parents are prone to creating problems that give their parents something to worry about. These problems are the equivalent of the mice that kittens proudly present at their parents' feet—a munificent offering designed to appease them. When we broaden our definition of who we are, we reassure our teens that there is "life after parenthood," which liberates both generations to develop more robustly.

ENLARGE YOUR GENERATIONAL PERSPECTIVE

Although a teen's grandparents and other antecedents may not be sitting in my office during treatment sessions, or even alive, I never feel like I'm doing my job unless I make sure that they are there symbolically. That is because it is much less likely that abiding change will come about unless parents' relationships with their own parents are included and examined as part of the process.

For one thing, I have worked with many parents who are astonishingly blind to the extent to which their relationship with their mother and father, or their in-laws, provides a template for their adolescent to emulate or spurn. One teenaged patient of mine said, with a glower, to her mother, "You don't even *talk* to your mother, but you expect me to open up to you. Why do you think I'm going to be any different than you? I'm just doing what you've taught me to." Another patient told his father, "If you think I'm going to live my life trying to keep you happy like you do with your parents, you can forget it. I'm my own man, Dad, not some chump like you are."

Also, the pattern of the particular family imbalance that is likely to emerge when our children become adolescents is invariably going to be an echo of an imbalance that occurred when we were growing up. In our easily fathomable attempt to avoid making the same mistakes our parents made and prevent our children from having the same hangups that we contend with, we tend to overcompensate in well-intentioned but frequently misguided ways and, in the process, magically create a mirror image of our own adolescence.

The father who felt that *his* father was oppressive and tyrannical may work so hard to be more tolerant and gentle with his son that he puts up with more than he should, resulting in an oppressive and tyrannical teenager. The mother who, as a child, had to mother her underresponsible mother may grow up to function as such a supremely competent mother that her daughter never has to develop an adequate level of responsibility, resulting in an underfunctioning teenager.

Finally, as we discussed in Chapter 1, imbalances that occur in one generation always ripple through the generations, provoking subsequent imbalances that create their own ripple effect up and down the generational ladder.

With this three-generational outlook in mind, it's wise for parents to pursue as much healing as they can with their own parents, alive or deceased, so that they don't imprison their children in their own past. Teens, without conscious awareness, often help us with this process by behaving in ways that remind us of how difficult we may have made it for our parents when we were growing up. More than one patient of mine has mused, "Now I understand what *my* parents were going through."

This identification with our parents may help us to understand and forgive them, and release them from the expectation that they should be, or should have been, perfect caregivers. It allows us to be more gracious and tolerant, and to conclude that whatever they did as caregivers, they did for their own reasons, to the best of their ability—or, as one patient of mine put it, "I realize now that my mother was doing all that she could with what little she had."

Forgiving our parents for their flaws will in turn help us to forgive our teens and instruct them in how to forgive us, so that they do not have to go through their lives hauling around the weighty millstones of resentment and guilt.

TREATMENT CONSIDERATIONS

Making decisions about whether to pursue psychological treatment is a particularly nettlesome prospect during adolescence. Because so much change is happening so rapidly, both for teens and for their families, it becomes difficult to distinguish between matters that warrant a consultation with a mental health professional and matters that may be worrisome and even unexpected but that turn out to be nothing more than harmless and transient nodal points in their development.

Is the discovery of an empty bottle of rum in the back of your daughter's closet a sure sign of incipient alcoholism, or simple evidence of from-time-to-time recreational experimentation? Is the histrionic codependence that your son is exhibiting with his girlfriend a harbinger of destructive relationships with the opposite sex down the road or an age-appropriate experiential workshop in fledgling intimacy, a chance to "work out some kinks"? Are your daughter's chameleonic hair color changes signaling deep emotional distress or a creatively symbolic way of chronicling her changing moods? Is your son's loss of interest in his usual activities the beginning of a clinical depression or part of the process of disinvesting from the childhood pursuits that he associates with his parents as a way of preparing to take on the young adult pursuits that feel more like his own?

In addition to the difficulties involved with assessing the seriousness of our teenager's behavior, there are other forces at work that may cloud our judgment as well. For example, because we have so narrowed the range of what is considered "normal" in our culture, parents may feel neglectful if they are not rushing to doctors' offices to diagnose and treat the latest emotional malady that, according to their friends or neighbors or the Internet or television advertising, is surely afflicting their adolescent. In our efforts to tend to our children, we seem to have effectively blurred the line between "discomfort" and "disorder" and then find ourselves overreacting to and overtreating conditions that are better envisioned not as diseases but as proverbial growing pains.

On the other hand, because there is still a stigma attached to addressing psychological matters, and some shame and embarrassment associated with the acknowledgment of family-based problems, parents may be reluctant to evaluate matters that truly do deserve, and would tend to rapidly respond to, therapeutic attention.

In an effort to help you to make a decision about whether, and when, to pursue treatment with a mental health professional, here are some guidelines to keep in mind.

First off, it's better to err in the direction of being too vigilant than not vigilant enough. Professionals like myself are available not just to treat but also to help determine whether or not treatment is even indicated. Just as fish cannot analyze the sea while they're swimming in it, parents find it hard to analyze family life while they're living in it.

For example, because your teenager has disclosed to you, during an unguarded moment, that he has had thoughts about killing himself doesn't mean that you should call 911 and have him immediately taken by ambulance to an inpatient psychiatric unit. On the other hand, it would be unwise to let a comment like this pass without obtaining an evaluation from a professional who could help you to determine whether he's truly at risk of suicide or, in reality, very unlikely to end his life but unable to find any other words to convey his strong feelings of frustration and despair.

One problem is that too many families, in my experience, have come to believe that "signing up" for psychotherapy means months of repetitive sessions without clearly stated and achievable goals, and with no real end in sight. I find that a good percentage of the families that come to meet with me do not need to return for many appointments at all. "Treatment" consists of nothing more than providing a way for the parents to understand what is happening, and implement some of the strategies that I have offered to get them on the right track. Even families whose difficulties are more complex and long-standing deserve to be thinking more optimistically and see tangible results after a few sessions, rather than feeling that they are locked into a sequential series of aimless conversations that don't seem to add up to anything substantial.

With this in mind, as you have probably inferred from the case material that I have presented thus far, I don't believe that real and enduring change is likely to come about when working with teens solely on an individual basis. It's only when change is catalyzed *within the system that they inhabit* that teens are able to risk and sustain changes on their own. When parents contact me asking if I work with adolescents, I always say yes, but, privately, my answer is no—truthfully, I work with families, not adolescents. After all, it is the family, not the therapist, that the adolescent ultimately returns to and lives with at the end of treatment.

It is because of this that I am generally exasperated when I hear from parents that their son or daughter has already been in "individual therapy" for months, if not years, and that even though they weren't seeing any lasting results, the therapist was busy assuring them that "progress was being made" without offering any details or actively including the family in the process. To me, that's not only an egregious waste of time, money, and energy, but worse, a process that actually interferes with growth, upholding the myth that the teen is "the problem" while absolving everyone else of accountability and opportunity.

I also don't believe that a therapist should become a teen's pal, someone for him or her to complain about his impossible parents to. When parents call to make an appointment for their adolescent because he or she needs "someone to talk to," one of the first questions I will be trying to answer is why no one else is currently fulfilling that role. The fact that an adolescent likes going to therapy does not, in and of itself, recommend it. Nor does it mean that the therapy is going to accomplish what it needs to. While there has to be some meshing, and a decent level of trust, between a teen and a clinician, they don't have to experience a deep affinity for each other for solutions to emerge and growth to occur.

In fact, it's much healthier for adolescents to turn to other, more naturally occurring connections for these relational purposes— parents, siblings, friends, teachers, coaches, religious leaders, employers, and mentors—rather than to rely on a therapist. And if individuals such as these don't currently play a salient enough role in a teen's life, then that, to me, should be one of the primary objectives of therapy, rather than promoting the teen's dependence on the therapist's nurturance and support. It may be appropriate to hire a tutor to assist your teen in a subject area that you have no facility for, but the same rule does not apply when it comes to growth and development. No therapy or therapist can ever be an effective substitute for a teen being able to enjoy and derive succor from a supportive family, school, religious organization, or peer group.

That is not to say, of course, that I never make time to meet with adolescents alone as part of our work together. After all, it's always important to hear what a child has to say and to learn more about what is on her mind without any other adults in the room. But even those individual encounters are used to create an overall framework through which to determine where the imbalance in the family system has occurred and how to realign it more functionally. That is why it's important for *all* family members to be available to participate in treatment sessions, because it's really the only way for the therapist to obtain a global perspective on the family and to better assess the role that the teen's problem is playing in all of their lives.

One additional advantage of conjoint participation in treatment is that it ratchets up the efficiency of the healing mechanism. The more individuals who are willing to get involved in treatment, the more progress is likely to be witnessed, and the more rapidly it will occur—and this doesn't mean parent and siblings only, but also grandparents, stepparents, friends, aunt, uncles, and cousins. As my erstwhile clinical supervisor Phyllis Stern often advised me, "If you get stuck, bring in more people."

But even when treatment is effective, that doesn't mean it should become the central component of an adolescent's life. For one thing, I have never observed a close correlation between the frequency of sessions and the rate of therapeutic progress. In fact, sometimes scheduling sessions too frequently can actually impede progress, promoting a dependence on therapy when what the family really needs to learn is how to engage, interact, and work things out on their own. That is why I usually provide patients with "homework" in between sessions. It forces them to put into action what we have worked on during our time together and gives them more "bang for their buck."

Ultimately, psychological treatment always holds forth the possibility of being quite helpful, but it should never be the place where the teen and his or her family reside. To my way of thinking, the therapist's job is to make him or herself obsolete as quickly as possible and empower patients to apply what they have learned during consultations to their real lives outside of the consultation room.

When it comes to the role of medication in the treatment of adolescents, there is no question that psychotropic drugs have reduced and ameliorated unnecessary suffering for many teens and their families, but there is also no question that we, as a society, have become dangerously reliant on treating developing teens with pharmaceutical remedies without fully understanding the risks and complexities involved.

We seem to have decided, with the enthusiastic support of the pharmaceutical and health insurance industries, that any disturbing, mysterious, or confusing behavior that teens display must be the irreducible outcome of a "chemical imbalance," and that the only legitimate clinical response is to rebalance through medicine.

I am reminded of the teenaged patient who recently came into my office, took a seat, and said, "I want whatever drug it was that they advertised on TV the other night that made everyone feel so good." Who could blame her?

Here are some thoughts to help you gain perspective on this matter. First, there is no reason to think that using medication is taking the easy way out, or masking the problem. There *are* disorders that adolescents are vulnerable to, and if these have been thoughtfully and appropriately diagnosed, medication may in fact be an important and necessary part of the treatment plan, in the same way that medication might be used as part of the treatment plan to address any other kind of disorder, such as elevated blood pressure, high cholesterol, cancer, heart disease, and diabetes. Being disappointed in yourself or your child for wanting to consider the curative properties of medication when symptoms are chronic and severe is both archaic and unwarranted.

On the other hand, *all* medications have side-effects—some minor, but some quite serious—and there is no medication that does not have some potential for psychological or physical addiction. Many of the medications that are currently being prescribed for teens have not been studied longitudinally, meaning that we don't know what long-term impact they may have on still-growing bodies and minds. Meanwhile, not only have FDA studies demonstrated that at least half of all children treated with psychotropic medication get better on placebos, but there is also evidence that drug companies, contaminated by financially based conflicts of interest, do not always publish studies that point to the ineffectiveness and potential risks of their elixirs.

Inappropriately prescribing medication for adolescents may also have far-reaching and disturbing non-medical side-effects.

For example, it can inadvertently prevent them from digging down deep and marshaling hitherto unknown strengths and resources that deserve to be summoned to take on a challenge or manage a crisis. It can reinforce, in the same way that individually based therapy may, the counterproductive belief that the "problem"— whatever it is—inheres within them, rather than within the family and cultural system. And it may suggest to them that it's always best to first look for the quick fix when difficulties arise—even though many psychiatric medications may not work all that quickly—which increases the likelihood that they'll be just as quick to resort to illegal street drugs to address these difficulties.

Taking these factors into account, while I never rule out the possibly helpful role that medication may play, I tend to be chary about recommending it, and if I do, I make sure that patients are evaluated and closely monitored by an adolescent psychiatrist or by a pediatrician with psychiatric training.

And while I don't believe that fear or ignorance should lead to teens being deprived of a trial of medication after a complete workup points to the potential efficacy of one, I also don't believe in the use of medication to "improve" teens who are already doing okay, who are not suffering from a diagnosable disorder, but who could, in their parents' eyes, "be doing better." Providing adolescents with psychostimulant medication on an as-needed basis when important tests in school are coming up, or with PRN antianxiety agents if an interview or oral presentation is approaching, or with sleep enhancers to regulate an uneven sleep-wake cycle is dangerous medicine and sends them the wrong message about their responsibilities and capabilities.

Likewise, just because there may be a neurochemical basis for some behavioral or emotional problems doesn't mean that these problems have to be treated solely through neurochemistry. Research has demonstrated conclusively that there are many non-medicinal practices that have tremendous and long-lasting impact on our neurochemistry, such as exercise, meditation, acupuncture, prayer, yoga, and creative expression. To convey to teens the belief that medication is the only intervention that alters our inner physiology is ill-advised, the result being that we may, to paraphrase Francis Bacon, "cure the disease but [psychologically] kill the patient."

Finally, there are limits to what any medication can accomplish. The ways in which medication often seems to be most helpful to my adolescent patients is when it frees up energy that had previously been absorbed by the need to fight off a disorder, energy that can then be more effectively funneled into addressing important issues, solving individual and family problems, achieving objectives, and moving forward with their lives.

EXERCISE 7

To help families find workable balances during the transitional stage of adolescence, I often ask them to take some relational snapshots of where they've been, where they are, and where they'd like to be. This helps everyone to gain some perspective on growth that has already been occurring, as well as providing some hope and direction for growth that is still to come. Here's one way to do this.

1. Make a list of all the aspects of your teen's life that he or she is solely in charge of. This will vary from family to family and might include choice of clothing, hygiene issues, selection of friends.

2. Make a list of all the aspects of your teen's life that you as parent are solely in charge of (financial issues, assignment of chores, etc.).

3. Make a list of all the aspects of your teen's life that the two of you are conjointly in charge of (deciding how summers are spent, what classes to take in high school, how much studying time there should be, etc.).

4. Now, do the same exercise but looking at how things were *one* year ago and *five* years ago.

5. Now, do the same exercise, but looking at how you'd like things to be *one* year from now and *five* years from now.

6. You can also ask your son or daughter to do the same thing, and compare the lists that you come up with.

EIGHT

THE GOOD ENOUGH MARRIAGE

The compensation for growing old . . . was simply this: that the passions remain as strong as ever, but one has gained—at last!—the power which adds the supreme flavor to existence, the power of taking hold of experience, of turning it round, slowly, in the light.

—Virginia Woolf, *Mrs. Dalloway*

amily therapists have come to understand that a family system's two most unstable times occur whenever there is an addition to or a subtraction from that system. My first book, *Things Just Haven't Been the Same: Making the Transition from Marriage to Parenthood*, explored the impact that the arrival of children had on the marital relationship. This chapter will look at the effect of the imminent departure of children on the marital relationship.

Despite the very high rate of divorce, the many negative perceptions of marriage, and the gradual social sanctioning of single life and cohabitation, 90 percent of individuals will still choose to marry at some point. And married couples who have children will find that parenting brings out the true nature of the marriage in ways that no other aspect of shared life—sex, finances, division of labor, in-laws—can ever do.

By the time one or more of our offspring move into adolescence, we are usually well into our marriage and carrying a mixture of feelings about wedlock. On the one hand, there is the shared pride we experience in having survived our offspring's early and middle childhood and guided them safely into adolescence. This is accompanied by the heartening belief that an end to childrearing is now in sight, and that new opportunities to enjoy our hard-won freedom await us as our teens empty the nest and begin soaring away on their own. As we become less necessary as caregivers, we are finally able to consider turning our attention to our spouse, as well as to the many individual and joint pursuits that have been put on the back burner for years while we tended to the tasks of parenthood.

On the other hand, raising adolescents can send even the most solid marriage into a tailspin that can take years to pull out of, if it's pulled out of at all, making our union feel much more like an ordeal than an ideal. This stage can mark one of the deepest valleys in a couple's relationship, as what were small relational fractures widen into chasms and chasms open up into a yawning, terrifying abyss. Let's take some time to discuss why this is.

For one thing, after years of having made little time to focus on our marriage as we dutifully dealt with the utilitarian functions of family life—cooking, housework, carpools, colds, quarrels, bills, car repairs, report cards, family vacations, school conferences, doctors' appointments, music lessons, homework, parent meetings, etc.—we may find that the bonds that initially held us together have frayed, if they haven't disappeared altogether. We discover, to our dismay, that we have slowly become sealed off from each other, disenfranchised from the very soul of our marriage, and out of contact, physically and/or emotionally, with our spouse, who may feel more like a ghost than a lover.

"What did I *see* in him?" we sadly muse. "Where is the woman I fell in love with?" we wonder. "Sometimes it feels like I'm living with a stranger," we mournfully admit. At times, our life together feels like mere co-existence, two well-socketed fugitives in the same home, the years slowly dissolving into what may seem like little more than a pointless, captive blur as one or both of us focus more and more on our individual pursuits or on the only common denominator of our union, our children.

Added to this, we may have gotten into the habit of focusing on our partners' shortcomings, trying to rearrange them in a futile attempt to make up for our discomfort with ourselves or our relationship. The outcome is a sludge of petty arguments, nursed grudges, and ancient resentments that have never been fully resolved or put to rest, and that have gradually hardened into a sour mortar that binds us unhappily together.

Differences of opinion when it comes to childrearing may also come to the fore at this stage, as important decisions that deeply and directly affect our teen's future need to be confronted: what his high school schedule should be, whether he should be allowed to get his driver's license, how late he can stay out, who's going to pay for his car insurance, whether he should be allowed to have an after-school job, when he can date, what the consequences are when he flouts authority, and, perhaps most importantly of all, what he should plan on doing once he graduates high school.

As we have seen, we generally choose a parenting style that either validates or rejects how *we* were raised, based on how we believe we turned out. The issue of whether or not our partner agrees with our parenting style tends to be less of a consideration when it comes to explaining or defining our childrearing behavior. So because we and our spouse were reared in different homes and have different appraisals of the outcome of how we were reared, rare are the husband and wife who are likely to come up with the same, or even similar, answers to all of these childrearing questions.

Meanwhile, one persistent question that we have been asking of ourselves as parents—"How are we doing?"—slowly distills into a much more gut-wrenching one when our child becomes an adolescent—"How did we *do*?" As we assay our teen's grades, or friends, or behavior, or college acceptance letters, and are forced to compare the results with other families', we may be prone to look to our marriage partner as the one to blame for disappointing results or stymied progress.

"If you had supported me in pushing our son to take advanced placement classes in his high school, maybe he would have gotten into the college he really wanted to go to," a wife will acerbically conclude for her husband. "If you had ever been able to stick with a job, we would've been able to afford a move to a better school district, and our daughter wouldn't have found so many skate-punk boys to waste her time with," a husband will rail at his wife. The combination of divisive disagreements about what is best for our teen, added to our readiness to engage in chronic finger-pointing for past miscalculations and misjudgments, can quickly lead to a heightened state of conflict and increased marital disenchantment.

From a social standpoint, when adolescents start to date and experience the magic of new romance, it highlights the decline in passion and sexual energy that we may be, or for some time have been, experiencing, and creates aching feelings of loneliness, jealousy, and loss. Filled with longing as our smitten teenager floats on an iridescent cloud of infatuation, ardor, and lust, even if we know that what we are seeing is bound to quickly pass, we are reminded of the waning of our youth, the old passions and desires that suddenly seem so quaint and foreign, the aging that, no matter how hard it is fought, will continue until it ultimately prevails and brings us to our final demise.

Parents sometimes find themselves responding to this chain of events not by trying to create a new, richer adulthood, but by trying to create a second adolescence, unconsciously competing or keeping up with their son or daughter in an effort to stay eternally young. Naturally, the results can be embarrassing, if not ruinous, with one parent's sudden self-absorption usually alienating the other and exacerbating their mutual feelings of neglect, distance, and dissatisfaction.

One patient of mine shared with me her frustration with her husband, "who's trying to be like teenager again. He sees my son all happy-go-lucky, and now he's the same way, buying clothes from stores I've never even seen, listening to radio stations I've never heard of. It's like he's trying to recapture his youth—and, to my amazement, my son's going along with this, mostly because my husband won't discipline him anymore, he's so busy trying to kiss up and be all buddy-buddy with him. So of course I'm not handling it well at all. It's like my husband's regressed back to being a fifteen-year-old, and I'm acting like Psycho Mom, constantly yelling at both of them for being so impossible."

Furthermore, as we have already seen in numerous case examples, adolescents, in their hunger for power, will never hesitate to bump hard against the marital relationship in an effort to disrupt its course and cash in on its weaknesses. New or old differences of opinion will be exploited as teens adroitly discover and traverse our seams and fissures, and attempt to conquer us through shrewdly capitalizing on our dissent and disunity.

The father of a 14-year-old patient admitted, "She knows just how to play us off of each other. It's as if she's got some secret guide to our marital workings, like the kids can get for their video games. She comes to me if she wants to be able to do something with her friends, because she knows that I think that having a good social life is very important, and that I'll stand up for her against my wife if there's some restriction in place that needs to be circumvented. And she goes to my wife if she wants to be able to just beg off on some commitment that she's made, because she knows that her mother will always go easy on her and stand up for her against me when I'm busy insisting that everything has to be followed through on. She's constantly pitting us against each other so that she can get what she wants, and then my wife and I wind up doing the fighting with each other while she goes off and does her thing."

Also, as part of their cognitive and emotional development, adolescents become more capable of carefully observing, and less hesitant about caustically evaluating, the intricacies of their parents' matrimony, heartily tendering the opinions and critiques that we may not want to have to endure. Already experiencing our own doubts and regrets about our marriage, we're not likely to be enthusiastic about having to hear their assessment of our conjugal failings as well.

One mother wearily observed, "I'm *so* tired of hearing my daughter tell me that I'm just a doormat for her father and that I should speak up for myself sometimes. The reality is, I know that I should, I've given in to my husband and let him have things his way for far too long in far too many ways—but I just don't want to have to hear it from *her*. It makes things that much worse for me, having it thrown up in my face all the time."

Meanwhile, individual or marital problems that have been fermenting just below the surface—from dared affairs to chemical dependencies, differences in sexual desire to destructive tempers, conflicts with in-laws to financial problems, depressive episodes to long periods of emotional disregard—begin to clamor for our attention as the children who knowingly or unknowingly distracted us from these problems by being buffers, companions, or lightning rods begin to pull away from us.

That seems to be why I usually get a surge in telephone calls from individuals requesting couples counseling in the autumn months. Often these are parents whose child has just left home and who are now forced to contend with marital problems that have been at a low boil for years and have finally begun to bubble over. Likewise, when parents contact me about a young adult who is having a difficult time making it on his or her own at college, it is often because their son or daughter remains preoccupied with or concerned by marital or family dilemmas at home that they sense, with their unerring radar, have continued or worsened in their absence.

One young man, a freshman at college who had been a 4.0 student in high school, was now struggling to keep his grades at a 2.0 level. While part of this was due to his difficulty adjusting to the increased academic expectations of university life, it also became clear, as we spoke, that he wasn't able to funnel his full energies into meeting his academic demands because he was upset about the tension that seemed to have broken out at home after he'd left.

"I try not to call home because whenever I do, my little sister gets on the phone and tells me that my parents aren't talking to each other, and how impossible they are. I mean, I knew that things weren't great between my mom and dad when I left, but I feel bad for my sister, who's stuck there with them. And I can just *feel* the coldness, like when my parents get on the phone at the same time to talk with me, it's like ice."

Many parents of teens are also forced to confront issues related to aging, ailing, or dying parents, adding to the many strains existing on their marriage. The enormity of the grief that we are compelled to consider will always stir up old family-of-origin dramas that have a powerful impact on our connection with our spouse. Realizing, with greater recognition, that our parent is never going to be the ideal parent, we may turn to our marriage partner to make up for what we never received during our childhood, a hopeless but insistent habit that is basically the equivalent of slamming a torpedo into the hull of the marital ship.

And finally, as our children move through adolescence, we are forced to ask ourselves the most frightful question of all, the one that we have been so gingerly able to step around until now: *What next?* How can we be husband and wife if we're not busy being father and mother? What endeavors could we possibly immerse ourselves in that would even come close to the consuming, rewarding, incandescent intensity of everyday parenthood? Without our children at home, what will we do, what will we share, and what in god's name will we find to *talk* about? How will we tolerate the thunderous silence that will soon roll through the house when there are no more wailing guitars, blaring stereos, ringing telephones, and shrill squabbles to fill the air? And if we have secretly or openly "stayed together for the sake of the children," what do we do when the children have grown and are no longer around to *need* us to stay together?

Every marriage is tossed and turned by the mountainous waves that swell in response to these profound and cavernous questions. Adolescence is indeed a stage during which our familiar marital navigation points disappear, when we take stock, face a new reckoning, and find that everything about and within our relationship is up for grabs.

Of course, that's only one side of the story. Not only does raising adolescents influence a marriage, but a marriage influences how we raise our adolescents. No matter what the nature of the relationship between a husband and wife, it will perpetually provide a prism through which our teens' development is refracted and understood.

For example, teens who are concerned about their parents' marriage, and who want it to be in tip-top condition so that they feel more confident and less guilty about leaving home, will attempt to nurture and heal it in a variety of inventive ways. Some may try to be perfect, hoping to mightily weld their parents together through the sheer heat of their astonishing achievements. Others may take a different tack and create so many difficulties that their parents' dismembered marriage has no choice but to reconsolidate in an effort to deal with them all. Still others find themselves intuitively attempting to force to the surface their parents' long-buried and highly classified feuds, secrets, and fears so that these can be disinterred, eventually allowing for new life to be breathed into the marriage. And some take on (or are invited to play) the role of relational circuit-breaker, constantly inserting themselves into the marital sphere in an effort to prevent it from overheating, but in the process putting themselves at risk through their exposure to dangerously high levels of emotional voltage.

Parents who remain at odds with each other, who continuously repel each other like magnets turned wrong-end round, and who are unable to speak in a unified voice to important family matters, may wind up triangulating their teens and placing them in pernicious loyalty binds. If they dare to heed one parent, they automatically alienate the other. These cross-generational triangulations create a climate of emotional infidelity and effectively undermine an adolescent's sense of security and sanctuary, since there is the constant threat of rejection, along with the dangling albatross of guilt.

Several likely outcomes will result from these marital splits, none of which bode well for an adolescent's development. In one scenario, he may be invited to enter into a coalition with one parent against the other, enjoy his temporarily elevated status, but then suffer immeasurably when he finds that his relationship with his other parent, as well as his own evolution as an individual, are both impaired by this inappropriate alliance. In another scenario, a teenager may try to avoid these coalitions by becoming immobilized, refusing to move in the direction of either parent, which will prevent painful betrayals, but simultaneously preclude growth.

In a third scenario, toxic marital conflict is detoured through the adolescent, and the intent focus on his or her "problem behavior" enables a couple to find reasons to sidestep their own struggles, maintaining a vicious cycle. For example, a diffident husband may find it easier to be angry with his daughter than with his wife, whom he is still intimidated by, even after 20 years of marriage. Sensing her father's discomfort, the daughter, without knowing why, begins to graciously offer him a variety of reasons to, in fact, *be* angry with her—her grades and neckline both plunge noticeably, and she gets lippy when asked to help out around the house—all of which keeps this dysfunctional three-way collaboration intact.

Or a lonely wife, angry and frustrated by years of being unable to connect with her aloof and isolated husband, gives up and instead devotes herself to trying to have "good conversations" with her 15-year-old son "before he's left home and it's too late for us to get to really know each other." Her son is actually not as withdrawn as his father is, but he's not at a stage in his life during which an exchange of intimacies with his mother over a cup of coffee is eagerly anticipated. Of course, the more this mother pursues her son for the contact that she should be having with her husband, the more her son distances from her, quickly reducing the fairly reasonable amount of contact that they originally had and leaving her feeling excluded by two males now, rather than one.

Having a better understanding of the vicissitudes of marriage during the stage of raising adolescents, let's take an in-depth look at a couple who responded to a crisis provoked by their teen in ways that ultimately led to marital, and family, growth.

Calvin's parents got in touch with me because of his propensity for sexual acting-out. He had been caught receiving oral sex from a female classmate in the back of the bus while returning from a band field trip; his parents had twice found him with his girl-friend, Carla, in his basement bedroom in the middle of the night; and he had stolen one of their credit cards and run up a bill of almost $1000 visiting pornographic websites and calling phone sex lines.

Always trying to keep things as simple and straightforward as possible, I recommended two fairly self-evident interventions after hearing what they had to say—allowing him no more unsupervised us of the telephone and computer and moving him back to an upstairs bedroom. When two more incidents occurred within the month after these guidelines had been established—his parents had been called by a hotel clerk while he and Carla were trying to book a room there using *her* mother's credit card, and one afternoon his English teacher noticed him insistently trying to get a female classmate to notice the erection that was bulging beneath his pants—it was clear that there was more texture to this story.

Part of the problem was that Calvin looked more 19 than 15. He was tall and well-built, with broad shoulders and thick facial

hair, and although he was a ninth grader, he would have no difficulty passing for a college student. His parents acknowledged
that this had been an issue since he had started middle school:

"He was just very precocious. His voice and complexion
started to change by the end of elementary school, he was shaving
by the time he was in seventh grade, and it's like there was just no
stopping him. His pediatrician never thought there was much to
worry about. It's just that puberty seemed to hit him like a truck,
and quite early on," his mother, Carolyn, related.

"I had a similar experience," his father, Wallace, recalled.
"My growth spurt hit me before my buddies back in junior high
school, even though everyone eventually caught up with me by the
beginning of high school. So I know what it's like."

"What was it like?" I asked him.

"Well, you sort of feel like a big man, which is kind of nice,
really. I remember the girls really getting off on the fact that I was
already shaving when most of my friends didn't even have any
peach fuzz! They'd all take turns at lunch rubbing my cheek to
feel my growth, oohing and aahing. And I was good at sports,
too, like Calvin, so it served me well there. In junior high
wrestling, I was just more developed than most of the guys I'd go
up against, so I was winning just about every match. Of course,"
he added with a rueful smile, "that changed by the time I got to
high school."

Wallace's recollection fit in with what adolescent research has
shown, which is that while it can be a social liability for girls to
enter puberty earlier than their peers—a source of shame and embarrassment—a young man will often find it to be a social advantage. And Wallace, like his son, hadn't hesitated to capitalize on
this.

Part of the problem, then, was that a fairly large gap had
opened up between Calvin's sexual maturity and his emotional
and intellectual maturity. The oceanic urges being stirred by his
rapidly developing body were probably far exceeding his capacity
to chart and regulate them, resulting in behaviors that showed
impulsivity and an absence of good judgment.

Still, the extent to which his actions exceeded his family's,
and society's, norms, was notable. Plenty of kids mature sooner
than their peers, or ripen sexually before they ripen emotionally,

get into some trouble because of it and gradually learn to rein in their behavior. In this case, things seemed to be getting worse, not better.

I brought his parents in to get some more perspective, discovering that Carolyn and Wallace had been married for 23 years, that Calvin was the oldest of their three children, with two younger sisters, and that, aside from their eldest's sexual acting-out, he was basically a good kid.

"He's no genius, but he does well enough in school, mostly B's, a couple of C's here and there. His teachers like him, his friends are pretty nice, and he's a *very* good athlete," Wallace reported. "He was playing varsity football this past fall, starting at tight end, one of only three freshmen on the squad. And he did great at wrestling last year. This'll be his first year in high school wrestling, and I know the coach is expecting big things of him."

"I agree with my husband. Calvin has never really given us much trouble, aside from the usual stuff—you know, tormenting his sisters, not always staying on top of his schoolwork, sloppy room, nocturnal on weekends, stuff like that. So we really don't know how to handle what's been happening. And the fact is, we don't really have much control over him once he leaves the house. Let's face it, we can keep him off the computer and the telephone, but how do we keep him from doing the things that he's been doing in school or on the bus or even at a hotel?"

"Wallace, you had mentioned that you had also matured faster than your peers. Being that you've had this experience, how have you helped to educate Calvin about the possibilities and pitfalls?" I inquired.

"I think I've done a pretty good job with that."

"Would you agree with that, Carolyn?" I asked.

"Sort of. Well, not really. I mean, Wallace, I don't think you've been as on top of this as I think you should have. I've been talking with the girls about development since they were little, and our middle daughter recently started getting her period, but she was ready for it, at least emotionally, because I'd prepared her for it. I'm not sure you've been as vigilant with Calvin."

"Guys are different, though, Carolyn," Wallace countered. "We just don't talk about things the same way. We don't *do* things the same way. You can't compare your relationship with the girls with my relationship with Calvin."

"How do you see the two as different, Wallace?" I asked.

He thought for quite some time before answering. "Fathers and sons just don't talk that way. That's the only way I know how to explain it."

"How did *your* father handle your sexual education?" I queried.

He chortled. "*My* sexual education? My sexual education was *Playboy* magazines and some stag films that one of my older brother's buddies got hold of and showed us in his basement one night. That, and the little that they taught us in school, which was mostly strange-looking drawings of the reproductive system."

"So did your father try to educate you at all?"

"Well, one time there was this very awkward, 'If you have any questions, son, I'm here to answer them,' but that was about it."

"So it must have been a challenge to consider dealing with Calvin differently than you were dealt with."

"That's for sure. I guess, now that we're talking about it, I still don't really know how to talk about it with him."

One thing that had already become clear was that Calvin had not been instructed as much as he should have when it came to puberty and its attendant emotional and physiological changes. Still, not every over-mature under-educated ninth grader was busy trying to book hotel rooms and engage in oral sex on school field trips. I went back to further explore their role as parents.

"What do you think that Calvin has learned about sexuality from the two of you?"

"What do you mean?" Carolyn asked, warily.

"All of us provide our children with a certain template for sexual behavior, one that is rooted in how we treat each other. That doesn't mean, of course, that they know specifically what we do or don't do in our bedroom, but even small children, and certainly adolescents, are able to pick up on the sexual energy or connection that exists between their parents, even when it's not literally observable."

Carolyn looked at Wallace and Wallace looked at me, as if asking for help.

"Maybe I ought to ask how things have been going between the two of you when it comes to your intimate life," I proposed.

"Not very well," Carolyn finally blurted out. I looked at Wallace to see if he wanted to comment, but he remained mute.

"In what way have things not been going well?" I pursued.

"There's just not much happening between us anymore. I mean, we never had a *great* sex life, but at least it was consistent, at least we could turn to each other in that way. But now things are worse than they've *ever* been."

"How about for you, Wallace?"

"I'd have to agree," he said, curtly. "Not very good."

"How long have things been this bad?"

Again, Carolyn took the lead. "For a while now. I mean, there was the normal dropoff in sex once we had kids. We kind of expected that, and we're not imagining that things are going to be like they were when we first met. But as the three of them got older, we were able to kind of resume our sex life, get it back on track. Until about a year ago, and then it's like the bottom fell out completely." She looked at Wallace pleadingly, but he avoided her eyes.

"How do the two of you understand what's happened?" The rapidly rising tension level in the room suggested that this was treacherous, and probably unmapped, territory.

"I don't know. I've asked Wallace what's going on, but I don't get any answer. He just doesn't seem interested in me anymore. I don't know what's changed." Her eyes brimmed with tears.

"What about on your end, Wallace? How do you understand the decline in intimacy between the two of you?"

"I guess things have just changed. I don't know how to explain it. I don't know what to say. I suppose after more than twenty years of marriage—and having known each other almost twenty-*five* years . . . well, let's just say it's hard to keep the interest going."

"I think you're right about that," I agreed. "It can sometimes be hard for a long-married couple to find ways to continue to be attractive and stimulating to each other after all that time. What have the two of you tried to do to keep your interest in each other as sexual partners percolating?"

Again, silence. Then Carolyn spoke, with tears running down her cheeks: "I don't know what else I can do. I tried to arrange a weekend away for us, but he's canceled out both times, saying he couldn't get coverage at the hospital where he works. For Valentine's Day I bought us one of those little 'love packages' they sell at the store—you know, massage oil, wine, that kind of stuff—and it's still sitting in the drawer. It's a little humiliating, really, I've never had to work this hard to arouse his interest in me."

"How about from your end, Wallace? What have you done to try to resurrect your sex life?"

"Look, I've tried too, but it just doesn't seem to be happening."

Carolyn exploded: "*You've* tried too?! What exactly have you *tried*? Have you tried holding me? Have you tried kissing me? Have you tried just coming to bed at the same time that I'm in bed, rather than watching TV all night in the family room? Have you tried taking me out to dinner? Come on, Wallace, you haven't even *looked* at me in months!"

Wallace sat perfectly still. The more emotional Carolyn became, the more stone-faced he appeared.

Aware, now, that this pattern had been in place for some time, but not being sure why, I was reluctant to prescribe any changes until I knew more about its genesis. As an assignment, I asked them simply to observe the ebb and flow of their erotic energy as they moved through their day, hoping to at least bring the issue of sexuality back up to the surface where it could be addressed and dealt with.

I also invited them to return in a couple of weeks for a session without Calvin, telling them that I felt that it was possible that there was some connection between his sexual inappropriateness and their parched sex life. However, Carolyn called me just a few hours before that session to tell me that an emergency had come up at Wallace's work, and he would not be able to attend.

While I usually cancel a couples treatment session unless both partners are available, I decided to bring Carolyn in by herself to see if any new ideas emerged without Wallace present. Often, when one spouse cancels an appointment, it is because he or she has some ambivalence about an issue that might leak out during the appointment, half wanting to keep the matter under wraps by not showing up, half hoping that his or her spouse and I will discuss the problem together.

After Carolyn described the absence of intimacy in a little more detail, I asked her whether she had ever thought that another woman might be involved.

"I've thought of that, yes, but just don't see it as a possibility. That's just not Wallace's way."

"Have you ever asked Wallace?"

"Yes, one time I did. My cell phone was out of power, and I went into his briefcase to get his and saw, on the 'recent calls' listing, the same phone number over and over again, a number that I didn't recognize. I asked him about it, but he said it was just a patient of his. But that didn't make sense, really, because I don't know that he ever gives his patients his cell phone number. Usually he has them page him."

"Did you believe him?"

"Well, basically, yes. I mean, I do have to wonder how he would have the *time* to have an affair. He's quite busy at work, and he's pretty involved with the kids when he's home."

"But you would have to agree that that might explain the sudden atrophy in your physical contact with each other, wouldn't you?"

"I guess. I just don't see it. He said it was a patient of his, and I really have no choice but to believe him. I mean, maybe he's got some kind of physical problem."

"That could be, as well," I concurred. "But then the question is, why wouldn't he be dealing with this or telling you? After all, you've been together for a quarter of a century, now. It would be an odd thing to try to keep hidden."

"Well, maybe he's ashamed."

"Have you asked him whether there's a medical problem that you're not aware of?"

"I asked, and he denied that, too."

We spent the rest of the session considering other possibilities, and I asked her to have Wallace call me to set up an individual session for himself as well, in an effort to keep things balanced between the two of them in terms of their work with me. I did not hear from Wallace, however. In fact, the next call I got was from Carolyn again.

"I think you might be right about what we were talking about last week," she said, choking back sobs. "I checked Wallace's cell phone bill when it came in yesterday, and I saw the same number I had seen before on his phone showing up a hundred other times—sometimes it's like five or six times a *day*. His patients never call that often. So anyway, I called the number, and a woman answered, but I hung up. And then I went on-line and looked over his credit card statement, and I saw that there were all these things that he's paid for that I've never seen—flowers, lingerie from Victoria's Secret, books and CDs, hotel rooms—so I think he's got to be seeing someone. And I don't know what to do, I don't know what to say, but I feel like I was kicked in the stomach."

We spent some time on the telephone strategizing how to proceed, and I offered her the option of bringing her findings up with Wallace on her own or in my office. She chose the former, not being certain that he would want to return after he'd already canceled one session. The next day, she called back, telling me that she had told him what she had found, that he had eventually confessed to an affair, and that they had both agreed to return to my office together to see if they could figure out a way to rebuild trust and salvage their marriage.

As is usually the case when I help couples to heal the betrayal of marital intimacy that infidelity signifies, there was much hurt and anguish to sort through. I made some time to speak with Wallace alone, and he explained to me that he had been feeling more and more distant from and neglected by Carolyn over the years. "She went on and on in our last session about what she's done in the last year to try to rekindle our sex life, but for a number of years before that, *I* was the one who was trying to keep the spark alive and she was the one who always had an excuse not to do anything. I would suggest going away for a vacation together, without the kids, but we could never agree on who would watch the kids, it's like no one was ever acceptable. And we were always so busy with the kids and their events, just going out to dinner as a couple was difficult. There was always a reason not to go, or to have to bring the kids along. And I'm not just talking about sex—this was in general. Plus, there just weren't many kind words from her, and she was certainly quick to criticize me. I would never hear that I looked nice, or that she appreciated me, or that I mattered to her. I felt very taken for granted, and after a while I got tired of it."

"How did you try to address this with her?"

"Well, I guess that's part of the problem, because at some point I suppose I gave up trying. I guess I decided that it just wasn't worth trying anymore. And then my partners and I decided to expand our medical practice, and all of a sudden there was a very attractive female doctor who joined us, and she looked up to me and thought the world of me, and it didn't take long for one thing to lead to another."

While the partner who goes outside the marriage to have an affair is always responsible for the violation of trust, *both* partners have to look at their contribution to the marital climate in which the affair came to be if their marriage is going to have the chance to grow from this painful experience. Setting things up as a victim-victimizer scenario, in which one spouse is completely guilty and the other is completely innocent, may temporarily simplify things but will always preclude true healing and real change.

Not surprisingly, as their couples therapy unfolded, the issue of how to address things with Calvin came up. Carolyn and Wallace had basically kept things under wraps but had agreed to tell all three of their children, at my suggestion, that they were working with me in an effort to get along with each other better and create a warmer relationship. As I had originally suspected, though, it became clear that Calvin's behavior had not occurred in a vacumn but was a direct response to the hitherto subterranean crisis in his parents' marriage.

I had continued to schedule separate family meetings with Calvin and his parents to make sure that his behavior stayed in check, which, for the most part, it had. There had been no major incidents in several weeks. At one point I asked Calvin, privately, if he sensed any changes in his parents' connection with each other, being that he was aware that they were also meeting with me on their own to address their relationship.

"It's different between them now, that's for sure," he observed. "I mean, they seem to be fighting more than they ever have before, but—and I know this seems a little weird—they seem to be getting along better, too. I'm not sure how to explain it."

I had the sense that Carolyn and Wallace were finally beginning to address the rifts that had opened up between them over the past several years, and were experiencing and displaying the heightened intensity that is a handmaiden to this endeavor, intensity that usually expresses itself in both negative and positive ways.

"Do you have any sense of what had gone awry in their relationship that led them to want to improve things?" I wondered, curious to know what he'd venture forth with.

"I actually have a guess, but I've never said anything about it."

"Do you want to try your guess out on me?"

"Is this confidential, just between you and me?"

"Sure, just between you and me. Although I'm sure you understand that what your parents are working on with me is also just between the two of them and myself as well."

"That's okay. I'll tell you what I think. I think my dad's been screwing around on my mom."

"What has led you to conclude that?" I asked, forced to encounter, as I have countless times, how astute adolescents are when it comes to family dynamics, and how they have an uncanny way of speaking "sideways," with their actions, to what their parents have tried to leave unspoken.

"Well, it was kind of weird, really, but a buddy of mine has a job as a doorman at a hotel near my dad's office. And one time he came up to me in school, sounding all creeped-out, and said, 'I saw your dad at the hotel yesterday, and he was walking a woman out to her car in the parking lot and kissing her good-bye, and, dude, it *wasn't* your mom.' So that really shook me up. It definitely made me wonder."

"Did you ever think of asking your father about this?"

"My father? No way. I didn't want to believe it, and even if I was sure, I couldn't say anything. Although I'll tell you, it's been hard, sometimes, not to just blurt something out, like when he and my mom have been fighting recently."

"Anything else that made you wonder whether he's been having an affair?"

"Well, I probably wouldn't have thought a lot about this if my friend hadn't told me what he saw, but there was one time at home after that when I happened to walk past his bathroom, and

I heard him on the cell phone in there, and he was sort of talking real low, but sounding kind of upset. I couldn't make out what he was saying, but that made me wonder, too—I mean, why would he be on a cell phone in the bathroom almost *whispering* to someone unless something was going on?"

"Do you feel that you would like to address any of this with your parents now?"

Calvin chewed his gum thoughtfully for a moment. "Would you tell me what's been going on?" he asked, hopefully.

"No," I replied. "You can ask them yourself. Or I'd be happy to help you ask them, if you'd like—but it's their business. It wouldn't be right for me to share any of that with you unless they wanted me to."

"Let me think about it, then," he suggested, and I agreed.

Wallace plopped down in his regular chair and began our next family meeting with an angry pronouncement: "Well, he's gone and done it again. Why don't you tell Dr. Sachs what's happened *this* time, Calvin?"

Calvin just studied his father with neutral eyes, saying nothing.

"*Tell* him," Wallace repeated.

"*You* tell him," Calvin said, a lethal tone suddenly lacing his voice.

"All right, I will," Wallace said. "My brilliant son has gotten his girlfriend pregnant. Carla's mother called me last night and told me. I thought she was going to leap through the phone and throttle me, she was so mad. And if I were in her shoes, I'd probably feel the same way."

Carolyn was tearful. "What are we going to do now? These two kids can't raise a child. Wallace and I certainly don't want to. The poor girl doesn't even have a father, and right now her mother is saying that they don't believe in abortion, and that her daughter is going to carry the baby to term and then give it up for adoption. I can't believe my fifteen-year-old son is going to be a father. I can't believe we're going to be grandparents. I can't believe *any* of this is happening!"

"Here I thought we were making progress," Wallace said, disgustedly, "and now *this*. You couldn't keep from screwing up now, could you, son?"

"Apparently, *you* can't either, Dad."

A stunned silence filled the room.

"What do you mean?" Wallace asked, while Carolyn clenched her fists and closed her teary eyes.

"I think you know what I mean, Dad," Calvin said, in a measured way.

His parents looked to me for direction.

"It sounds like Calvin is feeling that it's time to bring some things out into the open," I offered. "Did you want to address his comment directly?"

"Is it appropriate?" Wallace asked, tentatively.

"At this juncture, I think you're better off being straight with him," I advised.

Wallace took a deep breath. "Calvin, I am very sorry to tell you that I've been having a relationship with another woman over this past year. I've put an end to it, but it's caused your mother great pain, and I'm trying to see if we can put it behind us."

Calvin glared at his father.

"Did you want to add anything, Carolyn?" I asked.

She wiped her eyes and took her son's hand. "Yes. What your dad has done has hurt me tremendously, but what we're discovering is that we *each* had let the other down. I wasn't the wife that your father wanted me to be, and he wasn't the husband that I wanted him to be. But we both want to stay married, and we both want it to work, and while we can't make any promises, we're going to give it a try. We didn't want you to have to know the details of our relationship, but I guess you're old enough, now. We would appreciate it if you'd keep it from your sisters, however. I don't think that they need to know anything."

Now it was Calvin who filled with tears. "How could you *do* this, Dad?"

"I'm trying to figure out the answer to that one, Calvin. I have some ideas, but mostly, I regret it terribly, and wish that I could push the rewind button and just do the last year over again."

"Perhaps you're wishing that Calvin could do the same thing," I wondered, trying to bring the focus back to what had initially brought them here.

"I guess you're right," Wallace said, wearily. "It's been a really horrible year. And I feel like I've been a fake, coming down on Calvin's behavior when my behavior has been just as reprehensible."

"Well, I don't think there's any question that some of the forces that were driving Calvin's behavior originated with your own behavior, behavior that he had a sense of or feeling for, but couldn't quite put his finger on. I think that that's what prompted him to act in such attention-getting ways."

"I guess it worked," Carolyn admitted, with a wintry smile.

"It did. His behavior was what got the two of you into my office, which might be a turning point in your marriage. It may seem odd to hear this, but I believe that Calvin was trying to sacrifice himself for the good of your marriage. Now, the question is, do you need him to continue to do so?"

"No," Wallace said, firmly.

"Then you need to tell him that. He has to hear that the two of you can take care of your marriage by yourself, that there won't be any more secrets, and that he's to go back to living the life of a normal teenager, not one who has to constantly shake his parents into an awareness of their dangerously drifting marriage."

"Calvin, I'm sorry for whatever we've done that led you to think that you needed to worry about our relationship," Wallace began. "The best thing you can do for us now is to let us work things out and stay out of trouble yourself. You're in a deep hole right now, and we're here to help you out of it, but we don't want you digging any new ones."

I turned to Carolyn. "What do you have to say about this to Calvin?"

"Honey, I should've known what was going on, and I'm angry at myself for not paying closer attention. But your father and I are going to learn from this, and we're not going to repeat any mistakes, just like we'd like you to learn from these last few months, and to not repeat those mistakes, either."

The rest of this session, and the several subsequent family sessions, were devoted to helping Calvin be as responsible as he could while his girlfriend proceeded through her pregnancy. I invited Carla and her mother into a session with Calvin and his parents, and we discussed together what was expected of these two young adults for the remaining months of gestation. Carla's mother remained opposed to an abortion but made sure that Carla took her prenatal care very seriously, which she did, and Calvin's parents insisted that Calvin join her for a couple of her obstetric appointments, which he did.

Meanwhile, Wallace was able to find a couple who were willing to adopt the baby, and who met with Carla and her mother several months before her due date. Carla eventually gave birth to a healthy baby girl, and the adoption went through with no more than the understandable amount of ambivalence on Carla's part.

Wallace and Carolyn continued to work with me to heal the betrayal of intimacy and restore love and trust, and eventually recommitted to each other with a renewal-of-vows ceremony that coincided with their twenty-fifth anniversary. Seeing that his parents were taking care of their own business, and having weathered the sobering experience of his girlfriend's pregnancy and childbirth, Calvin finally settled down and was able to keep himself in check.

The behavior that had at first seemed so outlandish to everyone had accomplished what Calvin had subconsciously meant for it to accomplish, and so could finally be foresworn and atoned for.

We have seen, in this case study, how teens are more likely to be, and to be seen as, good enough if they are being raised by two individuals in a good enough marriage. Here are some additional thoughts on how to go about creating such a marriage while ushering our children through adolescence:

FOCUS ON HORIZONTAL, RATHER THAN VERTICAL, LOYALTIES

Marriages function best, and children are most likely to thrive, when a couple's *horizontal* loyalties—those that exist specifically between the two of them—take precedence over their *vertical* loyalties—those that extend a generation up (to our parents and grandparents) or down (to our children).

An adolescent has to see that the primary filiation at home lies safely between her parents, rather than between her and her mother or her and her father, or between her parents and any of *their* parents. One of my first jobs with many of the families that I see is to gently begin lancing the cross-generational coalitions that have been cropping up for years, and that are probably at the root of the adolescent's presenting problem. In so doing, I often find that the presenting problem quickly disappears.

For example, in a situation in which a mother and father are constantly complaining about each other's parenting, providing ample opportunities for their devious teen to divide and conquer, I'll ask each of them to spend a week taking note of what his or her spouse is doing as a parent that appears to be appropriate, effective, or useful. Sponsoring their collaboration as partners helps to strengthen the horizontal loyalty between husband and wife and dilute the vertical loyalty between parent and child that has likely been undermining growth.

RECOMMIT TO YOUR MARRIAGE

Most of the parents of teens that I work with who are having difficulties with their marriage have been over-involved either with meeting their own needs of the needs of their teen. In both cases, however, the needs of the marital partners have been seriously neglected, and the relationship is crumbling as a result.

What I tell such couples is that if you really care about your teen, you'll make sure that you take care of your marriage, because of all the ingredients that we have control over as parents, a positive marital relationship is the one that may turn out to most significantly promote our teens' growth and our capacity to see them as good enough.

In Chapter 5, we looked at how trust results from a balance between how much we give and how much we receive in a relationship. Modeling a trustworthy marriage is a priceless gift to teenagers, and enormously enhances their ability to create their own trustworthy relationships. When the emotional exchange rate between a husband and wife is even and equitable, everyone in the family is the beneficiary.

To do this, however, we have to revisit the accumulated sins and hurts of our marriage in an effort to right old wrongs, redress old grievances, and settle old injustices. We have to realign the skewed and imbalanced aspects of our relationship so that we move back into a state of symmetry and parity. We have to challenge each other to resuscitate the forces that first attracted us to each other and restore them to their original luster. We have to take the risk of sharing more of our inner lives with our partner than we have ever done before so as to preserve and strengthen the relationship that is freighted by the burdens of arriving at midlife and raising a teenager.

Couples who actively take on the task of revitalizing their middle-aged marriage usually find that the process of raising adolescents can be gratifying rather than punishing, filled with satisfactions and rewards that more than compensate for the inevitable losses that need to be faced at this stage. Released from the day-to-day shackling that the rearing of younger children entails, we can experience our teens' growing separation from us as an opportunity to begin injecting our energies back into the marriage, rather than into childrearing, the opposite of what happened after childbirth. Our teens' sexual energy becomes something more than a destructive force that needs to be restricted and curtailed. Instead, we can tap into it as a motivating reminder that serves to rejuvenate our erotic liaisons, rather than a souvenir of what has been missing and is likely to remain lost.

Even the best marriages experience a myriad of small emotional divorces over the years, but couples who use their adolescents' impending departure as an awakening event are usually able not only to avoid divorce but just as importantly to reanimate the marital bond that has resolutely withstood the test of time.

BREAK OLD PARENTING PATTERNS AND START NEW ONES

In previous chapters, we have seen the many ways in which an individual's actions occur in a context rather than a vacuum, how our behaviors do not simply emerge from within us, but are engendered by the behaviors of whoever we are in relationship with, and vice versa. By the time that our children are teenagers, many of these reciprocal patterns within our marriage have been in place for a good amount of time and may have long outgrown their original purpose and value.

For instance, one spouse may "over-emote" and carry most of the feelings in the marriage while the other spouse "under-emotes" and carries very little. Or one spouse may "overfunction" and shoulder the lion's share of the childrearing responsibilities in the marriage while the other spouse "underfunctions" and shoulders almost none. Most spouses who have arranged themselves into assemblages of this sort will be quick to complain about all of the problems that result from their *partner's* tendencies, while maintaining the capacity to completely ignore their own tendencies, thus missing the ways in which each of them actually elicits the very behaviors that they find so aggravating. The result is that two parents may find themselves working very hard at parenting, but accomplishing absolutely nothing, because they are basically working at cross-purposes.

In one family I consulted with, a father who complained about his wife's leniency with their teenaged son persecuted him so relentlessly and aggressively that she felt she had no choice but to protect him from his father's wrath. But her mothering was so indulgently solicitous that her husband felt that he had no choice but to come down even harder on their son to ensure that he grew up to "become a man" and "learn some discipline." Of course, the harder Dad worked to toughen up this teenager, the harder Mom worked to soften him, and the mutually agitating conduct that each parent found so dismaying in the other was being propagated in the fertile breeding ground born of their clashing tactics.

Knowing that these patterns are common but generally poisonous to adolescent development, the best thing for a couple to do is to identify them, and for each partner to do some careful observations of what he or she might be doing that is contributing to the pattern. That is often all that's necessary to begin disrupting it, allow new, more balanced, and productive patterns to take root.

On a similar note, it's important to work together as much as possible; this reinforces not only your authority but also your marriage. Making sure that you don't abandon your spouse if he's in the midst of a skirmish with your teen, or that you don't back off to such an extent that you leave her "hung out to dry," will go a long way toward keeping a healthy hierarchy intact, as well as building a sense of marital teamwork.

Likewise, helping your partner disengage when he's sinking into another marathon dogfight will be of immense help. One couple I worked with came up with the ingenious idea of pushing buttons on the microwave when one had the feeling that the other was having their "buttons pushed" by their crafty daughter. Their good-natured solution helped stave off many a struggle and got them feeling more in league with each other as well.

FIGHT THE RIGHT FIGHTS, AND FIGHT THEM RIGHT

In the cartoon strip *Frank and Ernest*, Frank asks his therapist how he can stop being his own worst enemy and is told simply to "get married." Every working marriage needs to have a way of addressing and resolving conflict, but this is particularly true when raising teenagers, since both the frequency and intensity of conflict during this stage of life are likely to be quite high. Most couples in struggling marriages resort either to avoidance or eruption when contention arises.

As we saw amply demonstrated in Calvin's family, the worst conflicts may come about as the result of our efforts to avoid the smaller, more solvable conflicts that have been cropping up all along. Marching through your marriage in a clench of unuttered anger while resentments stealthily extend their malign influence, year after year, is one certain way to lay the groundwork for an unsatisfying marriage. In fact, in one study of divorcing couples, 70 percent were not identified as "highly conflictual," suggesting, to me, that these spouses had spent so much energy avoiding conflict that they must have eventually drifted so far apart that nothing was left between them anymore.

On the other hand, exploding with rage every time a disagreement arises doesn't make for a healthy marriage, either. Time and again, I have seen in my office the catastrophic effects that emotional combustibility has had on all family members, and how difficult it is to ever regain trust when physical and psychological boundaries have been violated by spousal or parental rage.

Adolescence is the stage in family development when parents finally need to find ways to settle their differences equitably, to negotiate the respectful compromises that don't leave either partner completely satisfied but still meet each partner's basic needs, and to show teens that differences of opinion between individuals can be assets, rather than liabilities, a source of relational growth and pleasure.

FORGIVE YOUR PARTNER AND YOURSELF

One of my supervisors in graduate school once commented that we should all be grateful for our spouses' flaws, because without them, our partner would probably have gone on to find someone better than us. This realization can serve as a humorous reminder that the lessons of forgiveness that we discussed in the context of childrearing apply to marriage as well. Just as our teens will quite dependably disillusion us, so, too, will our spouses, and the solution to both of these quandaries lies not in choosing to marinate in a stew of frustration and disappointment, but in releasing our partners from the expectation that they devote *their* lives to satisfying and completing *ours*.

The path toward marital forgiveness follows the same path as the one toward parental forgiveness—acknowledging the realistic and unrealistic expectations that we have been imposing on our spouse, finding a balance between give and take so that obligations can be met without either partner feeling angry (from *giving* too much) or guilty (from *getting* too much), and speaking the right words and performing the kind actions that will help us anneal our wounds. Marital forgiveness ultimately requires not just the capacity to remember but also the capacity to forget, or at least to not remember every single insult and injury quite so vividly.

Just as there is no perfect adolescent out there, waiting to gratify us, there is no perfect soulmate, either, but that doesn't mean that a marriage can't thrive nonetheless. In fact, it is in allowing our marred and incomplete selves to be revealed to each other, an ongoing enterprise that can only take place in an ongoing relationship, that we become most fully conscious and alive. Marriage may be the most humanizing haven that we will ever be privileged to construct and inhabit. When we take on the duties of love, suffer through its complex irreconcilabilities, and remain bound in the embrace of our imperfect but everlasting devotion to each other, we create the best of all possible worlds in which to care for and raise our imperfect teen.

There are numerous exercises that help to build better marriages when couples have reached a crossroads. Here are two that many of the parents I have worked with seem to have derived benefit from.

EXERCISE 8

1. Each of you is to make a list of what you believe your partner has done that has contributed to a state of martial conflict or stagnation.

2. Each of you is to make a second list of what you believe that you have done that has contributed to a state of marital conflict or stagnation.

3. Compare your lists and take note of where the overlaps and the gaps occur.

4. Pick *one item* from the first list that you'd like your partner to work on for a week.

5. Touch base in a week's time and see if these changes have made a difference.

EXERCISE 9

We have seen how our teens' problems often serve a function in their and their family's lives. Marital conflict is a problem that serves a relational function as well. It's often a way to help a husband and wife calibrate the balance between separateness and togetherness, a dynamic that is constantly in flux.

After all, fights are very versatile mechanisms. Through their heightened intensity, they can serve the purpose of bringing two people closer together by clearing the air and restoring connectedness. Or they can serve the purpose of pushing two people farther apart by stirring hostility and hurt feelings. In fact, it is not an unusual situation for me to hear a couple describing a fight and help them to realize that the same fight has had the opposite effect on both of them, one feeling warmer as a result, the other cooler.

I have often worked with couples who engage in chronic combat because they have come to rely on their fights to iron out, rather than talk out, their differing needs for closeness or space.

In this exercise, you are to check in with each other at least once a day for two weeks and observe yourself, take note of what level of closeness or separateness you are wanting, and share that information with your spouse. If you'd like, you can quantify it in a simple way on a scale of 1 to 10, 1 being a desire for complete separateness, such as "wanting to be left alone," 10 being a desire for complete engagement, such as "wanting to take a long walk together" or "wanting to make love." See if you can get a clearer sense of your and your partner's needs and how they ebb and flow over time.

When you do have a fight, try to view it through the lens of its function by asking yourself and each other these three questions.

1. Looking back at the time leading up to the fight, would you say that one or both of you wanted more separateness or more closeness than you were getting?

2. What impact did the fight turn out to have on your level of engagement? Did it accomplish what you (might have) wanted it to accomplish? How about for your partner?

3. In retrospect, would there have been any other way to establish a mutually satisfying balance between separateness and togetherness besides fighting? What did you try? What *could* you have tried, but didn't?

NINE

THE GOOD ENOUGH DIVORCE

It doesn't much signify whom one marries, for one is sure to find next morning that it was someone else.

—SAMUEL ROGERS

If you took everything that I have said about the challenges facing married parents who want to raise a good enough teen and raised it to the *n*th power, you'd have an understanding of the challenges facing parents who have divorced. Because of the complexities involved when parents gradually or abruptly dismantle a marriage, separate, embark on single parenthood, date, and contemplate new courtships and marriages, the expected developmental issues associated with adolescence can become quite fearsome, and the problematic ones can become absolutely hair-raising.

When confined in the crucible of a divorce, I have witnessed some parents who had previously been eminently sensible and judicious become absolutely septic with unappeasable anger. I have watched other parents who have had enormous experience and expertise dealing with emergencies and crises in their professional lives basically go limp and become totally avoidant and ineffectual. But worst of all, I have seen numerous healthy, vigorous teens go down in flames, immolating themselves on the blazing altar of their parents' failing, or failed, marriage.

This is not to say that a divorce has to be a disastrous trauma for an adolescent. For one thing, marriages that are abusive, high-conflict, stagnant, or altogether loveless weigh heavily on teenagers, and present neither an optimal climate for psychological growth nor a resplendent model for the intimate relationships that they are considering or actively pursuing.

Also, single-parent and stepfamily households have certain advantages for teens. Single-parent households, for example, can be run along cleaner, more efficient lines, as there is no need, in an everyday context, for negotiation between a mother and father. Executive decisions can subsequently be made that much more quickly and autonomously, and a (single) parental hierarchy established with greater calm and constancy. Also, the absence of the "other" parent, one whose presence had most likely contributed regularly to friction, can lead to the creation of a different kind of closeness between a single parent and a teen that hitherto might not have existed or even been possible.

Stepfamily arrangements can provide benefits, as well. The presence of stepparents can provide teens with new, unsullied adult role models whose commonsense composure enables them to function as mentor, advocate, adviser, affectionate "aunt or uncle," or a human balance to stabilize the family system that may still be experiencing emotional fluctuations in the aftermath of the divorce. A caring, patient, open-minded stepparent, one whose appeal may not yet have been sanded down by the unavoidable abrasions of years of daily contact, also gives teens the chance to play some different parts and experiment with innovative ways of engaging with, and being like, a new adult.

Because we have seen how adolescents worry about their parents and want to make sure that they're doing alright so that they can differentiate from them without undue guilt and anxiety, a remarriage can also help to emancipate teens and diminish their sense of obligation and concern. As one 16-year-old patient remarked to me privately, "Now that my dad's getting married, it's like I can *breathe* again. I'm not that crazy about his fiancée—she's too preppie for my liking—but at least *he's* happy with her, and that makes me happy. I used to feel so bad when I'd go out with my friends on weekends, and he'd watch me leave from the screen door, looking sort of sad, and then I'd come home and he'd be sitting there by himself in the dark, watching TV. Now I don't have to feel guilty, because he's finally got someone."

Likewise, stepsiblings offer opportunities as well. If there are younger ones, teens may benefit from the chance to develop a mentoring or counseling role themselves, guiding a younger brother or sister through the step-transition, a process which usually circles back and helps them with their own adjustment as well. If there are stepsiblings who are the same age or older, they can not only provide a thicker web of mutual support but also offer exposure to a broader peer network, as well as to different interests, activities, and ideologies.

Finally, while divorce tends not to be coveted or desirable at any stage of development, adolescents are often better suited to navigating its more treacherous rapids than younger children, and may consequently be more immune to its potentially damaging effects. Because they are at a point in their lives when they are already attempting to separate from their parents, they may display a stronger motivation and capacity to separate themselves, in a healthy way, from pernicious parental conflicts. They are usually able to more clearly identify and articulate their desires when it comes to custody and visitation arrangements, and even to begin to understand the complexity of working these out to everyone's satisfaction. And their ability to independently drive, bike, or use public transportation may allow them to more self-reliantly maintain their relationships with all family members and eliminate the pickups, dropoffs, and rendezvous that can become emotionally and logistically problematic for everyone involved. These factors all raise the likelihood that teens will master the crisis of a divorce and complete their childhood in sound and solid ways.

But there is no question that divorce can have a detrimental impact on teenagers. One reason for this is that the potential for increased separateness from at least one parent makes it difficult to do the intergenerational striving and struggling that is a developmental necessity during adolescence. The teen who only sees his mother or father every other weekend or less loses the continuity necessary to dive into conflict and then find a way out of it, to experience relational rupture and rapproachement on a regular basis.

The blurring of generational boundaries that is a typical but troublesome outcome of divorce can also impede adolescents' adaptation to and completion of their normal developmental tasks. For example, the coalitions that we spoke of in Chapter 8 can become that much more compelling and constraining under the dominion of a divorce. A socially isolated father may find himself growing inappropriately attached to his teenaged daughter, looking to her for the companionship and support that he now knows his former wife will never offer him. A hurt and vulnerable mother may hoist her adolescent son up into a spouse-like or peer relationship, hoping he'll join her in vigorously castigating and ostracizing her ex-husband, praising him if he does so, but punishing him if he dares not.

An embittered father may have difficulty distinguishing his 16-year-old son's snotty attitude from the condescension that characterized his former wife, mentally merge the two of them into the same unlikable individual, and then react to him in the same negative ways in which he reacted to her. A fed-up mother, having finally extracted herself from her dismal marriage to a life-long alcoholic, may find herself responding to her daughter's age-appropriate experiments with alcohol with misdirected rage and ill-considered consequences, thereby creating a tension-filled rift in their relationship at a time when support and understanding are critical.

A wrathful father may assume that his daughter's mood swings are signs of the same "psychiatric illness" that he believes his ex-wife should be diagnosed with, and asks the pediatrician to "put her on medicine" rather than looking at the ways in which his own biting taunts and retaliations consistently provoke outraged reactions in *both* females. A beleaguered mother may see no point in even bothering to set limits with her violent son when he tries to threaten and intimidate her into submission. After all, she never really had any impact on his savage and bullying father, either. So she simply capitulates, defining his aggression as "like father, like son," subconsciously hoping that they both wind up *in* jail and *out of* her life.

With all of these distorted reflections displayed in the family looking glass, is it any wonder that seeing teenagers as good

enough seems well-nigh impossible when a divorce makes it difficult to see them clearly at all?

But if all of these generational crossovers weren't bewildering
enough, we may then have to factor in the additional travails associated with beginning a stepfamily, the complications of which
can easily push a barely manageable stress level right over the top.
The etymological origin of "step" in stepfamily is rooted in the
middle-English word for bereaved, and a stepfamily still signals
an irrevocable loss to children. It is the final nail in the coffin that
contains the fantasy of their original parents' reconciliation, and
the termination of what may have been at least a workable, and
possibly desirable, arrangement with their unattached parents.
Every teen's reaction to her mother or father's remarriage will always include, to some degree, the fear that she will never be important to her parent again.

Because single parents tend to be more on the permissive and
indulgent side than married parents, the arrival of a stepparent
will unavoidably collide with teens' predictable wish to maintain
the chummy atmosphere that they had gotten used to and had
been enjoying. This clashing of cultures will be exacerbated when
stepparents eagerly envision their new marriage as a long-awaited
opportunity to finally become involved with rearing a child, or as
a second chance to overzealously rectify the childrearing mistakes
that prevailed during a previous marriage.

Meanwhile, territorial disputes can materialize as mothers and
fathers feel encroached upon by stepmothers and stepfathers, and
as new spouses experience the need to establish firm, impermeable
boundaries between their current marriage and their partners'
previous marriage. The triangulating conflicts that ensue can reproduce at a positively dizzying rate.

For example, a mother doesn't think that the new stepmother
should be allowed to set limits with her teenaged daughter when
her daughter is over there, while the father feels that his new wife
should be entitled to impose discipline when required. The
mother not-so-subtly tells her daughter that she needn't listen to
her stepmother. The daughter, of course, is delighted to act out
this sanctioned sedition, which prompts the stepmother to become angry with the father for not backing her up and wielding

firmer authority. The father, sensing his ex-wife's role as provocateur, subsequently attacks *her* for trying to incapacitate his new wife, which further cements the bond between mother and daughter as they rally around their dislike of the interloping stepmother and cast her in the role of rigid martinet.

In another case, a stepmother, who had an affair with her husband that ended his first marriage, strives to eliminate any contact between her husband and his ex-wife because (at some subconscious level) she still feels guilty and worries that he'll (justifiably) return to her. Feeling that he's too "soft" with his ex-wife, and that constantly giving in to her requests for greater child support or "extra funds" for kids' activities is reinforcing the cycle and keeping the two of them too connected with each other, she advises her husband to take a get-tough approach with his ex-wife, or to cut her off altogether, a step that he, out of his own guilt about the affair, is unlikely to take. When his 14-year-old son comes to him and says that "Mom can't afford" the pricey music camp that he has already been accepted to (without his father ever being told that he was auditioning), Dad is caught in the middle. Agreeing to subsidize the camp will surely antagonize his current wife and weaken their already strained relationship, but refusing to do so is likely to antagonize not only his ex-wife but his son as well, something that he is understandably loathe to do.

So it's easy to see how adolescents can feel afflicted by all these multiplying tensions, and try to mitigate them and resolve their divided loyalties in typical teenaged fashion—either by precipitously choosing sides (often, the side of the parent or stepparent that they feel is most vulnerable and dependent), or by desperately playing one side against the other, maneuvers that all family members are now less protected from.

Of course, these territorial disputes do not seethe solely at the adult level. Teens and their stepsiblings may find themselves at war as well, fighting battles that are actually echoes of ignored, denied, or unresolved conflicts that exist between their parents and stepparents.

For example, adolescents may feel that their parents unfairly compare them with their pristine, impeccable stepsiblings, who, as new rivals on the scene, and without any unhappy history or reminders of despised former spouses, may be more than a little appealing to a teen's mother or father. Naturally, they'll address this problem by working diligently to expose their stepsiblings' blemishes by complaining about them, provoking them, or setting them up.

So a daughter will complain to her father that her stepsister went into her room and took her CD player without asking, and insist that Dad bring this up with the stepmom. When Dad does so, he'll learn from his wife that *his* daughter "started it" by going into *her* daughter's room without permission and using her makeup. His daughter, of course, will deny having done so, or defend it by saying that, prior to that, the stepsister had taken one of her favorite sweaters and worn it to school, then left it crumpled in a heap on the floor. If Dad is a big enough glutton for punishment that he brings this up with his wife, she'll be quick to report that his daughter told malicious lies about her daughter at school, implying that she was a slut and ruining her burgeoning relationship with her boyfriend. Where will it all end?

And finally, no stepfamily is conceived without sexual conflicts crystallizing around it. Adolescents whose parents are moving toward or into remarriage have to deal with the disturbingly conspicuous uncovering of their parents' sexuality and find ways to contend with it to a greater extent than they probably would have if their parents had remained celibate or were still back in their comfortably familiar previous marriage. So at a juncture when they might need their same-sex or opposite-sex parent's interest in and support of their own sexual development, or when they just might not want to have to deal with the realities of their parents' sex life at all, they are forced to witness parents who may overtly be cultivating their sexual renaissance, and who perhaps may even be in unspoken competition with their teenager regarding whose sexual activity is more fulminating and adventurous. The unsettling possibility that sexual desire may also be stirred between a teen and his or her stepsiblings or stepparent further confounds family clarity and supplies another dose of anxiety for an already perturbed and fumbling federation.

Experiencing unmistakable resentment about this intricate matrix of post-divorce shifts in their *old* roles and relationships, teens are likely to display flagrant resistance to taking on the *new* roles and relationships that are being foisted on them. Parents who are enthusiastically pushing for much sought-after cohesion and conformity in a stepfamily when their teens are hell-bent on differentiating and distinguishing themselves from this family are cooking up a surefire recipe for disaster.

As we saw in Chapter 6, when families do not find ways to successfully adapt to necessary growth, teenagers are often the ones who call attention to the obsolete, outmoded equilibrium through their problematic or symptomatic behavior. One of the challenges of a divorce is that family members tend to become more obdurate and unyielding at a time when elasticity and accommodation are really what are called for.

Let's take a look at one family that was struggling to make a successful post-divorce adjustment, and some of the adaptations that they eventually learned to make.

Jacob contacted me by telephone to schedule an appointment after he noticed a series of raised scars on his daughter, Fatima's, calves and forearms. When I suggested that the initial meeting include Fatima's mother, he told me that they were divorced, that he had sole legal custody, and that Fatima had asked him to promise not to tell her mom what he had discovered. He also disclosed that there was a long and acrimonious history between him and his ex-wife, and that he didn't think it would be productive for them to be in the same room together at this point.

I agreed to meet with Fatima and him without her mother for an initial evaluation, but made it clear to him that, should they continue working with me, I would at some point be including her mother in the treatment. Jacob reluctantly agreed to this plan, reminding me once again that it was Fatima's wish that her mother not know anything and implying that his ex-wife wouldn't participate even if she were invited.

During the first interview, Fatima appeared unnervingly matter-of-fact as she detailed how frequently she resorted to self-mutilation, and she calmly lifted her shirt sleeves and pants legs to show me the long streaks of red welts.

"I really only do it because it feels good. It feels better than anything I know how to do. It's the only thing that makes the pain go away. It's the only thing that makes me forget."

"What is it that you want to forget?" I asked.

Her eyes brimmed. "Everything, pretty much."

"How did you first come up with the idea of carving yourself to feel better?"

"One of my friends does it, and I noticed her arms, and I asked her about it, and she told me. And so I started doing it. What's so bad, really? Some girls put on makeup or color their hair or have all these piercing. I slice my arms and legs."

"So when did you start slicing your arms and legs?"

"Almost a year ago."

I turned to Jacob to get some perspective from him.

"When did you become aware that Fatima was carving herself?"

"Only last week, right before I called you."

"So she was able to keep this a secret from you for almost a year?"

"I guess so," he admitted, looking uncomfortable.

"Was there anything in particular that was going on a year ago that you think might have contributed to Fatima coming up with such an unusual way of expressing herself?"

"*Expressing* herself? You call this expressing herself? It makes me sick, absolutely nauseous, to think of my beautiful daughter slicing up her arms and legs. What could she possibly be expressing by *destroying* herself?" he asked, incredulous.

"I guess that's what we're here to figure out, but I think we have to begin with the assumption that Fatima's trying to express something. After all, a moment ago she said that she doesn't see a whole lot of difference between what she does and what other girls do to create a 'look'—so, to her, this might be just another form of divulging or accentuating or adorning some aspect of herself, kind of like lipstick or nose rings or orange hair might do." I smiled at Fatima, who looked at me quizzically.

"Fatima, do *you* have any sense of what was going on about a year ago that might have led to your decision to starting carving yourself?"

Her forehead puckered as she thought about my question. "Not really," she replied after a few moments. "Like I said, it was more that one of my girlfriends was doing it."

I turned back to Jacob. "When did you and Fatima's mom separate?"

"Well, things started falling apart a while back, but we didn't actually separate until three years ago."

"And when did the two of you divorce?"

"I guess the divorce became final about a year ago." I waited a beat for either one of them to acknowledge that that was about the time that Fatima had started mutilating herself, but neither seemed aware of this.

"Have either of you remarried?"

"*I* haven't," Jacob said, "but her mom . . ." He looked over at Fatima, who stared back at him, narrowing her eyes angrily.

"Go ahead," she urged her father, with an edge in her voice.

"Fatima's mother wants to be with women—that was the reason our marriage ended. Right after we divorced, her partner moved in with her. So I guess you could say she's *sort of* remarried, but who knows how long this one will last."

Jacob then asked if he might have a few minutes with me alone to delineate his marital history without Fatima present. His daughter stalked off to the waiting room, muttering imprecations and slamming the door on her way out. He went on to explain that his ex-wife, Carmen, had always struggled with her sexual identity but that after their second child was born, Fatima's younger brother, Felix, Carmen found it too hard to continue "living a double life" and began actively dating women.

Jacob explained that he initially tried to see if they could still make their marriage work, but it eventually became too difficult. "She was spending all of her time with her lesbian friends, going to lesbian bars and spending all night in lesbian chat-rooms on-line, and a husband can take only so much. She was never unkind to me, but there just wasn't anything left between us after a while, if you know what I mean. By the time we separated, our marriage had been over for years."

"How was it decided that you would retain custody of the kids?" I wondered.

"Not very easily. There weren't really any property disputes between Carmen and me, but custody was a big bone of contention between us. I just didn't think the children should be raised by someone who's so busy cultivating her social life that she doesn't have any time for them. My focus is on the children, and it always will be. I date now and then, but I don't know that I'll *ever* consider remarrying. I can't say the same thing for their mother."

"So how did the two of you resolve your disagreement?"

"Well, the reality is, she didn't put up much of a fight. At least not much of a legal fight. I hired a very good attorney and gave her a lot to work with, and she made a very strong case for my having custody when we went to court. Over the last few months of our legal battle, Carmen didn't even have an attorney, she was representing herself, probably because she ran out of money. In any case, the judge took my side and awarded me full custody. They visit her every other weekend and one evening a week, and spend a couple of weeks with her in the summer."

"How did your children react to the decision?"

"They basically went along with it. I mean, in a way it meant less change for them. They got to remain in the house, because Carmen was the one who moved out, and, like I said, I run a pretty stable ship. I often work from home, have a lot of flexibility, and really put myself out for the kids. So they were pretty much okay with it. Even when Carmen has the kids for weekend visits, she doesn't put her social life on hold. She'll have parties and the kids'll stay up later than they should with all those people over, or she'll take them out with her to go to a movie with her friends, and they won't get back home until close to midnight."

"How did Carmen react to the custody decision?"

"She was frosted—didn't handle it very well at all. Our separation had been fairly amicable, but once we went through court, it really set us apart from each other. We haven't communicated well since then. But I did what I had to do. I did what I believed was best. I made plenty of compromises during the marriage, but I wasn't going to make any when it came to the kids' welfare, I can tell you that."

"Have either of the children ever expressed an interest in having more time with their mother?"

"No," he snapped, "and I'm not sure I'd agree to it anyway, even if they did." The tautness of his tone suggested to me that perhaps this was an issue that might be fermenting more than anyone had thus far let on.

I then asked for some time alone with Fatima in an effort to see what she might share with me without her father in the room.

"How's the current arrangement working out for you in terms of time with your mom and time with your dad?" I began.

"*What* time with my mom? I almost never get to see her."

"You'd like to see her more than you do?"

"*Duh*—you think it's fun for a girl to live only with her father and younger brother?"

"Have you brought this wish up with anyone?"

"Why bother? My dad'll never agree to it, and my mom's not strong enough to take him on, so she's not going to do anything."

"Except that, at your age, I think it's natural to want to have some say in how your time is spent. I haven't met many adolescents whose parents are divorced who don't have some thoughts from time to time about how to modify a custody or visitation arrangement."

"Oh, I'd love to have some say. But you obviously don't know my dad. He'd hit the ceiling if I told him I wanted to be with my mom."

"That must put you in an awkward bind—wanting to spend more time with your mom, but not sure that she would support it or your dad would agree to it."

Fatima grew quiet. I noticed her slowly stroking the jagged scars on her arm.

"You know, I mentioned earlier that I viewed cutting yourself as a form of expressing yourself. I'm wondering, being that you started doing it around the time that your parents divorced and your mom's partner moved in with her, if it might be related to some of your strong feelings about all of these changes."

A tear rolled silently down Fatima's flushed cheeks. "I never thought that before," she murmured softly.

"Maybe it's worth pursuing," I suggested. "I don't know how you wouldn't have some very hurt and angry feelings about how your family life has played out, but if you don't feel like you're entitled to voice these feelings or that you're going to be listened to, these feelings might just get buried. Then, you'd kind of have to hack or scratch away at the surface to get at them—in your case, literally."

At this point Fatima burst forth with a bundle of pent-up thoughts, telling me that part of her really wanted to live with her mom, not just visit her, but that she wasn't sure that her mother wanted her there, that she felt guilty because her dad "works so hard to give us a good home," and that she was still trying to make sense of her mother's sexual preference and had some fears that she might "catch gayness" if she spent too much time with her mom. When I asked her if she might like me to intervene and see if I could promote some discussions of these important matters with, and between, her parents, she nodded happily. I also invited her to give some additional thought to my hypothesis about the origin of her self-harming and to observe and keep a journal of what she was feeling when she sliced, or felt like slicing, her arms.

As I anticipated, Jacob wasn't happy when I brought him back into my office and explained to him that, to be of some help, I would need to meet Fatima with her mother, as well, "to get the whole picture." But when he asked Fatima what *she* thought about a meeting with her mom, and Fatima told him that she thought it would be "cool," he relented and provided me with Carmen's phone number.

I began my session with Carmen and Fatima by asking Carmen if she knew why Fatima's father had initially contacted me. "I'm guessing Fatima's having some problems, but I also know that Jacob likes to see himself as Superdad, overreacts to everything, wants to blame everything on me, and keep me out of the loop at the same time. From my perspective, there's *no* problem that he can't somehow tie back into my being gay or my decision to end the marriage."

"Fatima, did you want to fill your mom in on what your dad's been concerned about?"

"Do I *have* to?" she asked, not sounding entirely resistant to the idea.

"Well, she's going to find out one way or another. I'd just as soon she heard it from you."

Fatima quickly rolled up her sleeves and pant legs and displayed her scars to her mother. A slight smile crossed her lips as she sat back to watch the reaction.

Carmen was almost too horrified for words. "What . . . when . . . Fatima, what's been *happening* to you? What is this all *about*?"

"I've been cutting myself. It makes me feel better. I've been doing it for about a year, now. Dr. Sachs thinks I do it because I'm upset about how things have been going and haven't been able to talk about it to anyone." I had to admit being impressed with her concise summary of our previous conversation.

"But what's got you so upset?" Carmen's face was still registering shock.

"I've been thinking about that, and here's what I've come up with," Fatima began confidently. She had clearly done her homework. "I'm upset because you guys are divorced. I'm upset that you guys can't even talk to each other because you're still so mad at each other. I'm upset because I'm stuck living with Dad and Felix, and Felix *really* gets on my nerves. I'm upset because you seem more interested in being gay than being my mother. And I'm upset because I've been slicing my arms for almost a year and you never even noticed."

Carmen stared at her in disbelief, trying to digest this powerful condensation of her daughter's hitherto unspoken feelings. Gradually gathering her thoughts, she began to try to explain herself.

"Fatima, I would've liked nothing better than to have gotten custody, or at least *shared* custody, of you and Felix and to have had you guys living with me and visiting your father, instead of the other way around. But your dad was so convinced that you kids were better off with him, and he was more willing to fight this in court than I was. I just didn't have the heart or the money to put you guys through a protracted court case, and have to have you interviewed by attorneys and judges and therapists. It just didn't feel right to have to fight for you, and I decided I'd just try to make the best of it.

"I know that your father is very angry with me for leaving him, and when I first married him, I really hoped that I could be happy with him. He's a good, kind man, and part of me will always love him despite how angry I am with him. But I simply couldn't hide from myself anymore, year after year. I was getting more and more sick and more and more depressed. I hope that you never have to live a lie, *ever,* because it's an absolutely terrible way to live."

"But you just don't seem that *interested* in me, Mom, you seem like you've got your own life now, and there's no room for *me* in it."

"Honey, I *so* want you in my life, you don't know how much I want you in my life. But you haven't seemed very interested in me, either. When you come over, all that you do is hole up in the bedroom with your headphones on or fight with Felix. You never seem to want to talk to me or do anything with us. I know that it's awkward now that Sheila is living with me, but you could at least be *nice* to her, at least say hi to her—she'd love to get to know you. How could I possibly know that you want to spend more time with me when you seem to shut down during the time that you already spend with me?"

Fatima started to cry. Carmen looked at her helplessly.

"When your daughter becomes tearful, what is it that you'd like to say or do?" I asked Carmen gently.

"I just want to go over and hold her and make it all better."

"Then maybe you should try."

"Would that be all right with you, Fatima?" Carmen asked, gingerly.

Fatima nodded silently, Carmen went over to hug her, and they rocked in each other's arms, and wept. After a few minutes, they smilingly brushed away each other's tears, and Carmen went back to her seat.

"How are you feeling now, Fatima?"

"Better," she said, shyly.

"There's a lot of connecting that the two of you have to do," I proposed, "and it doesn't all have to take place in my office. Maybe it's time to become reacquainted with each other so that you know each other better and can decide what you think is best."

Carmen agreed. "Fatima's right, in a way. I really haven't been there in the way that I should be for my daughter. But sometimes it's easy to forget that she might need me. I see her so infrequently, and she's so independent."

"A daughter *always* needs her mother," I observed, "especially when she's in the midst of adolescence."

"You can say that again," she concurred. "I would've loved to have had my mother more involved in my life when I was Fatima's age, because I was struggling with this whole sexual identity thing, knowing inside I was gay but not feeling like I could tell anyone. So I know how lonely I felt, and how much I envied those girls who were close with their mothers, who could *talk* with them."

"But that's how I've felt with you, Mom," Fatima interjected. "I'd love to be with you more, but it never seemed important to you, or at least not as important as other things were."

Carmen looked stricken as she considered the unfavorable parallels between her mom and herself that she had apparently not recognized before. "Well, maybe it's finally time for that to change," she said, assertively.

"Just out of curiosity, Fatima," I asked, as we were finishing up, "do you have much of an urge to cut yourself right now?"

She thought for a second, as if taking her own emotional temperature, and then grinned. "Not at all. I guess there's nothing like a good cry."

"I guess not. Maybe we were right, maybe the cutting was the best way you knew to express yourself, but now that we've found another way, cutting may not be so necessary anymore. It looks like you found a way to 'go below the surface' that didn't involve using a knife."

Carmen and Fatima agreed to do some additional talking about their relationship, and what they wanted with and from each other at this point in their lives. Meanwhile, I brought Jacob back in for a follow-up session to see if there was much room to maneuver.

When I summarized the content of my session with his daughter and ex-wife, his predictable response was, "I *knew* that was going to happen. That's why I didn't want her involved. Look, Dr. Sachs, you may have a good reputation, and I don't mean any disrespect when I say this, but I don't think you've met anyone like Carmen before. I'm sure she put on a good show for you, and I'm sure she said what you wanted to hear about what kind of mom she wants to be, but you don't really know the history here. You don't know the extent to which I've been in charge of the kids all these years. You don't know how many nights she was out with her lesbian pals while I was home, working on the kids' homework and making sure they did their reading and brushed their teeth and took their showers."

"Jacob, I don't want to underestimate for a moment how much of an anchor you've been for the kids over the years, and it's impossible for me to know what things were really like when you were married to Carmen. I certainly *can* say that we'd all be better off if there were more fathers like you who were so actively involved in their children's lives.

"But I can also tell you that it's quite common for teenagers whose parents have divorced to, at some point, desire to live with or spend more time with their non-custodial parent, even if their custodial parent has been doing a fine job. And this desire is especially strong when teens are the same gender as their non-custodial parent. I'm not saying that Fatima should or shouldn't live with her mother, or should or shouldn't spend more time with her. What I *am* saying is that Fatima doesn't feel that she can have an honest conversation with you about this issue because she's afraid you'll be hurt or angry with her. And until she can have an honest conversation with you, she's likely going to speak her mind with her knife, rather than with her words."

"So I'm supposed to just give in and send her off to her mother? I know what you're saying about adolescents and their same-sex parent, but what about when their same-sex parent is gay? Don't you think that Fatima might have some mixed feelings about living with her mother and her mother's female lover?"

"I'm sure she does. And as I said before, I'm not recommending or discouraging a change in her living situation. That really isn't the answer. The answer is in her knowing that you love her so much that you are willing to hear her out, even if what you hear is not what you *want* to hear. And when she knows this, no matter where she lives or who she spends time with, she'll be less likely to cut herself and more likely to grow up in a healthy way. But if she continues to believe that she can't speak with you honestly, you may always have her in your home, but she'll never feel that you've had her in your heart."

Jacob and I continued to bat this around for the rest of the session. During our discussion, one interesting thing I learned was that he had an older sister who had been killed in a car accident when he was 12 and she was 15. In fact, he had named Fatima after this sister, Faith. It took great courage for Jacob to consider the possibility that some of his reluctance to "let go" of Fatima (who was now the age that Faith was when she had died) had to do with his unresolved grief for his sister and his (admittedly irrational) fear that, as with Faith, once he "let go," he'd never see Fatima again.

Several more sessions followed as the family worked to sort things out. I brought Felix, Fatima's younger brother in, to get his take on things. I had Fatima and Carmen back to continue to work on healing their relationship with each other. I invited Fatima and her father back to promote a more direct dialogue between the two of them about her needs and wants. I brought Carmen and her partner, Sheila, in, to discuss the logistics and realities of Fatima being there more often. I scheduled a session with Jacob and Carmen, in an effort to promote more of an understanding between the two of them and enable them to come up with a modification to the current custody-visitation arrangement without having to return to court.

After some time, with more trust having been built, I also scheduled a session with Jacob, Carmen, and Sheila, so that they all could become acquainted with each other, and so that some of Jacob's fears could be put to rest. Coincidentally, Jacob and Sheila were both engineers, which provided them with a bridge that helped ease the awkwardness of their relationship with each other.

In a couple of individual meetings with Fatima we discussed other ways for her to purge her anger that did not involve self-mutilation. Harking back to her initial metaphor of slicing being like "putting on makeup," we decided that whenever she had the urge to cut herself somewhere, she would color that part of her body with lipstick. She would then slice a lemon or grapefruit instead and suck out the juice. This would help to mimic the intense, bracing feel of the self-harming without her having to do any actual harm.

Eventually, it was agreed that Fatima would spend one week living with her mother and one week living with her father. Carmen was pleased that she would have more of a chance to get closer to her daughter, Jacob was pleased that he wouldn't have to give up Fatima entirely; Felix was pleased because he got more alone time with his father without his big sister in his hair; and

Fatima was pleased that she was able to preserve her relationship with her father while deepening her relationship with her mother.

It also meant a lot to Fatima that her mother and father resumed contact with each other. In a final meeting with Fatima and both of her parents, she confessed, "You guys don't know how terrible it was for me to know that you couldn't even talk to each other, that neither of you wanted to pick up the phone even if it was just to figure out who was going to pick Felix and me up. It made me want to scream."

"It makes me think, Fatima, that your cutting yourself had another level of symbolism to it, which is that it signified the division between your parents, a division that, you must have known, was not healthy for any of you. I was never pleased with your decision to cut yourself, but I have to say that I was always struck by your commitment to trying to convey your feelings, directly or indirectly. You've worked very hard, sometimes at your own expense, but hard just the same, to help your parents get past their old hurts and move forward."

Meanwhile, with much more out in the open and the family finally having found a way to adapt successfully, Fatima's problem—self-harming—diminished entirely, and we finished up our work together.

An epilogue occurred about a year later, when Jacob called to tell me that he had begun dating again and wanted some advice on how to address this with Fatima and Felix. During our appointment, he did acknowledge that the process of addressing Fatima's buried feelings about the divorce had helped him to see that he needed to move on, too. "I realize, now, that I was pretty frightened about starting to date, and wondering if there was something wrong with me for having selected a spouse who was gay. As you said, maybe I was holding on to Fatima a little too closely because of that business with my sister's death, which I think is a good point. But maybe I was *also* holding on to the kids as a way to keep myself safe, to have an excuse not to get out there and try again, which really isn't very fair to them."

Meanwhile, around the same time, Fatima sent me a poem that she had written in her English class that contained the following stanza, one that captured the meaning behind her symptom with astonishing clarity.

The knife that cut my family
Became the knife I used to cut me
Their blood was my blood,
My blood was their blood
With each slice
I said my sad little good-bye

Fatima's ability to nudge the family into saying some "sad little good-byes" had allowed all of them to say hello to some new and enlivening possibilities.

Here are some additional steps to take in the direction of creating a family life after divorce that does not ensnare adolescents and compromise their growth and that instead contributes to the development of good enough teens.

COMPLETING THE DIVORCE

Many parents I've worked with are legally divorced but still emotionally betrothed combatants who have not been able to negotiate a truce with peace, a cease-fire with disarmament. This situation can manifest itself in different ways, but they are all basically identical, like flip sides of the same coin. Some parents maintain an emotional entanglement with their ex-spouse, reacting just as strongly to the pinpricks, button pushing, and outright manipulations as they did when they were living together. Others work overly hard to create a *fraudulent* sense of cohesion and closeness as if to mask the reality of the divorce. They interact as if they are merely geographically separated and never experienced any of the dissatisfactions and differences of opinion that led to the end of the marriage. Some find themselves in continuous conflict with their former spouse around even the most benign, neutral issues, while others cut themselves off entirely as a way of trying to manage continuous conflict and allow no communication at all to cross their tightly guarded borders.

The unresolved hurt and anger that fuels all of these states is a powerful emotional adhesive that continues to bind a mother and father together, and until a couple finds a way to dissolve the ad-hesive, they will remain fused, to their own and their teenager's detriment. As we have already seen in this and previous chapters, adolescents will take matters into their own hands when they feel that their parents are stuck, or in this case stuck *together,* and en-gage in what might be debatable and dubious efforts to get them *unstuck.* When a divorce remains psychologically unfinished, everyone is held hostage by the old hostilities.

Adolescents become more confident that there has been a suc-cessful resolution of a divorce only when they can see that their parents are usually able to be courteous and respectful to each other, to be in proximity to each other without anyone being overly uncomfortable, and to effectively exchange childrearing in-formation and address conjoint parenting decisions through open, honest, and emotionally unimpeded channels.

They do not have to see you in warm and constant contact with their other parent (although, fortuitously, that sometimes can happen) or witness you getting to the point where you go out for coffee with your ex's new spouse, or develop a doting relationship with your ex's new birth or stepchildren. In fact, when divorced parents work too hard to concoct an artificially engaged or en-dearing relationship with each other in a well-intended effort to protect their children from the realities of the divorce, it generally winds up confusing everyone, making it harder than necessary for each individual to grieve for the loss of the original family's unity and move on.

In situations in which the marital climate was openly and un-relentingly contentious, or when the separation process was pro-longed and highly litigious, simply being decent to and disengaged from each other may be all that's achievable. This is fine as well—and often quite a remarkable accomplishment. In these cases, it may have to be understood that the air will *never* be cleared, and that animosity may forever cloud the family's horizon, but that a complete breakdown of civility and dialogue can still be avoided. This might mean confining communication with each other to e-mail or voice-mail messages, or sitting apart from each other at events, games, and performances so that flareups do not occur, while still being able to nod to each other in recognition and re-tain the capacity to quietly share in parental pride.

Under no circumstances should the teen be placed in the middle, such as by being asked to take sides, ferry messages back and forth between parents, or protect either parent from discomfort with the situation. This not only places an adolescent at tremendous risk, it keeps an extremely dangerous equilibrium in place and actually prevents the essential completion of the divorce from ever taking place.

RESTORING AND PRESERVING THE HIERARCHY

No matter what the status of the relationship between a teen's parents, there still needs to be a working hierarchy in place, one in which all the caring adults maintain executive leadership and no one's authority is sabotaged for any reason. Adolescents, as we have seen, are mercenaries and won't hesitate to exploit an unstable situation for their own short-term gain. When they sense gaps in the parental system—and believe me, if gaps are there, teens will know it—they'll scamper through them in the blink of an eye.

If you are a single parent following a divorce, you must watch the very strong tendency to relinquish your sovereignty over the family's jurisdiction and promote your teen to peer, or near peer, status. After all, who better to ease the loneliness of solo parenthood than the children you are raising, particularly when the children are becoming more adult-like, and are delighted to enjoy the benefits of their suddenly elevated status.

Likewise, it's equally tempting to try to mobilize your teen around you, to persuade him to sympathetically side with you against your evil ex-spouse so that you are better able to deal with the fact that you are still smarting from the demise of your marriage. The problem here is that the two of you will wind up behaving more like a pair of victimized siblings than like a functional, hierarchically intact parent-child system.

While these kinds of arrangements have obvious short-term appeal for both generations, they always backfire. This can happen when you finally decide that you actually do need to set some limits and invoke some consequences that are bound to make a teen unhappy, when he realizes that, with or without justification, you have been misappropriating his allegiance so that you can better deal with your own frustration, or when you decide to remarry and wind up alienating your previously close teenage confidante by becoming close with your new partner.

Adolescents generally do not take very kindly to parental efforts to "turn back the clock," and trying to abruptly shift from a permissive state of affable indulgence to one of strict vigilance or emotional disengagement will not be tolerated without a fight. Better to avoid that kind of enmeshment in the first place, because once it takes hold, it's very hard to wrest free.

By the same token, whether the parental system consists of just two parents or two parents with a stepparent or two added into the mix, all of the parents have to work hard to speak together in one, unified voice. Otherwise, the chorus of competing, cacophonous voices will essentially cancel each other out, and the teen will hear nothing.

While stepparents, due to their relative freshness, objectivity, and emotional neutrality, may contribute in meaningful ways to the redesign of the family hierarchy, that doesn't mean that the responsibility of maintaining it should be handed over to them. Ideally, both of the original parents should be entrusted to continue, amplify, or improve whatever alliance they originally had in place when they were married, and then find ways to gradually invite their new partner(s) into the reconstructed administration.

TEENS SHOULD GET A *VOTE*, NOT A *VETO*, WHEN IT COMES TO DECISIONS THAT AFFECT THEM

One result of an ineffective hierarchy, as we have learned in previous chapters, is that adolescents will always fight for power, but when too much power is ceded to them, they become anxious and are prone to acting with impaired judgment. In divorced families, teenagers will insist on having their *say* when it comes to issues that intimately affect them, such as visitation, custody, and remarriage, but that doesn't mean it's always in their best interest to get their *way*. Parental boundaries must always be clearly in place, with the understanding that the adults are responsible for making any final decisions.

I have worked with families in which mothers or fathers asked their teenaged sons or daughters to "approve" of their prospective spouse, making it clear that "I won't marry him unless my children are comfortable." I have seen situations in which a parent leaves a visitation arrangement entirely up to the adolescent, with no expectation that a legal agreement that was signed by both parties in court after months—maybe even after years—of negotiation should be upheld.

Of course, it is appropriate for children to be given increasing input into the decision-making process as they grow. For example, Dewey had enjoyed his every-other-week Friday-Tuesday weekends with his two children, Max, 16, and Shana, 14, since he and their mother had separated six years before. Now, however, Max had a weekend job that started at 7 A.M., stocking shelves at a grocery store that was only a few minutes from his mother's house but that was a good half-hour from his father's house. He also had a girlfriend who he generally got together with on Friday and Saturday nights and who also lived much closer to his mother than his father.

Max told Dewey that he'd rather be able to stay at his mother's house on Friday and Saturday night so that it'd be easier for him to see his girlfriend, and so that he'd be able to sleep in a little bit longer on Saturday and Sunday before heading out to work, an arrangement that his mother had already agreed to. Dewey was initially disappointed that his twice-monthly visits from Max were going to shrink in half, from four nights to two. He was also concerned that Shana would soon follow suit and want to reduce her visitation time.

However, he also understood what a good thing it was for Max to have a job and realized that a 16-year-old boy with a girlfriend isn't likely to want to hang around with his father and younger sister on weekend evenings, anyway. So he proposed a compromise. Max could stay at his mother's on Friday and Saturday nights, but he was to reserve Sunday afternoon, once he was done work, for the three of them to do something special together.

At first, Max balked at this, not wanting to tie up his Sunday afternoons either, which were usually when he caught up on his homework. However, Dewey promised that no matter what they did, they would be home by late Sunday afternoon so that Max would have the rest of the evening to study or complete his assignments. He also reminded Max that he didn't have to go out every Friday and Saturday·night if he had particularly heavy academic responsibilities on certain weekends, and that Saturday afternoon was a time that he could get some work done as well.

Everyone eventually agreed to the compromise, and while Dewey had to get used to seeing less of Max, he realized that that he would be seeing less of him even if Max lived with him full-time, because he was becoming more social, more a part of the world outside of the family. Interestingly, Shana did not initially ask for a subsequent reduction in her visitation time. In fact, she seemed to enjoy the visits with her father a little more than usual now that her brother, who was somewhat attention-hungry, wasn't always there to hog their dad. However, seeing that her father and brother were able to renovate their visitation schedule in a mutually satisfying way reassured her that the same process could take place down the road for her, should she initiate it.

CUSTODY AND VISITATION DISPUTES

Over the years, I have worked with numerous divorced parents who have custody of their children and who want to limit the contact that their children have with their noncustodial parent. Others in similar situations justify, support, or perhaps even quietly (or not so quietly) celebrate their teen's detachment from or lack of interest in the "other" parent, mostly because they don't want her to be overly exposed to or influenced by the ex's "malignance."

Interestingly, however, what I generally see over time is that the parent that teens are most detached from, for whatever reason, is generally the parent that they either become most similar to or the parent whom their eventual intimate partner most closely comes to resemble. This means that, paradoxically, if you don't want your child to become too much like your ex-spouse, the best way to prevent this is actually to support, rather than limit, their contact with each other. The exposure from these visits may enable your teen to "immunize" herself against whatever bad influence may exist in the present, so that she's less likely to be seriously infected by it in the future.

Remember that, aside from situations in which there is outright abuse or flagrant irresponsibility, the damage that you fear that your adolescent will sustain from your flawed ex-spouse is generally going to be less than the damage sustained if your ex-spouse is not present at all or if your adolescent continues to idealize this parent, which is likely to be the ultimate outcome of thwarted contact during the teenage years. (Also keep in mind, as we saw earlier in the case of Fatima, that the desire to spend some time living with one's non-custodial parent is a normal part of an adolescent's identity formation and to be expected.)

In these highly charged circumstances, it can become very easy for one parent to get finagled into a conflict that involves the teen and the other parent, but it is always best to avoid destructive triangles of this sort. For example, just because your ex and your son send out an SOS during their visit and insist that things are going so poorly that you must drop everything and pick him up before the visit is officially over, that doesn't mean that you should rush to the rescue. Or just because your daughter regularly complains about her non-custodial parent as she prepares to leave for a visit or upon her return doesn't mean that you have to feel committed to easing her pain or solving her problem. Staying as disengaged as possible, difficult as it may be, is the best solution for everyone.

I have also worked with many families in which adolescents consistently refuse visits with their noncustodial parent. This may have been going on for some time, or it may have surfaced recently, but the scenario is usually the same.

On the one hand, the custodial parent does not want to be in the position of "forcing" his or her teen to visit the other parent. "It's fine with me if he wants to visit his father, but he's fourteen years old, now. I can't make this happen—it's for the two of them to work out." On the other hand, the spurned parent believes that the teen's refusal to visit is in fact a response to manipulation by the other parent. "This is my ex-spouse's doing, not my son's. It's her way of getting back at me through my son. How dare she!"

Often, one or both partners will resort to litigation in an effort to sort things out, which, despite everyone's best efforts, tends to make things worse. The parents' attorneys go to war, guardian ad litems are appointed, social workers are assigned, therapists are deposed, and within no time at all a sometimes irretrievable breakdown of trust among all parties ensues. Rarely is a courtroom going to be the setting for dealing with these vitriolic altercations because the issue seems to be more *soul* custody than *sole* custody.

The tangled topography of these predicaments best deserves a chapter, if not a book, all of its own. While each scenario of this sort is unique in its own way, they are all linked together by one thing: unresolved issues between the parents that *each* have a role in, even though they will both very convincingly assign to the other parent, rather than accept for themselves, any responsibility for this very damaging state of affairs.

Custodial parents will tend to ignore the strong possibility that they are sending mixed messages to their adolescent, saying that he's "free" to visit his noncustodial parent, but signifying in important ways that this would be a severe betrayal, a violation of trust. I have observed dozens of parents telling their teenagers, "Of *course* I want you to have a good relationship with your mother," but everything about their body language and follow-up actions conveys just the opposite.

Non-custodial parents will tend to ignore their own contribution to this state of affairs, and by refusing to acknowledge this, wind up further alienating and antagonizing the adolescent, for whom no comment could be more insulting than, "I know you're not speaking your own mind here, you're simply a mouthpiece for your father." These parents find it infinitely more convenient to accuse their ex-spouse of subverting the situation than to examine their own behavior and try to heal whatever hurts their teenaged son or daughter has experienced over the years and is attempting to address.

When I have been able to help parents make a shift and understand that the stalled visitation arrangement is a barometer of their unfinished marital business, workable compromises, even in these perplexing quagmires, tend to emerge. If this doesn't happen, however, teens' overall development, along with their relationship with *both* parents, becomes severely affected.

The anger at their custodial parent for keeping them trapped (anger that may take some time for them to recognize and understand, at which point it's sometimes too late to successfully sort out), and at their non-custodial parent for being unwilling to take their concerns seriously and at face value (anger that is usually no more intense than their anger at the custodial parent, but more immediately accessible), builds to monumental proportions, and then is likely to be played out in various ways in the years to follow. Whenever there is wrathful competition for a teen's heart, no matter what legal outcome eventually emerges, the teen is always the one who loses.

TOLERATE AND EMPATHIZE WITH MIXED FEELINGS

Divorced parents do themselves and their teenagers a disservice when they don't allow for the complete bandwidth of emotions to be experienced and expressed, and instead believe that they can make everything alright. Anger, sorrow, guilt, resentment—all of these feelings and others can be expected to be part of the normal family process during and after a separation and divorce. Parents who learn to tolerate this range of conflicting and competing emotions without taking them all personally will find that they make a difficult situation somewhat easier to manage.

When we are engaged to be married, we all fantasize about the perfect marriage, even though we know (or at least are told) that it is never to be had. Likewise, separating couples fantasize about the perfect divorce—the sudden and permanent passing of gray and stormy conflict, replaced by the cool, comforting breezes of serenity and congeniality. But such a state is just as eternally elusive as is the perfect marriage.

And of course if we embark on another marriage, the same exact fantasies will optimistically rear themselves. *This* time I'll get it right, *this* time it'll work, *this* time it'll be better than it ever was; we'll defy the odds and emerge as one big happy, blended family, the kind that newspaper and magazine articles, movies and sitcoms, are based upon. So when our fantasies are revealed as just that, how much harder it is to settle for clumsy reality, with its wearisome allegations and accusations, its grueling skirmishes and squabbles. The myth of the perfect stepfamily always dies a particularly gruesome death.

But rather than becoming demoralized that things are not

working out perfectly and irritably censuring your own and your teen's frustration, it's better to allow all parties a chance to speak their mind, remembering that the more room that you allow for negative emotions, the more room there will also be for positive emotions as well.

Along similar lines, your teen, as we have seen, may sometimes gravitate toward you and other times toward your ex-spouse. These shifting loyalties are perfectly normal and would be played out in one form or another even if you were still married. But it's important to remain balanced, to not take these shifts too personally, and to not overreact in either situation, such as by responding with jubilation (to the former) or with despair (to the latter). Maintaining your flexibility will help adolescents to maintain theirs and get what they need from both parents without feeling as if they're betraying either.

ACKNOWLEDGE THE LIMITS OF STEPPARENTS

While the task of building a solid stepfamily during any developmental stage is difficult, we have seen how, during adolescence, it can become one of Herculean proportions. If a stepparent has been part of a teen's family for years, since early childhood or elementary school, and if trust has slowly been built and a benevolent bond has gradually developed over those years, then it's possible for the stepparent-stepchild relationship to survive and even prosper during adolescence. After all, stepparents offer unique gifts to the family system and can observe and intervene in ways that would be impossible for the original parents to duplicate.

However, in situations in which a remarriage occurs close to or during adolescence, the likelihood of a very warm and positive relationship blossoming between stepparent and stepchild drops significantly. A new marriage may be a gain for the parent, but it always signals a loss for the teen, and presents her with another authority figure to contend with and differentiate from. Because of this, she will often express her feelings by directing indifference, resistance, or hostility toward her parent or her parent's new partner.

Of course many parents of adolescents are understandably relieved to finally be married again and given another opportunity to construct a happy family. From a marital standpoint, they avidly anticipate the additional support inherent in a two-adult household and hope that their new spouse will cheerily take on an equal distribution of parental labor, even in situations in which the spouse has dependent children from a previous marriage. Sometimes parents will even expect that the stepparent will take over and replace them altogether so that they can retreat into the auxiliary role that they had carefully crafted for themselves in their previous marriage.

From a family standpoint, parents may be just as eager for their teen to connect with their new partner in a relaxed, close, and convivial way, so as to validate their having chosen wisely (this time), to mitigate some of their guilt for having "put their child through" a divorce, and to enable them to feel better about the prospects for survival of the new family.

Despite the good intentions behind such hopes, they are still likely to be dashed on the rocks of reality. Expecting your teenager to gleefully receive a new parent at a point in her life when she is trying to unhook herself from parental controls is destined to lead to hurt feelings all around.

What may be more important, and more realistic, than plotting to insert your new spouse into an authoritative or intimate stepparenting relationship with your teen is to simply strive to model a healthy marriage for her. This not only takes the pressure off the stepparent-teen dynamic; in many cases it will automatically improve it. It also provides teens with a working prototype for intimacy that may make up for the marriage that couldn't survive and teaches them that we almost always get the chance to learn from our mistakes and try, try again. Focusing on and succeeding in this goal will yield solid returns down the road and keep all of you from experiencing unnecessary frustration during an already arduous period of time.

KEEP THINGS IN PERSPECTIVE

A child's well-being does depend less on the structure of the family and more on the quality of the relationships that comprise the family. So just because your teen complains bitterly about how you've ruined her life by getting divorced doesn't mean that you should assume that she's right, that that's her only feeling about it, or that she wouldn't have alternative complaints about how you ruined her life if you were still married.

Many parents come to me certain that the problems that they are encountering with their adolescent are the result of a divorce, when it's likely that some or all of these problems would be surfacing in one form or another anyway. And while a divorce is never a day at the beach for a family, impaired marriages, as we have seen, carry their own developmental risks for teens as well. No relationship, or teenager, is perfect.

Adolescents are happy to induce whatever guilt they can in an effort to make things work to their advantage, and making it clear that you're vulnerable to their guilt won't do any of you any good. You're entitled to wish that your marriage could have worked, as you initially hoped that it would, but if it didn't, you're not entitled to wallow in self-pity and self-loathing to the extent that you imperil your ability to stand your ground and do your job as a parent.

Remember, too, how we have seen that it is the normal course of events for old issues to be churned up as adolescents prepare for their new, independent lives. This is often the case when there's been a divorce. One adolescent patient of mine who was going through a very ill-humored phase surprised his father by ending his dyspeptic litany of laments with the announcement that "and I'm still angry that you and Mom divorced," even though the divorce had occurred 13 years before, when he was only 3.

"You probably can't even remember Mom and me living together? How could you possibly still be upset about this?" Dad wondered, with not a little annoyance.

"Because things would have been different if you had stayed together," he responded, honestly, and, the fact, is, he was right. Whether or not things would have been better for him if his parents had remained married was open to debate, but there was no doubting the importance of his answering the question, "What would I be like if my father and mother had remained husband and wife?" as a way of coming to terms with that loss and further defining his identity.

As part of this coming to terms, adolescents may also want to revisit their parents' explanation for the divorce, feeling like they deserve, and are ready to understand, a more sophisticated exege-sis of a decision that had such significant ramifications for them. General statements that may have served a useful purpose earlier on—"We divorced because we just weren't happy together in the way that a husband and wife ought to be"—may need to be leav-ened with additional insights as teenagers attempt to grasp the complexities of an intimate relationship and apply their parents' lessons to their own lives.

This can get tricky, because you don't want to use this opportu-nity to demonize or vilify your ex-spouse, detailing all of his or her flaws and foibles, and the ways in which it was "all his/her fault" that things didn't work out. Better to take this opportunity to pro-vide a primer in the reciprocity of every relationship, so that your teen has as balanced a view of what happened as possible, and so that he can make sense of your marriage, as well as your divorce. This will serve the additional purpose of preventing him from blam-ing himself for the marital breakdown, if any self-blame still exists.

"I found your father's temper impossible to live with, and decided I could no longer go on being married to him. But I also realize, now, that I didn't make it very easy for him by just pulling away whenever he was angry, rather than dealing with things more directly. I think my 'disappearing act' probably made things as difficult for us as did his tem-per, and I wish, in retrospect, that I could've been able to handle it better, even though there's no guarantee that we would still be together even if I had."

"Your mother was very depressed for a good deal of our marriage. I know that she's spoken with you about this, I know that she's doing much better now that she's gotten treatment, and I'm pleased that she is happier. However, even though she's not depressed anymore, her being de-pressed did our relationship a lot of damage, and it was hard to repair all of it. I probably didn't make things any better by getting as upset with her as I did when she was de-pressed, but I felt helpless and frustrated, and didn't always manage it the best way. I still wonder what things would've been like if we had gotten on top of all of this sooner, and it

makes me sad to think that we couldn't make it work, but sometimes you have to make the best decision you can at the time and live with it, and that's what I tried to do."

"You're free to talk with your father about this, if you'd like, but I felt like I needed to be the number one person in his life, and I didn't always feel that way. I attempted to live with this, but after a while, I felt like I was selling myself short. I know that I'm not perfect, and I'm sure there were things about me that made it hard for him to want to be with me only. But, to my way of thinking, a good marriage depends on trust and commitment, particularly when you have to live with your partner's imperfections, and I didn't believe your father was trustworthy and committed to the marriage in the same way that I was, and in the way that I wanted him to be. I felt like I deserved to be treated better, which is why my marriage to your stepfather seems to be working out better for me, even though you're not that thrilled with him."

Try to keep in mind that it's not just the words you use, but the tone that you adopt as you address these topics that is most important. Conversations like these, difficult as they may be, communicate your growing respect for your adolescents' maturity, provide them with a wonderful opportunity to deepen their relationship with both of their parents, and lay the groundwork for their capacity to commence healthy intimate relationships with their peers as well.

One other issue that's often difficult to keep in perspective after a divorce is when a teen displays some of your ex-spouse's worst qualities, stirring your fears that he or she will turn out to be just like your former partner. To keep yourself from overreacting to this, bear in mind that adolescents will often take on the least appealing attributes of someone who is important to them, not because they necessarily want to become like that individual, but because they want to understand that individual better, or because they want to keep their connection with that individual alive and intact.

Becoming alarmed by these parallels—"This is why I couldn't live with your father, because he was angry all the time just like you are!" or "You and your mom are like two peas in a pod, always seeing the worst in everyone!"—is certain to create more bad feelings than necessary. Better to view this as just another stage in your teen's development, and to remember that, over time, he or she is just as likely to take on your ex's stronger, finer virtues as well.

KEEP CONFLICT CONFINED

In *The Good Enough Child*, I detailed some of the dramatic strategies I have felt the need to invoke over the years to help divorced parents understand how devastating it is for children when they are unable to quarantine their anger at their ex-spouse, allowing it to seep poisonously down into the next generation. At times, and without meaning to, separated or divorced parents may act like they are more in love with their legal positions, or with their lawyers, than with their children, or appear more invested in getting even with their ex-spouses than in getting close to their adolescent, The reality is that no matter how justifiable you believe your rage to be, any time you express negativity about your teen's other parent in a way that she can hear, or overhear, or even silently experience, you are inexcusably injuring her.

One 15-year-old patient of mine, who had made a serious suicide attempt by swallowing a bottle of Tylenol after she knocked back three bottles of beer, eventually disclosed to me that her effort to end her life was the result of finally realizing that she would never be able to calm the troubled waters that still roiled between her parents years after their divorce: "I get good grades, I'm in the National Honor Society, I play the French Horn, I don't use drugs, I don't have sex—and, tell me, what *good* has it done? They hate each other as much as they ever have, they still don't get along, my dad's not allowed out of the car when he comes to pick me up, my mom's not even allowed on my dad's property when she picks me up, I have to walk down the street to meet her! My mom can't accept the fact that I have a stepmother and constantly puts her down in front of me, my dad can't accept the fact that I have a stepfather and constantly puts him down, and I'm so fucking sick of it I think I finally just gave up."

What was amazing, and even more disturbing, to me was that both parents told me privately that they felt that they had been doing a "good job" of putting the past to rest and keeping their anger at their former spouse at bay. That they could believe this despite ample evidence of their scorched earth policies made it easy to see why their daughter had gotten to the point where she had completely given up hope.

For teens to maintain a positive self-image, they have to know that there were some positive things that attracted their parents to each other, and that these attributes can still be disinterred and acknowledged despite whatever conflictual history has ensued. Being able to say authentically positive things about an ex-spouse, and meaning it, is one of the great legacies that divorced parents offer their adolescents, and can be a form of parental restitution that expiates old guilt and makes up for the loss of the original family's integrity.

EXERCISE 10

As we just noted, there must have been something that originally drew you to your child's other parent, or you would not have gotten married in the first place. Sometimes, the toll that bitterness and heartbreak have exacted over the years, along with our anger at ourselves for having been seduced and deluded by our fantasies, erases from our memories all that had once been radiant with hope and promise. We lose sight of the essence of the individual whom we partook in the miracle of creating a family with, and the story of our marriage acquires the nap and weave of a repulsive fiction, rather than the delightful fairytale that we had envisioned for ourselves.

In many ways, our inability to recapture whatever was initially golden about our bond with their other parent causes teenagers great harm and anguish. They may not expect us to remain in love with each other, but they do expect us to remember and honor whatever qualities initially brought us together, because those become the very foundation for their positive self-image. Otherwise, this image is built on sand and will constantly be on the verge of collapsing.

Addressing these questions may help you to reclaim your respect for the sanctity of the bond that remains in place through the presence of your shared children:

1. What initially attracted me to my former spouse?

2. What prompted me to go ahead with the marriage, despite whatever ambivalence or reservations were surfacing?

3. What prompted me to go ahead and start a family, despite whatever ambivalence or reservations were surfacing?

4. What did my former spouse do that made me forget whatever was the positive basis for our bond with each other?

5. What did I do that made me forget whatever was the basis for our bond with each other?

6. What positive things would or do other people say about my ex-spouse?

7. Can I imagine that the things that my ex-partner is doing as a parent that make me unhappy emerge out of his/her love for our child, rather than out of his/her dislike of me?

8. Have I forgiven him/her for whatever he/she did that helped dissolve the knot of our marriage?

9. Have I forgiven myself for marrying him/her, and for whatever I did that helped dissolve the knot of our marriage?

TEN

CONCLUDING THOUGHTS

As the grandchild of indomitable immigrants, I grew up immersed in the sagas that my fore-bears told of their audacious and dangerous travels. Many times, as I am leading the families in my practice across their rough and uncharted emotional oceans, it has occurred to me that children and their parents enter adolescence as immigrants enter a new country—feeling both fearful and inquisitive, overwhelmed and adventurous, anxious and exhilarated. And of course it's always fascinating to see what immigrants, and young adults, choose to take with them and what they choose to, or are forced to, leave behind.

Here are some final thoughts that may help you and your teen to feel more at home as you embark upon the shores of the new, promised land to which you have arrived.

We must begin with the assumption that we have no choice but to fail as parents. In fact, it is our failures that are essential to our children's success. After all, if we were too good as parents, why would our children even want to leave us? This means that all parental emotions have to be seen as normal and acceptable during adolescence, even the hot, dark, and distressing ones, and that we are neither able nor expected to be perpetually gracious, nurturant, tolerant, and loving.

This also means that we shouldn't shy away from making mistakes, and instead should try to value them because they help us, and our adolescents, to grow. They become, in James Joyce's words, our "portals of discovery." *Vulnerabilities* should not be confused with *fragilities*—teens are generally supple, hardy, and resilient, and likely to survive just about all of our flubs and flops, our misfires, misconduct, and missed chances. Our goal is not perfection, but simply trying to be present to our imperfect selves at the same time as we remain present to our imperfect children. That will usually be enough to prompt teens to want to get moving with their own lives, which, of course, is the whole point. As Boris Pasternak wrote, "I don't like people who have never fallen or stumbled. Their virtue is lifeless and it isn't of much value. Life hasn't revealed its beauty to them."

We must also repeatedly bow to the mystery of child and family development. I have a pretty good success rate as a clinician, but I'm certainly not batting 1.000. I have presented to you in the preceding chapters numerous case studies in which there was a positive outcome, but I'd be less than honest if I didn't also admit that I have faltered as well and experienced plenty of clinical futility, miscalculation, and outright defeat. The reality is that children and families are infinitely complex, and despite the mental health profession's tireless efforts, there will always be childrearing questions that contain no completely satisfying answer, developmental problems that hold forth no ideal solution, and family conflicts that resist any comprehensive amnesty. The influential theoretician Wilfred Bion wrote, "However experienced we are we still know very little indeed about how to bring up children of whatever age. We are beginning to know that we do not know—that is something."

We have to remember, too, that teens need us the most when they are the least pleasant to be with. The times when we are confronted with their formidable will and wiles, their deft indictments of the family's thoughtfully constructed ethics and beliefs, their exhausting and inexhaustible need to test, their ceaseless "I don't care's" and "I hate you's" and "*Whatever*'s" and "I can't wait until I'm eighteen and can move out's" are, ironically, the times when they are actually most connected with us. It's just that the depth of their connection is making them scared and uncomfortable, so it comes out as an obnoxious screed. Rare are the teens who truly do not care about their families. The indignation or defiance or indifference they manifest are smokescreens designed to cover up the deep sense of shame they experience about still needing us.

Related to this, one of our most important endeavors is to help adolescents discover and become themselves, rather than who we want them to be, and to display admiration for who they already are, not for who we imagine they should be. All parents have plans for their children to become new and improved versions of themselves, but trying to graft our dreams and aspirations onto them is destined to create tension, distress, and plenty of adversarial interaction. As Touchstone, in *As You Like It*, observed, life may be "an ill-favoured thing, sir, but mine own." Adolescents are not here to carry out our hopes for the future—they have their own future to carve out.

We should also not be exclusively devoted to making our teenagers happy—that's neither realistic nor advisable. Change cannot occur without pain, discomfort, and disquiet, and our efforts to shield and rescue our children from this reality will handicap their growth and always do more harm than good. I often tell parents that adolescence may feel like a nightmare, but as with any nightmare, just about everyone eventually wakes up from it.

Of course, as parents we can't expect to be happy all the time, either, but despite whatever disappointment or disillusionment we are feeling about our adolescents, we should still try to celebrate, rather than repudiate or merely tolerate, their flaws, idiosyncrasies, and eccentricities. We must find ways to love them because of, not in spite of, their imperfections, and staunch the wound to our self-image that was inflicted when they chose not to follow the paths that we so carefully and assiduously laid out for them. As André Gide wrote, "It's better to be hated for who you are than loved for who you aren't."

Finally, we need to help teens to understand that, in the long run, it's not what you have and what you do but who you are and how you love that is going to make the difference. We should be emphasizing effort over results, process over outcome, authenticity over appearances. We should get teens thinking not just about how they're going to make a living, but about how they're going to live, not just about doing, but about being. We should enlarge our goals for them beyond engineering an impressive résumé of attention-getting accomplishments and focus instead on the enduring value of kindness, honesty, industry, and compassion.

That is why connecting teens up with religious or service organizations becomes one of the greatest antidotes to their feelings of melancholy, alienation, and nihilism—learning to be on intimate terms with meaning, purpose, and belonging is what's necessary to transcend the limitations of blindly compulsive, parent-pleasing achievement and acquisition. Self-worth cannot be taught or implanted, and ultimately comes not so much from doing well but from doing good.

Although I have tried to cover as many developmental bases as possible in The Good Enough Teen, the extraordinary range of issues, worries, dilemmas, and problems that parents of typical teenagers confront far exceeds my capacity to address them in a single text. Instead, I have offered you a framework that I believe has applicability to a wide variety of situations and scenarios.

However, because there are so many questions that I hear parents repeatedly ask me in my practice, and during my lectures and workshops—ones that I have not had the space to specifically tackle in the preceding pages—you should feel free to visit my website (www.bradsachs.com), where you will find a question-and-answer section that you can look over and contribute to.

As I write these final words, an 8-week-old puppy, Dasia, sleeps on my lap, snuffling and twitching her way through some dreamy canine narrative. The first "child" my wife and I had the pleasure of raising was, in fact, a puppy as well, one whom we affectionately named Bruce. Bruce was already 9 years old before our first son, Josh, was born, and died shortly before our second son, Matt, came along. We've had a couple of dogs since then, and one more child, Jessica, but I am intimately aware that just as Bruce is the dog who helped us to welcome parenthood, Dasia is the dog who will help us to say good-bye to parenthood, who will shepherd us through the sequential departures of our three children. I am certain that it is this apprehension that accounts for the tender tug of sadness I experience as I stroke her soft, Falstaffian belly and feel the ardent heartbeats thrumming within her stout little chest.

In fact, Josh, who is now 16 and a junior in high school, commented wistfully, as he played with Dasia on the floor the night we brought her home, that he didn't think he would get as close to this dog as he did to our other dogs because he'd probably be spending much of the rest of his life living away from her. This was a sobering, bittersweet thought that had not escaped me either, and one that has prompted much further consideration about all of the other changes that will occur as our children begin the inexorable process of leaving home.

Just a little while back, there was a phase during which I was routinely despairing about the prospects of finishing this book in an acceptable manner. For several nights in a row I awoke in the lonely silence of 3 A.M., unable to get back to sleep and plagued by the same persistent questions: How, after all this work and all these words, could I have said so little? How had I so grievously missed the essence—the misery and joy, the terror and exhilaration—of raising teenagers? How had I so trivialized the complex emotional circuitry of parenthood, the love and ache and longing that all harmonize elegiacally as teens unfurl the magic carpet that is for the sole purpose of soaring away and leaving us far behind? How could I have so meagerly limned the wondrous odyssey of adolescents, their rhapsodic peaks and agonizing valleys, the wrecks and wrenches of their passionate hearts, their remarkable passage of jumbled and jubilant drama?

During these dark nights, I gave serious thought to simply disposing of the hundreds of pages of manuscript that had already been completed, tearing up all of my notes, and just starting over from scratch (although I must confess that the realization that my wife might respond to this decision by strangling me served to keep this rash impulse in check).

As I reflected forlornly upon my blighted and baffled hopes for this book, however, it slowly began occurring to me that going ahead and finishing it despite my chagrin was akin to going ahead and finishing the work of raising an imperfect adolescent—books and children, like everything else we invest our hearts and souls in, will always feel somehow incomplete, inferior, and insufficient, no matter how hard we have tried, no matter how strong the desire to just start over. All that any of us parents can really do is give it our flawed, fumbling best, and then stand back, pray a little, hold our collective breath, and watch with heroic, undying love as our children take their leave and begin to row slowly out across destiny's vast ocean, brave oars creaking rhythmically, steadily within their locks.

Benjamin Disraeli once wrote, "The best way to become acquainted with a subject is to write a book about it." With this thought in mind, I hope that you have been able to embrace what I have written about my intimate acquaintance with imperfect humanity, and done so in the same spirit of acceptance, compassion, and forgiveness that I have invited you to bring to the life of your family. In so doing, perhaps you will come to decide not only that this book is good enough, but that your teenager is good enough, and, most importantly, that *you* are good enough as well.

ACKNOWLEDGMENTS

I extend my deepest gratitude . . .

To my parents, Claire and Herb Sachs—I haven't forgotten how difficult I may have made things for the two of you during *my* adolescence, but hope these pages help other parents of teenagers to manage with as much patience, perspective and humor as you did

To my mother-in-law, Selma Meckler, for so successfully raising the daughter who became my wife, and for her constant and clever re-arrangements of the furniture in our house (fortunately, when I'm not home)

To my brother and sister-in-law, Paul and Janet Sachs, and their children, Danny, Rachel, and Adam—ten points if, in the next ten minutes, any of you can locate the one place in this book where I used the word "deleterious"

To my brother and sister-in-law Lee Sachs and Deborah Pangle, and their son, Anatole—I present to you yet another Key-Limeless text (and readers should not forget to check out *www.deborahpangle.com* for elegant jewelry designs)

To my grandmother, Anne Sachs—here's hoping that you'll hang in there long enough to enjoy this book, and—what the hell—maybe the next one, too

To my uncle, Ken Sachs, who, after all these years, has never lost faith in Philadelphia's sports teams (*that* should tell you something)

To Tom Burns, for always supporting my "clinicoliterary" (or is it "literoclinical"?) efforts

To Roger Lewin, for encouraging me to tolerate my shortcomings with compassion, grace, and humor

To Phyllis Stern, whose wise and benevolent voice, even from miles away, still guides me

To my friends Greykell Dutton, David Gilberg, Norman Gross, Roberta Israeloff, Rick LaRocca, Eric Metzman, Steve (still *mio fratello*) Rosch, Scott Rosenthal, Paul Scimonelli, and Scott and Teri Strahlman

To our next-door neighbors, the Earle's (Sherri, Dave, Brady, Samantha, Jansen, Lucy, and Michael) on one side, and Jeanne Busch, Richard Robey, and Leo on the other, for helping to create such a child- and dog-friendly cul-de-sac

To *all* of the individuals who were so helpful and understanding during last year's medical crisis (and my apologies for losing track of all of those casserole dishes and lasagna pans), in particular . . .

The parents from the Long Reach Marlins Swim Team

The parents from the CSC Fury

The families of Kendall Ridge

To Gary Glisan, for somehow maintaining the functioning of the extensive Sachs computer network despite the porn, music videos, and viruses that were frequently and "mysteriously" downloaded

To Andrea Ohler, for helping us all to stay afloat

To Rabbi Gary Fink, Cantor Charlie Bernhardt, and Congregation Oseh Shalom, for providing a spiritual home during both difficult and joyous times

To the staffs of Deep Run Elementary School, Mayfield Woods Middle School, and Long Reach High School for their tireless efforts on behalf of our community's children

To George Martiyan, of Long Reach Parcel Plus, for making sure things always got to where they needed to go (including all of those comics during the summer)

To Katie Smith and the pet-loving staff of Patapsco Valley Veterinary Hospital

To Barry Trent, for inviting all of us into the world of double-reeds

To Coaches Jerry Fischer, Abby Bausman, and Wendy Epke for being such wonderful role models to young athletes

To Laurie Hill, for never getting bored with having to give me the same haircut, month after month after month

To the Howard County Public Library System

To my agent, Sarah Jane Freymann, for her adamantine faith in my abilities, and many thought-provoking discussions

To my editor, Sarah Durand, for (apparently) never tiring of my e-mails, for her open-mindedness, for her editorial acumen, for her college search ideas, and for treating me to some delicious lunches in New York

To all of the schools, parent groups, agencies, and institutions that have invited me to lead the workshops that shaped and stimulated my evolving thoughts and perspectives on family life

And to all of my patients, who inspire me every day with their commitment, their conviction, and their courage

A portion of the author's profits from the sale of this book will be donated to UNICEF—the United Nations Children's Fund

INDEX

BOOKS BY BRAD E. SACHS, PH.D.

THE GOOD ENOUGH CHILD
How to Have an Imperfect Family and Be Perfectly Satisfied
ISBN 0-380-81303-3 (paperback)

Respected psychologist Dr. Brad Sachs helps recognize unrealistic expectations placed on children and helps parents to free themselves from the crippling belief that a healthy family should be absolutely perfect.

Appropriate for the parents of toddlers to teens.

"Sachs provides clear and realistic guidance for all parents." —*Washington Post*

THE GOOD ENOUGH TEEN
Raising Adolescents with Love and Acceptance (Despite How Impossible They Can Be)
ISBN 0-06-058740-7 (paperback)

Sachs presents a developmental overview of what parents can expect from their children during adolescence, then delineates the five stages in the journey toward accepting a child for who he or she is. With prescriptive tools and strategies for parents, including checklists, quizzes, and exercises, and numerous case studies from the author's own practice, *The Good Enough Teen* is vital help for any parent with a teenager.